PITTSBURGH THEOLOGICAL MONOGRAPH SERIES

General Editor
Dikran Y. Hadidian

13

CRUX IMPERATORUM PHILOSOPHIA:
Imperial Horizons of the Cluniac
<u>Confraternitas</u>, 964-1109

CRUX IMPERATORUM PHILOSOPHIA:
Imperial Horizons of the Cluniac
<u>Confraternitas</u>, 964-1109

by

Robert G. Heath

The Pickwick Press

Pittsburgh, Pennsylvania

1976

Library of Congress Cataloging in Publication Data

Heath, Robert George, 1923–
   Crux imperatorum philosophia.

   (Pittsburgh theological monograph series ; no. 13)
   Bibliography: p.
   Includes index.
   1. Cluny, France (Benedictine abbey) I. Title.
II. Series.
BX2615.C63H42   255'.1   76–56099
ISBN 0–915138–17–4

271.1
H351
7804046

TO

CATHERINE AND EUGEN

MARGRETE, FREYA, CLOTHILDE

CONFRATERNITAS VIVORUM ET MORTUORUM

CONTENTS

PREFACE

Historians have long been aware of the close associations between monasticism and secular society in the Middle Ages, but they have tended to pay more attention to the political and economic than to the spiritual and liturgical aspects of the relationship. For most contemporaries, however, especially between the eighth and twelfth centuries, the *raison d'être* of monks and nuns was their work for the spiritual welfare of mankind. "The greatest hope of salvation for all Christians" lay in the life and chastity of monks, according to Charlemagne,[1] and in his letter *De litteris colendis*, which was addressed to the abbot, community, and "our faithful *oratores*" of Fulda, he remarked on the letters sent him by many monasteries signifying "that the monks living there were fighting for us in pious and sacred prayers".[2] Thus for Charlemagne the faithful monks fighting on the spiritual battlefield were the equivalent of the faithful warriors fighting for society in temporal warfare. Both groups were considered particularly responsible for the welfare of secular rulers. According to the *Ordines Romani*, the names only of living kings, princes, and priests were to be recited in monasteries on Sundays,[3] and in the collection from St. Martial at Limoges of the monastic legislation of Aachen, the times were laid down for the daily chanting throughout the year of five psalms "on behalf of the king and all catholics and familiars and givers of alms".[4]

In the post-Carolingian period this tradition of liturgical intercession for rulers and their subjects was particularly preserved at the great Burgundian abbey of Cluny, which was given to the Apostles by its founder, Duke William of Aquitaine,

> first for the sake of the love of God, then
> for the sake of the soul of my lord King Odo,
> of my father and mother, for the sake of my-
> self and my wife, that is the salvation of
> our souls and bodies, likewise for the sake
> of Hava who granted me this property [at
> Cluny] by testamentary right, also for the
> souls of our brothers and sisters and nephews
> and of all our relations of both sexes, for
> our faithful followers who are attached to
> our service, also for the sake of the status
> and integrity of the catholic religion.[5]

This mission of carefully graded responsibilities was never forgotten by the monks of Cluny, and over the years it was augmented by countless gifts made to the abbey in return for prayers and other services, such as burial, designed to promote the spiritual welfare of the donor both in this world and in the next.[6] The great customaries of Ulrich and Bernard, after referring to the union and confraternity with Cluny of many congregations of monks and clerics, go on to say (in the words of Ulrich, which closely resemble those of Bernard) that:

> There are many faithful followers of Christ,
> both rich and poor, who, when they come [and]
> are taken into our chapter, ask that they also
> may deserve our confraternity. This is granted,
> and with the book [of confraternity] they re-
> ceive part and community in all the goods which

are in any way performed either in prayers or
in alms not only by us but also in all the
places subject to our jurisdiction.[7]

The customaries then specified the prayers and good works to
be performed for these *confratres* both during and after their
lifetimes.

Secular rulers had a special position in the Cluniac
liturgy. The so-called customary of Farfa, or *Liber tramitis*,
included an *ordo* for the reception of a king or queen in the
monastery,[8] and in the customary of Bernard there are elaborate
regulations for celebrating the anniversaries of emperors, empresses, and kings "who have given something great to the
church".[9] Special mention is made elsewhere in the customary
of the Emperors Henry II and III, King Ferdinand of Spain, and
the Empresses Adelaide and Agnes and of liturgical intercession
on behalf of other kings.[10] In the twelfth century, perhaps
about 1138/9, Abbot Peter the Venerable wrote to the Emperor
John Comnenus asking him to restore the monastery of Civitot
and to protect the monks there "for the eternal salvation of
his soul", and at the end of the letter he added that:

> In order that we may give you something of
> spiritual benefit in return for these things
> which you do [for us], just as our predecessors
> and we ourselves have made the kings of the
> French, the kings of the English, the kings of
> the Spaniards, the kings of the Germans, the
> very emperors of the Romans, and your neighbors
> the kings of the Hungarians *confratres* and co-
> participants in all the benefits of the congre-
> gation of Cluny, so likewise we receive Your
> Sublimity fully and perfectly, inasmuch as
> possible, into the same spiritual benefits
> on behalf of omnipotent God and of the most
> blessed Mary, the eternally virgin mother of

> God, and of the holy apostles and of all the
> saints, in order that the omnipotent savior
> may both augment and conserve this temporal
> kingdom for you and may in the future bring
> you to the eternal [kingdom] with the sainted
> kings.11

The over-riding concern of Cluny with the welfare of
souls, both now and in the future, is the subject of the
present work, of which the particular merit is to look at
the relation of Cluny and the German emperors in the context
of contemporary attitudes and practices rather than in the
light of later events. The author sharply criticizes the
"false historical perspective" of seeing Cluny "mainly in
terms of the Investiture Contest" (p. 194 n. 51) and warns
in particular against the dangers of studying an age when
"the two strands of world and spirit, law and grace, Empire
and Church" were intertwined from the point of view of a
later age when these elements were sharply distinguished
(p. 61). In the early Middle Ages, as in Antiquity, religious rites and ceremonies were a central part of life and
should not be seen as something apart from the secular institutions of the time (pp. 112-113). The emperors, as the
heads of secular society, naturally looked at Cluny, as the
leading monastery in Europe, for liturgical intercession on
their behalf; and the Cluniacs equally naturally responded
by offering prayers on behalf of the emperors, and they kept
them up even during the Investiture Contest. Archbishop
Hugh of Lyons wrote in 1088 that he had discovered the previous year that, "The abbot [of Cluny] had publicly celebrated on Good Friday the customary prayer on behalf of the
emperor, which is now suspended on account of Henry's excommunication and deposition by the lord Pope Gregory."

The abbot apparently at first tried to excuse himself by saying that the prayer was on behalf of any emperor, but when the archbishop pointed out that it pertained especially to the Roman emperor, he was silent "but did not emend his acknowledged error by a due penance".[12] The letter of Peter the Venerable cited above shows that the spiritual association between Cluny and the German emperors continued into the twelfth century.

The Cluniacs were concerned with the spiritual welfare of the dead as well as of the living, and especially with the state of souls at the time of the Last Judgment, which became for them a time of fearful terror rather than of joyful anticipation. The increasing concentration on the themes of guilt and penitence, as the author shows, is symbolized by Abbot Hugh's suppression of the traditional prayer *"O felix culpa"*,[13] which reflected the older spirituality of glorification of Adam's sin as a source of good and of confidence in the ultimate salvation of mankind (pp. 98-99). The concern with the state of souls in the other world is also shown by the many stories in Peter the Venerable's *De miraculis* of visitations by departed spirits to living men in order to remind them of their duties towards the dead. "By forcing the individual soul to be exposed to lines of force emanating from the end of time and stretching back into his present life," the author says, "and extending this experience to all souls that had ever lived or would live, a Christian democracy based on overcoming death came into being. Cluny's confraternity made man conscious as never before of death as the unremitting equalizer between man" (p. 103).

These conclusions challenge various accepted views about Cluny and its relations with secular society, and some readers may disagree with them. The special concern for the spiritual welfare of rulers, for instance, which is stressed here, suggests that the democracy of souls at Cluny was less than perfect. Other evidence shows that Cluny was not unique in the monastic world of the ninth and tenth centuries. All the elements of annual commemoration of the dead were found in other monasteries before they were brought together in the feast of All Souls by Abbot Odilo in 998.[14] This step was so important in popularizing the practice, however, as the present work shows, that there is some justification for regarding Cluny as the fountainhead of the cult. More than any other contemporary monastery Cluny brought together all types of men and women--living and dead, great and small, rich and poor--into a single great *societas* of which the supreme religious value was generally recognized at least until the twelfth century. The importance of this *societas*, and the central position in it of the German emperors, is the subject of this book, which thus redresses the balance of scholarly research by putting the emphasis on those aspects of the social role of monasticism which were most important to contemporaries.

Giles Constable
Harvard University

1. *Capitularia regum Francorum*, ed. A. Boretius (Monumenta Germaniae historica: Leges, II; Hannover, 1883-97) I, 94-5.

2. *Ibid.*, p. 79.

3. *Initia conseutudinis benedictinae*, ed. K. Hallinger (Corpus consuetudinum monasticarum, 1; Siegburg, 1963) p. 72.

4. *Ibid.*, p. 561.

5. *Recueil des chartes de l'abbaye de Cluny*, ed. A. Bernard and A. Bruel (Paris, 1876-1903) I, 125, no. 112.

6. Cf. Willibald Jorden, *Das cluniazensische Totengedächtniswesen vornehmlich unter den drei ersten Äbten Berno, Odo und Aymard (910-954)* (Münsterische Beiträge zur Theologie, 15; Münster in W., 1930), on which see Johannes Ramackers, "Analekten zur Geschichte des Reformpapsttums und der Cluniazenser," *Quellen und Forschungen aus italienischen Archiven und Bibliotheken*, XXXII (1931-2) 30-2.

7. Ulrich of Cluny, *Consuetudines Cluniacensis*, III, 33, in *Patrologia latina*, CXLIX, 777a-778b, and Bernard of Cluny, *Ordo Cluniacensis sive Consuetudines*, I, 26, in *Vetus disciplina monastica*, ed. M. Herrgott (Paris, 1726) p. 200.

8. *Liber tramitis, dictae Consuetudines Farfenses*, II, 32, in *Consuetudines monasticae*, ed. B. Albers (Stuttgart--Vienna--Monte Cassino, 1900-12) I, 170.

9. Bernard, *Ordo*, I, 74 (27), *ed. cit.*, p. 272.

10. *Ibid.*, I, 51, *ed. cit.*, p. 246; cf. C. J. Bishko, "Liturgical Intercession at Cluny for the King-Emperors of Leon," *Studia monastica*, III (1961) 57-9.

11.   *The Letters of Peter the Venerable*, ed. G. Constable
(Harvard Historical Series, 78; Cambridge, Mass., 1967) I,
209, Letter 75. He concluded the letter, most usually, with
"Amen".

12.   *Patrologia latina*, CLVII, 515ab; cf. T. Schieffer,
"Cluny et la querelle des investitures," *Revue historique*,
CCXXV (1961) 69.

13.   Ulrich, *Consuetudines*, I, 14, *ed. cit.*, 663a.

14.   Cf. J. Leclercq, "Un ancien recueil de leçons pour
les vigiles des défunts," *Revue bénédictine*, LIV (1942) 23-4,
and H. R. Philippeau, "Contribution à l'étude du culte collec-
tif des trépassés," *Zeitschrift für schweizerische Kirchengeschichte*, LI (1957) 45-57.

FOREWORD

A study of the relationship between the medieval Roman emperors and the Cluniac *confraternitas* presupposes that a Cluniac confraternity did exist and, secondly, that imperial relations with it are of some marked significance for history. This study therefore has a two-fold aim on two converging levels of understanding. The first level concerns the confraternities themselves. What were they? How did they come into existence? What needs did they fulfill and what purpose did they serve? How did this particular form of communal association express itself at Cluny, what importance does it assume in the life of the monastery and society at large? In order to provide answers to such questions research will have to concentrate necessarily on the inner life of the Burgundian monastery.

However the very nature of the subject demands that this aspect of it be supplemented by another of equal importance, the relationship of the emperors to the confraternity. Here considerations of another kind must be introduced. Whereas the inner life of the Cluniac confraternity during the period of 964-1109 shows a general cohesiveness of development, its "life-style" so to speak, any question of the relationships between the monastery and the outer world introduces the need to appraise the external elements acting upon and transforming the very principles on which these relationships were founded. Consequently, what may appear at first glance to be a straight-forward problem shows itself to be an extremely complex one once the interrelationships between the imperial role and the

Cluniac movement are seen to be subject to changing historical circumstances requiring careful chronological definition.
In short it is one thing to juxtapose two categorically static
entities, Empire and monastery, and then compare the "relationships" between them. It is quite another to come to grips with
the changing intensity and effect of historical forces imping-
ing on institutional continuity in such a way as to recast the
roles of Empire and monastery in a new light. All too frequently is the former method employed in works on Cluny. Conclusions tenable for one period of its history are applied indiscriminately to other historical circumstances in a "time-
less", abstract manner.

Since this study is confined almost exclusively to the
use of Cluniac sources, it follows that our central point of
orientation is the inner life and character of the Burgundian
monastery. However limited such a focus may be, it offers
compensating advantages, not the least of which is a firm
basis for statements regarding essential concerns of the
abbey. Another advantage, awaiting verification of course,
may be anticipated: Seen from the "inside" the various lives
and writings of the abbots, supplementing other sources, provide significant information as to the abbey's orientation.
The absence of historical and biographical detail during the
abbots' long reigns, a source of annoyance and criticism to
many historians, receives quite a different interpretation
as a result. By orienting ourselves on a Cluny characterized
primarily by its own communal life of prayer we are better
placed to appraise its influence on events external to itself.

The main focus of our effort remains, however, the express
uniqueness of the imperial cult in a non-imperial, independent
abbey during the period extending from the accession of Majolus
to the death of Hugh. Before coming to the core of this prob-

lem two preliminary chapters have seemed essential. The first of these is an introductory survey of three aspects which provide necessary perspective: the range of literature on Cluny, a brief discussion of the sources used, a necessary historical acquaintance with the disintegrating and chaotic forces of the tenth century in which Cluny and the restored Roman Empire came to the fore. The next chapter focuses on the response made to this given situation on the part of monastery and Empire. The first part of this chapter will utilize one group of source documents which oblige us to focus on the primary mission of the abbots, as they viewed it, a facet of the monastery in need of emphasis. Starting from here we shall then be able to proceed to a first appraisal of the overlapping interests of abbots and emperors confined to the period ending in 1049. At that point we shall be prepared to utilize other sources to evaluate the depth and significance of the imperial participation in the Cluniac confraternity. It will become obvious in the latter part of this investigation why events after 1049 call for a realignment of historical perspective in order to evaluate the evidence of the sixty years which follow.

This study was begun during the spring of 1964. At that time my studies in Cluniac liturgy had already led me to utilize what is now identified as the principal Cluniac obituary source, that of Marcigny, and, by following the lead of Molinier, to recognize its value for the thesis of this book. These efforts were obliged to suffer a long interruption during which time a number of invaluable publications in this area have appeared. Although these have without question "opened the field", my own historical approach, then, as now, has been formed independently of them. However the delay has

allowed me to benefit from the very different kinds of helpful criticism and suggestions offered to me by Professor
Constable of Harvard University and Professor Werckmeister
of the University of California, Los Angeles, both of whom I
wish to thank on this occasion. Although my own teacher,
Eugen Rosenstock-Huessy (1888-1973), that true genius whose
Soziologie presents the long-awaited founding of a scientific
methodology in the social sciences based on the Word, and whom
Frederick Heer has recently called "the greatest historical
thinker of our time", did not aid directly in the composition
of this monograph, his presence throughout, both human and
scholarly, will be apparent. His only advice to me at the
beginning of this enterprise was a word from von Ranke:
"Meine Herrn, bilden Sie sich den Sinn für das Interessante
aus!"--*Satis superque*.

Robert G. Heath
California State University
Northridge, California

Easter, 1976

ABBREVIATIONS

AA SS	*Acta Sanctorum Bollandiana*
Albers	*Consuetudines Monasticae*
Ber.	*Ordo Cluniacensis* by Bernard
CF	*Consuetudines Farfenses (Liber Tramitis)*
DA	*Deutches Archiv*
DACL	*Dictionnaire d'Archéologie chrétienne et de Liturgie*
DHGE	*Dictionnaire d'Histoire et de Géographie ecclésiastique*
FS	*Frühmittelalterliche Studien*
Herrgott	*Vetus Disciplina Monastica*
HZ	*Historische Zeitschrift*
La Bibbia	*La Bibbia Nell' Alto Medioevo*
LTK	*Lexicon für Theologie und Kirche*
MIÖG	*Mitteilungen des Instituts für österreichische Geschichtsforschung*
MGH	*Monumenta Germaniae Historica*
NF	*Neue Forschungen über Cluny und die Cluniacenser*
NA	*Neues Archiv*
P.G.	J. P. Migne *Patrologia Graeca*
P.L.	J. P. Migne *Patrologia Latina*

QFIAB	*Quellen und Forschungen aus italienischen Archiven und Bibliotheken*
RB	*Revue Bénédictine*
RG	*Revue Grégorienne*
RHE	*Revue d'Histoire Ecclésiastique*
RHEF	*Revue d'Histoire de l'Eglise de France*
RHS	*Revue d'Histoire de la Spiritualité* (formerly *Revue d'ascetisme et de mysticisme*)
RM	*Revue Mabillon*
Sackur	E. Sackur, *Die Cluniacenser in ihrer kirchlichen und allgemeingeschichtlichen Wirksamkeit bis zur Mitte des elften Jahrhunderts*
SG	*Studi Gregoriani*
StMGBO	*Studien und Mitteilungen aus der Geschichte des benediktiner Ordens*
Udal.	*Consuetudines Antiquiores Cluniacensis* by Ulrich
ZKG	*Zeitschrift für Kirchengeschichte*
ZRG KA	*Zeitschrift der Savigny-Stiftung für Rechtsgeschichte, kanonistische Abteilung*

INTRODUCTION

1. The Problem of Cluny

The subject of Cluny, its particular significance, its
general and specific contributions to the history of the
Church and of the world and, above all, the impact of its
influence on social, institutional, political and religious
development during the reign of its major abbots remain a
matter of lively and thoughtful controversy among scholars.
This is not surprising. To one interested in casting light
on the debate waged on Cluny the contradictory aspects of his
enterprise soon became evident. Cluny's beginnings were un-
pretentious, taking root against an historical background of
anarchy, social chaos, war, famine and barbarism. Yet within the space of precisely two hundred years this abbey, become the most powerful and influential of Benedictine monasteries, had seen its efforts come to fruition, its fame established, its name spread across Europe. How to account for
this prolonged growth over such an extended period of time?

Neither environmental causes, such as the monastery's
favorable geographical situation in Burgundy, nor unsatisfy-
ing generalizations, such as a stricter observance of the
Benedictine Rule, seem adequate as explanations in spite of
their undeniable significance. Cluny's contribution to history had to be something far more specific in view of the

fact that the two centuries of its growth were witness to one of the most tumultuous periods of European history. Indeed profound transformation on a universal scale was to penetrate the most vital areas of European life at the very moment when Cluny was addressed by the pope, Urban II, "as shining on earth like another sun imbued with divine charisma" to which the word of the Lord applied: You are the light of the world.[1] Civil war unleashed as a consequence of the confrontation between Pope and Emperor, the concentrated response to the impulses of holy war focused in the general appeal of the call to arms at Clermont in 1095, the appearance of the first war of propaganda, fundamental questioning and reappraising of basic Church dogma signalled by the rise of the Berengarian Controversy, culminating in a new involvement of the intellect in the life of the universities, the creation of a new architecture and new standards of beauty, the end of the last threat of barbarian invasions and--the list could be extended quite easily --the re-opening of the Mediterranean to trade with the East: Cluny is a witness to this highly charged atmosphere of deep conflict and historical change.

Hence, during the period extending from the year of its foundation in 909[2] by the noble William III of Aquitaine to the death of St. Hugh, the last of three consecutive abbots recognized as saints, the role of Cluny has appeared to be at times enigmatic. Cluny was the addressee of both parties in the bitter conflict waged between Roman pope and Roman Emperor, itself an outgrowth of the long shadow cast by the renewal of the Empire in 962 and the synodal reform of the Papacy at Sutri in 1046, both events welcomed by Cluniac abbots. Lay investiture, the proprietary church and the evils of simony come to the fore as issues of the day in a world where Cluny's outstanding wealth lends itself readily to an economic interpretation of its role.[3] Knightly ideals express themselves throughout the Mediterranean area from Spain to the Orient coincident with the impulse given to Cluniac life by a chivalric nobility. It is a former prior of Cluny who directs as heir to his extraordinary predecessor, Gregory VII, himself a Cluniac,[4] the first Crusade. At the same time any attempt to connect Cluny with the genesis of the crusading movement by reference to popes subject to its discipline shows itself to be oversimplified when one recalls that it was Bernard of Clairvaux, outspoken in his condemnation of that same religious house whence Urban II came, who preached the Second Crusade. Consequently, the list of complications and apparent contradictions associated with Cluny is a long one. The resulting scholarly controversies are witnesses themselves to the scope of Cluniac studies.

Cluny's overriding importance in the history of Benedictine monasticism has been emphasized in the classic history by Dom P. Schmitz,[5] its significance for universal history is beyond discussion.[6] Yet no informed history of the abbey exists which can be considered satisfactory. Particularly is this true for that complex period which scholars in the majority feel to be the most creative in the abbey's development and therefore most worthy of interest, those years from its foundation in the first decade of the tenth century to its withdrawal from the center of the historical stage following the death of Peter the Venerable in 1156. An attempt to write such a general history was made in the previous century by Pignot who relied heavily on Mabillon.[7] The strong point of the book is generally agreed to be the biographies of the abbots. However, indispensable source documents were not utilized, many of them being unavailable or unknown

to be of Cluniac origin. Also Pignot's identification of
Cluny with papal reform colors his whole interpretation.
Sackur[8] reversed this all too blithely accepted view, that
Cluny was in league, so to speak, with the Roman popes in
their determination to remove kings and emperors to the
secular sphere of life whence they were considered as "in-
terfering" in the life of the Church. He insisted that
Cluny was not "anti-imperial", that its significance could
not be summarized by this facile interpretation, that there
existed a deep bond of cooperation between German emperors
and the abbots of Cluny.[9] This divergence of views from a
previous century on the relationship of Cluny to the Gregorian Papacy and the lines of historical force and moment which
either divide or separate them, has served as a focal point,
and continues to do so, for the wide range of Cluniac studies.
A general review of the literature under this rubric by Tellenbach[10] is instructive as to the extent to which scholarly
research has found itself obliged to concentrate on the issue
raised by Sackur many decades ago.

However, Sackur's book ended with the death of Odilo in
1049 and was limited to the areas of French Burgundy and
Lorraine, points all too often forgotten both by those who
take him to task for attributing to Cluny an influence beyond
measure, as well as by others who have opposed the results of
his research by reference to later times and historical conditions. A positive result of this divergence of views however has been to lead scholars down new paths of investigation
carefully appraising the evidence in multiple areas of Cluniac
life and activity.

Two deserve especial mention representing as they do major
undertakings, minute perusal of the sources, the presentation
of new evidence and new questions, valuable background informa-

tion and full bibliographies. The first of these sets as its
task an understanding of Cluny extending from the tenth to the
fifteenth centuries with the emphasis largely on the centuries
following the so-called "heroic period".[11] Its main focus is
the presentation of a detailed survey of Cluniac observances
and on this basis to discover the abbey's essence, found to
be liturgical prayer.[12] This insistence on the essence of
Cluny as being contained in daily liturgical observance, a
point without question which needs to be made, leads the
author,nonetheless,to stress the continuity in the evolution
of Cluny at the expense of any originality or newness generally assumed, or at least implied, in the Cluniac phenomenon.
Cluny is seen to stem directly in spirit and discipline from
a Carolingian prototype and serves only to extend throughout
the West the precepts and rigors of monastic observance.[13]
Also the relationships between Cluny and the monasteries subject to its order are regarded as reflecting those existing
between Cluny and the Holy See following the declaration of
Pope Honorius II in 1125 that Cluny and its monasteries were
dependent on him as his unique property, *ad speciale jus et
singularem proprietatem Sanctae Romanae Ecclesiae.*[14] As a
consequence of this evolutionary bias, based on an essentially
restricted view of Cluny, the element of changing historical
circumstances is hardly given its due.[15] Although de Valous'
second volume makes it clear that from the better part of the
twelfth to the fifteenth centuries Cluny had become increas-
ingly subject to papal power and jurisdiction, not every
scholar will welcome the conclusion that such conditions pre-
vailed in an earlier period of Cluny's history when the revolutionary principles of the papal monarchy were either non-
existent or in process of being formed.

    An impartial reader of de Valous' volumes might well be
led to the conclusion that the task of the monastic and Church

historian had become notably limited in scope. Once de Valous'
thesis of Cluny's unoriginal contribution to its own time and
historical circumstances was allowed to pass unchallenged, it
remained only to ask how the Cluniac movement differed from
other currents of monastic reform with which it was contemporary. In another book of extraordinary erudition this theme
of differentiation is developed between the various movements
within the whole area of monastic reform.[16] A comparison between the imperial monastery of Gorze and Cluny is carried out
in detail. That there were monastic reform movements operative
other than that of Cluny and contemporary with it is undeniable
but quite apart from the unassailable fact that the Cluniac
movement was the most extensive of them, the question remains
as to the content of their qualitative differences, which a
sympathetic, yet impatient, critic has indicated in a lengthy
review.[17] Not least of these differences is the monastery's
role within or without the imperial Church system (Reichskir-
chensystem) and its public services under the aegis of or in
alliance with the king. In view of Hallinger's conclusion[18]
it shall remain a task for scholars to spell out in greater
detail than before these qualitative differences that exist
between Cluny and the imperial monasteries.

The challenge and force of Hallinger's weighty tomes have
provoked admiration, qualified criticism and sharply opposing
views. The most pertinent and direct of these will be found
in a series of monographs edited by G. Tellenbach.[19] Hallinger's claim that Cluny embodied an anti-feudal movement is re-
futed in articles by J. Wollasch,[20] H. E. Mager,[21] and H.
Diener,[22] who reaffirms that Cluny was not a party to the conflict between popes and bishops but stood above and apart from
ecclesiastical struggles.

General and specialized studies include the older work of
Cucherat,[23] the general surveys of Joan Evans,[24] and L. M.

Smith,[25] as well as the work of Dom D. Knowles,[26] mostly devoted to England, but containing many thoughtful pages on
Cluny and its congregation. The book by Noreen Hunt follows
much in the methodological paths laid out by de Valous and is
largely devoted to the constitution of the abbey as contained
in the customals and the expansion of Cluny beyond the bounds
of Burgundy.[27] The continuing interest in the number and
variety of Cluniac studies is indicated by the series of international conferences begun in 1910[28] to commemorate the
founding of the abbey. One of these held at Todi limited itself to questions of Cluniac spirituality.[29] A congress was
held at Cluny in 1949 to commemorate both Saint Odo and Saint
Odilo.[30] Another dealing with more general aspects of Cluniac life was held at Moissac in 1963.[31] A conference on the
layman in the Middle Ages saw Cluny's name figure prominently
in the papers and discussions centered upon this theme.[32]

Works dealing exclusively with the lives of the three
abbots are relatively few in number, one each for St. Majolus
and St. Hugh.[33] The first of these is of a popular kind
while the latter, although at a far higher level of scholarship, is often limited in its scope. Odilo of Cluny has received the most attention in three serious works by Ringholz,[34] Jardet[35] and Hourlier,[36] all of which in varying degrees offer substantial portraits of the great abbot.

Also noteworthy in the context of this general survey
are the works of G. Schreiber,[37] P. B. Egger,[38] A. Brackmann,[39] Letonnelier,[40] Lemarignier,[41] which are concerned
with different facets of Cluniac life, organization and interpretation.

Of highest interest are further publications which indicate anew the unflagging interest in Cluny's role in the history of Europe, the West and the Church. Two of these are on
the Peace of God and the Truce of God both of which originated

with Cluny. Now we are told that communes are outgrowths of
associations formed under oath to preserve the peace originating in the *Pax Dei*.[42] H. Hoffmann has investigated anew the
Treuga Dei,[43] authored by Odilo of Cluny,[44] a movement from
which kings, the high nobility and the communes were to benefit. A landmark in medieval architectural history[45] has also
found its way into print after many years of preparation by
K. J. Conant. And the perennial question of the relationships
between Hildebrand, Cluny and the Papacy has been given new
impetus by the publication of a series of articles which
clearly and succinctly reviews sources and literature around
which the debate has drawn its lines.[46] The unending fascina-
tion of the subject of Cluny and the Papacy is also in evidence in the last full-length study devoted to the topic.[47]

Despite this extensive scope of Cluniac studies, the
topic of the present investigation, the relations of the
German emperors with the Cluniac confraternity from 964 to
1109, opens other vistas on the question of Cluny's relationship to the Empire. Since the Cluniac *confraternitas* was a
community of prayer centered on monastic life and liturgy,
it may be pointed out that intercessory prayer was not a
subject that interested politically-minded scholars of the
nineteenth century, nor their heirs, primarily interested in
questions of "Church and State". The obituary notices, necrologies and liturgical observances, which form an indispensable part of such studies, were of borderline interest
for the majority of investigators. Hence, discussions of the
relations between Cluny and the Saxon and Salian Kings were
inclined to minimize this aspect of matters, if not to leave
it out of account altogether. Although research dealing with
liturgical intercession for kings at Cluny has received little
attention as yet, some steps along this path have been taken.

Bishko's article is the only one thus far concentrating on a similar theme.[48] However, his study is confined to the king-emperors of Spain and, although valid in its main conclusion, needs to be supplemented with other sources and literature. The latter shall require separate discussion, all the more so in the light of further discoveries and reevaluations appearing in recent years. For the general study of the king in the liturgy several works are invaluable, among them those of L. Biehl,[49] E. Kantorowicz,[50] H. Hirsch,[51] G. Tellenbach,[52] C. Erdmann,[53] G. Ladner,[54] P. E. Schramm,[55] A. Sprengler.[56]

NOTES

1. Urbanus papa II in *Diplomate ad Hugonem abbatem Clun.*, *anno 1098, Bibliotheca Cluniacensis,* 250.

2. Following de Valous' article on Cluny in *DHGE*, XIII, 40 which places the date of the foundation in 909 rather than, as is customary, in 910 because of a faulty calculation of the indiction.

3. For example, E. Werner, *Die gesellschaftlichen Grundlagen der Klosterreform im 11 Jahrhundert*, (Berlin, 1953).

4. See Addendum.

5. P. Schmitz, *Histoire de l'Ordre de saint Benoît*, (Maredsous, 1948). Translation: *Geschichte des Benediktinerordens*, 3 vols., (Zürich, 1947).

6. F. Heer, *Aufgang Europas*, (Vienna, Zürich, 1949) and E. Rosenstock-Huessy, *Die europäischen Revolutionen*, (Stuttgart and Cologne, 1951). *Out of Revolution*, (Norwich, Vermont, 1964).

7. J. H. Pignot, *Histoire de l'Ordre de Cluny depuis la fondation de l'Abbaye jusqu' à la mort de Pierre le Vénérable, 909-1157*, 3 vols., (Paris, 1868). Mabillon's *Sancti Maioli Elogium* is found in *P.L.* 137, 709-744, his *Sancti Odilonis Elogium* in *P.L.* 142, 831-896.

8. E. Sackur, *Die Cluniacenser in ihrer kirchlichen und allgemeingeschichtlichen Wirksamkeit bis zur Mitte des elften Jahrhunderts*, 2 vols., (Halle a.S., 1892-1894).

9. *Ibid.*, II, 452f.

10. See Appendix III of G. Tellenbach's *Libertas; Kirche und Weltordnung im Zeitalter des Investiturstreites* (Leipzig, 1936) and the bibliographical additions in Appendix V of R. F. Bennett's translation (Oxford, 1959).

11. G. de Valous, *Le monachisme Clunisien des origines au XVe siècle*, 2 vols., (Paris, 1935).

12. *Ibid.*, I, 328, "L'âme de Cluny, on ne saurait trop le répéter, ce fût vraiment la prière liturgique".

13. *Ibid.*, I, 14, "Il n'y a rien en effet de véritablement neuf dans la réforme de Cluny et les mouvements rivaux de Xe siècle, l'essentiel en est constitué par le développement de la pensée de Benoît d'Aniane". Also *ibid.*, 19 and passim.

14. *Ibid.*, II, 12. Also in the same vein Paschal II flattered himself to watch over the monks of Cluny *tamquam oculi sui pupillam custodientes, ibid.*, II, 161.

15. Avoiding the whole question of whether the Gregorian party was influenced by, or responsible to, Cluny in any way, Cluny's mission is reduced to being merely an executor of the uniformity of observance proposed by Benedict of Aniane in 817. Although written for another historical context, the wise warning of Harnack still deserves our attention: "Ist man dazu noch mehr oder weniger gleichgültig in Bezug auf das Alter der Quellen aus denen man schöpft, so entsteht notwendig im besten Fall ein Wirrwarr, im schlimmeren wird durch diese 'Antiquitäten' das, was man erhellen wird, völlig verdunkelt." In *Sitzungsberichte der Preussischen Akademie*, Phil.-hist. Kl. (1926), p. 215, n. 4, hereafter *SBdAkW*.

16. K. Hallinger, *Gorze-Kluny*. Studien zu den monastischen Lebensformen und Gegensätzen im Hochmittelalter, 2 vols., (Rome, 1950-1951). Monastic research owes much to this scholar. However, Harnack's criticism, n. 15 above, is also applicable to this book and the article by the same author, "Neue Fragen der reformgeschichtlichen Forschung," *Archiv für mittelrheinische Kirchengeschichte*, 9, (1957), pp. 19-32.

17. T. Schieffer, "Cluniazenische oder gorzische Reformbewung," *Archiv für mittelrheinische Kirchengeschichte*, 4, (1952), p. 32f. which rightly points out the abandonment of historical presentation by the author in favor of one that limits itself to analysis of factual material in a purely systematic manner based often on overly subtle distinctions.

18. "Gorze und Kluny...sind eigenständig." "Die Allgemeingeltung Klunys wird...um einen entscheidenden Grad herabgemindert." *Gorze-Kluny*, I, 11.

19. G. Tellenbach (ed.) *Neue Forschungen über Cluny und die Cluniacenser*, von Joachim Wollasch, Hans-Erich Mager und Hermann Diener, (Freiburg, 1959), hereafter *NF*.

See also "Zum Wesen der Cluniacenzer," *Saeculum*, 9, (1958), 370-378.

20. *NF*, "Königtum, Adel und Kloster im Berry während das 10. Jahrhunderts," p. 118f.

21. *NF*, "Studien über das Verhältnis der Cluniacenzer zum Eigenkirchenwesen," where it is expressly denied that Cluny is in conflict with the proprietary church system of laymen, p. 207.

22. *NF*, "Das Verhältnis Clunys zu den Bischöfen vor allem in der Zeit seines Abtes Hugo 1049-1109." Also "Das Itinerar des Abtes Hugo von Cluny," p. 394: Hugh did not allow his order to become involved in the Investiture Contest which can be seen in his voyages.

23. M. F. Cucherat, *Cluny au onzième siècle; son influence religieuse, intellectuelle, et politique*, (Autun, 1873). Preferable to the 1854 edition.

24. J. Evans, *Monastic Life at Cluny, 910-1157*, (Oxford, 1931).

25. L. M. Smith, *Cluny in the Eleventh and Twelfth Centuries*, London, 1930. *The Early History of the Monastery of Cluny*, (Oxford, 1920).

26. M. D. Knowles, *The Monastic Order in England*, (Cambridge, 1963).

27. N. Hunt, *Cluny under Saint Hugh, 1049-1109*, (London, 1967).

28. *Millénaire de Cluny*, (Annales de l'Académie de Mâcon ser. 3, XV, 1910).

29. *Spiritualità Cluniacense*, (Convegni del Centro di Studi sulla Spiritualità Medievale, Todi, 1960).

30. *Congrès Scientifique de Cluny 9-11 Juillet 1949 en l'Honneur des Saints Abbés Odon et Odilon*, (published by the Société des Amis de Cluny, Dijon, 1950).

31. "Actes du Colloque International de Moissac, 3-5 mai 1963," in *Annales de Midi*, LXXV, no. 64, (Toulouse, 1963).

32. *I laici nella societas christiana di secoli XI e XIII*, (Settimane internazionale de studio, 3rd, Passo della Mendola, 1965, Milan, 1968).

33. L. J. Ogerdias, *Histoire de S. Mayeul abbé de Cluny*, (Moulins, 1877). Dom A. L'Huillier, *Vie de S. Hugues Abbé de Cluny, 1024-1109*, (Solesmes, 1888).

34. O. Ringholz, O.S.B., *Der heilige Odilo von Cluny*, (Münster, 1885).

35. P. Jardet, *S. Odilon sa vie, son temps, ses oeuvres*, (Lyon, 1898).

36. Dom J. Hourlier, *Saint Odilon Abbé de Cluny*, (Bibliothèque de la Revue d'Histoire Ecclésiastique, Fascicule 40, Louvain, 1964).

37. G. Schreiber, *Gemeinschaften des Mittelalters*, (Regensburg, Münster, 1948). *Kurie und Kloster im 12. Jahrhundert*, 2 vols., (Stuttgart, 1910).

38. Dom P. B. Egger, *Geschichte der Cluniazenser-Klöster in der Westschweiz*, (Freiburger Historische Studien, III, 1907). Although this book is devoted to a study of Cluniac priories in Switzerland, it contains much of wider interest as well.

39. A. Brackmann, *Zur politischen Bedeutung der kluniazensischen Bewegung*, (Darmstadt, 1955). "Die politische Wirkung der kluniazensischen Bewegung," *HZ*, 139, (1929), 34-47, "Die Ursachen der geistigen und politischen Wandlung im 11. Jahrhundert," *HZ*, 149, Heft 2 (1935), 229-239.

40. G. Letonnelier, *L'Abbaye exempte de Cluny et le Saint-Siège*, (Archives de la France Monastique 22, Ligugé and Paris, 1923).

41. J. F. Lemarignier, "L'exemption monastique et les origines de la réforme grégorienne," in *Congrès Scientifique* etc. n. 30. "Structures monastiques et structures politiques dans la France de la fin du Xe siècle et des débuts du XIe siècle," in *Il monachismo nell' alto medioevo e la formazione della civiltà occidentale*, (Settimane di Studio del Centro italiano di studi sull' alto medioevo IV, Spoleto, 1957), 357-400.

42. A. Vermeesch, *Essai sur les origines et la Significa-tion de la Commune dans le Nord de la France (XIe et XIIe siècles)*, (Études présentées à la Commission Internationale pour l'Histoire des Assemblées des Etats, no. 30, Heule UGA, 1966).

43. H. Hoffmann, *Gottesfrieden und Treuga Dei*, (Schrif-ten der Monumenta Germaniae Historica, vol. 20, Stuttgart, 1964).

44. *Ibid.*, p. 167.

45. K. J. Conant, *Cluny, Les Eglises et la Maison du Chef d'Ordre*, (Mâcon, 1968). Publication no. 77 of the Medieval Academy of America.

46. Dom A. Stacpoole, "Hugh of Cluny and the Hilde-brandine Miracle Tradition," *RB*, LXXVII, nos. 3-4 (1961), 341-363. "Hildebrand, Cluny and the Papacy," *Downside Re-view*, LXXXI, (1963), 142-64; 254-72. Also Dom P. S. Schmitt, "Neue und alte Hildebrand-Anekdoten aus den *Dicta Anselmi*," *SG*, 5, 1-18.

47. H. E. Cowdrey, *The Cluniacs and the Gregorian Reform Movement*, (Oxford, 1970).

48. C. J. Bishko, "Liturgical Intercession at Cluny for the King-Emperors of León," *Studia Monastica*, 3, (1961), 53-76.

49. L. Biehl, *Das liturgische Gebet für Kaiser und Reich*, (Goerres-Gesellschaft, Heft 75, Paderborn, 1937).

50. E. Kantorowicz, *The King's Two Bodies*, (Princeton, 1957). *Laudes Regiae: A Study in Liturgical Acclamations and Medieval Ruler Worship*, (Berkeley and Los Angeles, 1946).

51. H. Hirsch, "Der mittelalterliche Kaisergedanke in den liturgischen Gebeten," *MIÖG*, 44, (1936), 1-20.

52. G. Tellenbach, "Römischer und christliche Reichs-gedanke in der Liturgie des frühen Mittelalters," *Sitzungs-berichte der Heidelberger Akademie der Wissenschaften*, 1 Abh. vol. 25, (1934), 4-71.

53. C. Erdmann, "Der Heidenkrieg in der Liturgie und die Kaiserkrönung Ottos I," *MIÖG*, 46, (1932), 129-143. "Das ottonische Reich als Imperium Romanum," *DA*, 6, 412-441.

54. G. Ladner, "The Portraits of Emperors in Southern Italian Exultet Rolls and the Liturgical Commemoration of Emperors," *Speculum*, 17, (1942), 181-200.

55. P. E. Schramm, "Die Krönung in Deutschland bis zum Beginn des salischen Hauses, 1028," *ZRG*, 55, *KA*, 24, (1935), 184-332. Also *Die deutschen Könige und Kaiser in Bildern ihrer Zeit*, (Leipzig, 1928).

56. A. Sprengler, *Gebete für den Herrscher im frühmittelalterlichen Abendland und die verwandten Anschauungen im gleichzeitigen Schrifttum*, (unpublished dissertation, Göttingen, 1950).

2. The Cluniac *Consuetudines*
and
Other Source Documents

Of primary importance among the sources which have escaped destruction are the documents describing the usages,
customs and the monastic discipline in force throughout the
liturgical year. It is to these *consuetudines*, customals,
customaries or consuetudinaries, that one must turn for any
deeper acquaintance with Cluniac norms transmitted by custom
and certified by tradition. They provide a crystallized description of the internal order of Cluniac life, the various
monastic observances and rites, the annual liturgical cycle,
the offices and duties of the monks in accordance with their
responsibility, the election of the abbot, in short the written aspect of the *ordo*, the law of the monastery, animated by
the spirit of the Rule.[1] To guide monks to union with God
by following the *ordo* is the goal of every abbot.[2] Cluny
of course was famous, as Peter Damian tells us, because of
its fidelity to its observances, its charity and the wisdom
of its monastic *consuetudines*.[3] It is in these sources then
that most of what might be called the basis of the constitution of the abbey is to be found.[4] A completely new edition
of these is now in an advanced state of preparation under the
editorship of Dom K. Hallinger.[5] For the time being earlier
editions shall have to suffice.

Dom B. Albers's five volumes make available editions of
the earliest Cluniac customals known to us.[6] The oldest of
these exists in two manuscript copies which are almost identical, one of which, the more ancient, is published as the

Consuetudines Cluniacenses Antiquiores, referred to as BB[1].[7]
This customal appears to date from the reign of St. Majolus
and possibly has precedents in a pre-Cluniac period; however
this speculation is not confirmed by any evidence. Another
Consuetudines Cluniacenses Antiquiores, designated by Albers
as C, is obviously inspired by the same source as BB[1].[8] It
is similar in length and can be dated within the confines
of the period 996-1030, that is, it falls within Odilo's
reign. In view of the doubt concerning the date and origin
of BB[1], C has to be regarded as the oldest Cluniac customal
we possess. Another incomplete customary has been found in
the abbey of St. Emmeram at Ratisbon.[9] However, it has not
been possible to identify the abbot under whose name it is
compiled.[10]

It is the customary C which links BB[1] with the *Liber
Tramitis*, better known as the Farfa Customary, so-called because of its discovery in the Sabine monastery of this name.[11]
Compiled between the years 1042-1049,[12] this customary is far
more explicit in content than these early texts. It owes its
origin to the visit of a disciple of St. Romuald, John by
name, who transcribed the observances practiced there.[13] As
a result they are an authentic version of the tradition observed at the mother abbey during Odilo's reign.[14] This is
the first Cluniac customal which contains detailed descriptions of intercessory prayers for imperial members of the
Cluniac confraternity. Another manuscript of this customary,
found at the monastery of St. Paul of Rome, has been published
by Marquard Herrgott.[15]

The most detailed descriptions of the Cluniac *ordo*
which we possess are those of the eleventh century by Bernard[16] and Ulrich.[17] No satisfactory identification of the
former has been made in view of the frequency with which the

name Bernard appears in Cluniac annals. However, a careful
study has been made of the life of Ulrich of Zell, the youth-
ful friend of William of Hirsau, whose varied travels took
him to the imperial court of Henry III, the monasteries of
St. Emmeram, Cluny, Grüningen and, of course, Zell before he
was canonized shortly after his death in 1093.[18]

There are other customals of Cluniac origin which may
be mentioned here. Herrgott's volume contains the customal
of Hirsau composed by its famous abbot William for the movement which followed Cluniac observances without being dependent upon the mother abbey.[19] The *Consuetudines Fructuarienses* reflect the efforts of St. Majolus' disciple, St.
William of Volpiano, abbot of St. Bénigne of Dijon, founded
circa 1000-1005.[20] Some fifty monasteries established for
men and four for women are certified by Albers's conserva-
tive count.[21] The liturgist Van Dijk has announced the discovery of a Cluniac customary used at St. Benedict's, Polirone (St. Benedict-on-the-Po).[22] However, his article and
that of H. Schwarzmaier[23] indicate that this monastery is
apt to be of borderline interest in a study devoted to the
relationship between Cluny and the emperors. Such a conclusion appears justified with respect to Fruttuaria whose
customary also appears to make no mention of emperors.

We may briefly summarize all of this, as it relates to
our purpose, as follows: of those customals which relate
directly to the practices and observances of the main abbey
itself we possess some early fragments and three customals
of major importance, the *Consuetudines Farfenses* and those
of Bernard and Ulrich. These three in their similarities
and differences indicate that the Cluniac community experi-
enced an organic continuity during its founding period while
seeking a uniformity of observance in its acceptance or rejec-

tion of previous usages.[24] Although a comparative study of
the process of change and selection evidenced in these various renderings and their significance for the eleventh century still awaits the scholar,[25] much concentrated effort to
analyze the content of these documents has been made by
Tomek,[26] de Valous,[27] Hallinger,[28] Hunt[29] and for the older
customals, Albers.[30]

As a consequence of the foregoing, the customaries of
most importance to us in our investigation and those referred
to the most frequently are those composed in the tenth and
eleventh century, particularly the so-called Farfa Customal
and its culminations in the works of Bernard and Ulrich.
With the appearance of these last two, the main canon of
Cluniac observance was fixed, as de Valous indicates, for
all time.[31] The question of which of these is the earlier
is a thorny one still awaiting a definitive study of the manuscripts.[32] As Hallinger sees it, Bernard made two renderings,
the first composed c. 1074, the second c. 1084-1086.[33] It is
the second version which is published in Herrgott. Ulrich
then used the first version of Bernard in answering the appeal
of Hirsau c. 1083.[34] As Bernard points out in his preface,
the increasing number of monks entering the monastery during
the reign of St. Hugh made further codification of the observances a necessity.[35] Also, if Hallinger's dating is correct,
all versions were likely written during the reign of Pope
Gregory VII (1073-1085). Bernard's customal follows the same
general form as that of Farfa. It is written in two parts,
the one dealing with the liturgical cycle, the other with the
customs and usages themselves. Ulrich's work is divided into
three books, the first dealing with the liturgy, the second
devoted to novices, indicating the importance this matter had
assumed, while the last book deals with all manner of subjects,

including the election of the abbots, the duties of the various monastic officials, the making of communion bread and the
usages practiced for the sick and the dying. It should perhaps be pointed out that the customals are not a comprehensive
statement of everything that went on in the monastery, Bernard
makes this clear,[36] but rather a selective choice of Cluny's
adaptation and interpretation of the Benedictine rule. Also
to be emphasized is that for those aspects of Cluniac life
not made sufficiently clear by the customals the abbot's decisions had the effect of legal decrees.[37] The difficulty
of translating living tradition into life is a perennial one.

Of equal, if not greater, importance as regards the customaries would seem to be the need to demarcate the new impulse to monastic life given by Cluny from those of previous
centuries. All too often we read that Cluny did not innovate
in any way, that the essence of its reform is already to be
found in the Rule of St. Benedict of Nursia or other precepts,
particularly those enunciated by St. Benedict of Aniane in
817.[38] Such statements are in contradiction with historical
reality. As Knowles says: "There is no evidence in any of
the sources that the Rule of St. Benedict was used exclusively
in any Roman monastery until after the first visit of St. Odo
in 936."[39] The Benedictines were not an integrated religious
order and the examples which give an idea of the haphazard
and gradual development of the Rule, especially with regard to
its adoption as a code, offer an essential guideline to understanding the change that appeared in the history of monasticism beginning in the tenth century.[40] It is from this period,
and not before, that the great constitutional development of
the monastic orders took place within a little more than two
hundred years from the abbacy of Odilo in 994 to the death of
St. Dominic in 1221.[41] By the time of the death of Majolus

only five houses depended on Cluny; in 1049 when Odilo died
there were about 60, whereas during Hugh's reign there were
said to be 2,000 houses dependent on the mother abbey, certainly 1,000.[42] No previous Benedictine congregation had
ever known, much less conceived of, such an expansion whereby the abbot of Cluny, indeed in actual contradiction to the
obvious intent of the Benedictine Rule, became the overlord
of all Cluniac abbeys and priories. The biting criticism of
Cluny's "kingdom" by Adalbero of Laon[43] reflects the shock
at the extent of a monastic organization founded on the basis
of the new federal and corporative principle. What may be
called the Cluniac pyramid of authority was held together by
the rule of a single abbot, often named by his predecessor,
imposing its customs and observances on those subject to its
independent jurisdiction.[44] However, it cannot be too strongly stated that with the new organizational principle represented by Cluny a great step forward was taken in terms of a
unity extending over a large territory animated by a single
spirit and discipline embodied both in the rule of the abbot
and the monastic discipline described in the customaries.[45]
It is in the light of the refounding of the very idea of
what a monastic community is that Nalgod's observation on
the importance of the customals needs to be understood. He
said that it was from the pinnacle of Cluny that the stream
of regular precepts and monastic discipline became widespread
throughout the countries of the West.[46]

Thanks to the collection of monastic charters which have
withstood the ravages of time[47] there exists a sound basis
for deeper understanding of the bonds, spiritual, economic,
political, between Cluny and dependent houses linked to the
main abbey either by being annexed or as a new foundation.
The names of kings and popes often figure prominently there

as do lesser figures. Another area is marked out for the
scholar by the series of papal bulls and other privileges
granted to Cluny, that of exemptions.[48]

For the *vitae* and other writings of and by the Cluniac
abbots the editions of Migne were used and shall be noted
as part of a fuller analysis of their content that would be
out of place here. There are of course many references to
Cluny in non-Cluniac sources only a minute fraction of which
could be brought to bear on the discussion.

Any quest into the inner workings of Cluniac life, experience and effectiveness must depend on two groups of
sources, as supplements to the customals and those collections of documents already mentioned. These are documentary
sources of the Cluniac liturgy and necrologies containing
obituary notices. In both cases the deficiency of available
manuscripts and documents is extensive. Of what must have
been an extraordinary number of liturgical manuscripts once
extant, only a minute proportion seems to have survived. Dom
P. Schmitz has described the extent of the loss.[49] The
nécrologue historique by the monk Georges Buyrin, reported
by Delisle[50] has been lost although its existence was confirmed as late as 1876.[51] As regards the use and value of
necrologies, their importance is such that they shall have to
be analyzed and appraised separately.

NOTES

1. U. Berlière, *L'ascèse bénédictine des origines à la fin du XIIe siècle*, (Paris, 1927), pp. 11-14.

2. *Ibid.*, p. 14.

3. *Idem.*

4. N. Hunt, *op. cit.*, pp. 30-123.

5. *Corpus Consuetudinum Monasticarum*, ed. Dom K. Hallinger, (Siegburg, 1963f.).

6. *Consuetudines Monasticae*, ed. B. Albers, 5 vols. (Stuttgart, 1900 and Monte Cassino, 1903-12), hereafter referred to as Albers, followed by volume number and page.

7. *Consuetudines Cluniacenses Antiquores*, Albers II, 1-30. See also B. Albers, *Untersuchungen zu den ältesten Mönchsgewohnheiten*. Ein Beitrag zur Benediktiner-Ordensgeschichte des X.-XII. Jahrhunderts, (Veröffentlichungen aus dem Kirchenhistorischen Seminar München. II Reihe, Nr. 8, Munich, 1905), XII-132. *Idem*, "Le plus ancien coutumier de Cluny," *RB*, 20,(1903), pp. 174-184. Also U. Berlière, "Coutumiers monastiques," *RB*, 29, (1912), pp. 357-367. "Les coutumes monastiques," *RB*, 23, (1906), pp. 260-267 and *L'ascèse etc.*, pp. 29f. for the general subject.

8. Albers II, 31-61 and *Untersuchungen*, pp. 44-71.

9. Albers II, 65-116.

10. See Albers's commentary, "Les *Consuetudines Sigiberti abbatis*," *RB*, (1903), 420-433. He finds that the first half of the eleventh century is the earliest date for their composition. Since the observances described indicate only an indirect relationship to Cluny and may possibly be more closely allied to other monastic centers, Albers hints at the possibility that these may be the primitive costumals of Lorraine.

11. *Consuetudines Farfensis*, Albers, I.

24

12. V. Mortet, "Note sur la date de la rédaction des Coutumes de Cluny dites de Farfa," *Millénaire de Cluny* I, 142f. Also A. Wilmart, "Le couvent et la bibliothèque de Cluny vers le milieu de XIe siècle," *RM*, 11, (1921), pp. 123-124, who uses circumstantial evidence to date the customary's composition ca. 1042-1043.

13. I. Schuster, "L'Abbaye de Farfa et sa restauration au XIe siècle," *RB*, 24, (1907), pp. 374-384 and J. Hourlier, "Saint-Odilon, Bâtisseur," *RM*, 51, (1961), pp. 303-324.

14. I. Schuster, *ibid.*, p. 383 and Hourlier, *ibid.*, p. 315.

15. M. Herrgott, *Vetus Disciplina Monastica*, (Paris, 1727), pp. 37-132, hereafter referred to as Herrgott.

16. *Ordo Cluniacensis* in Herrgott, pp. 133-371, hereafter referred to as Ber. followed by book, number, page.

17. *Consuetudines Antiquiores Cluniacenses*, hereafter referred to as Udal. followed by book, chapter, page. *P.L.* 149. Also in Luc d'Achery, *Spicelegium*, vol. 2, (Paris, 1723).

18. E. Hauviller, *Ulrich von Cluny*, (Kirchengeschichtliche Studien III, 3 Heft, Münster i.W., 1896).

19. *S. Wilhelmi Constitutiones Hirsaugienses* in Herrgott, 371-571. It was at this abbot's request that Ulrich composed his own version of the *consuetudines* at Cluny. *P.L.* 149, *Prooemium*, 643-644.

20. Albers IV.

21. *Ibid.*, pp. 263-271.

22. S. J. P. van Dijk, "The Customary of St. Benedict's at Polirone," *Miscellanea Liturgica in honorem Cuniberti Mohlberg*, 2 vols., (Rome, 1949), II, pp. 451-465.

23. "Das Kloster S. Benedetto di Polirone in seiner cluniacensichen Umwelt," *Adel und Kirche* (Eds. K. Schmid und J. Fleckenstein, Freiburg, Basel, Vienna, 1968), pp. 280-294.

24. H. R. Philippeau, "Pour l'histoire de la Coutume de Cluny," *RM*, vol. 44, (1954), pp. 141-151.

25. Above all K. Hallinger, "Kluny's Bräuche zur Zeit Hugos des Grossen (1049-1109)," *ZRG, KA*, 45, (1959), pp. 99-140, which supersedes Wilmart, *DACL*, 3, pt. 2, 2089.

26. E. Tomek, *Studien zur Reform der deutschen Klöster im elften Jahrhundert*. I. Teil: Die Frühreform, (Studien und Mitteilungen aus dem Kirchengeschichtlichen Seminar, Vienna, 1910) whose excellent study is limited by his sole reliance on Ulrich's customary.

27. *Op. cit.*

28. Both *Gorze-Kluny* and "Kluny's Bräuche".

29. *Op. cit.*

30. See note 7 above.

31. Not only were no further Cluniac customaries composed after the eleventh century but seven centuries later, when the congregation, long since outrun by events, tried to reform itself by imposition of a uniform observance, it could imagine no other expedient in its attempt to enforce monastic discipline than to republish the texts of Bernard and Ulrich. G. de Valous, I, 3.

32. K. Hallinger, "Kluny's Bräuche," p. 110f.

33. *Ibid.*, pp. 137-140.

34. *Idem.* For further references on the dates of the various Cluniac consuetudinaries and the usages influenced by them, infra p. 150, n. 8; G. Constable, *op. cit.*, p. 29, n. 25-27, p. 30, n. 30-32.

35. Ber., preface, 134, and Hunt, *op. cit.*, p. 34.

36. *Haec pauca ut memoriae occurrerunt de multis dicta sunt,* Ber. I, 19, 179.

37. *De qua consuetudine dubitatur, quidquid ille inde definierit decretum quasi pro lege tenetur,* Ber. I, 137. See N. Hunt, *op. cit.*, pp. 37-46 and G. Constable, "Monastic Possession of Churches and *'Spiritualia'* in the Age of Reform," pp. 307-308, in *Il Monachesimo e la Riforma Ecclesiastica (1049-1122)*, Mendola, (1968). Constable notes that in the tenth and early eleventh centuries Cluniac charters emphasize that custom (mos) is law, although unwritten.

38. For example Tomek, *Studien*, p. 201, Berlière, "L'ascèse," 29f. and infra n. 13, p. 11.

39. Dom D. Knowles, *From Pachomius to Ignatius: A Study in the Constitutional History of the Religious Orders,* (The Sarum Lectures, 1964-1965, Oxford, 1966), p. 7, n. 3.

40. *Ibid.,* p. 7.

41. *Ibid.,* p. 2.

42. *Ibid.,* p. 11.

43. G. A. Hückel, *Les poèmes satiriques d'Adalberon,* (Bibliothèque de la faculté des lettres de Paris, 13, 1901), p. 129f. Also C. Erdmann, *Die Entstehung des Kreuzzugesgedankens,* (Stuttgart, 1935; reprinted 1955), p. 338f.

44. G. de Valous, *op. cit.,* II, p. 27.

45. "Jamais peut-être la recherche de l'unité dans l'observance ne se manifesta d'une façon plus vive et plus complète qu'aux Xe et XIe siècles." U. Berlière, "Les coutumiers" etc., p. 262.

46. *Vita S. Maioli,* I, c. 10, 661, *Acta SS,* May, II.

47. A. Bruel, *Recueil des chartes de l'abbaye de Cluny,* 6 vols., (Paris, 1876-1903).

48. P. Simon, *Bullarium sacri ordinis cluniacensis,* (Lyons, 1680). The studies of Letonnelier and Lemarignier are devoted to the question of exemptions. However, their conclusions regarding Cluny and the Papacy are too one-sided to be acceptable.

49. P. Schmitz, "La Liturgie de Cluny," *Spiritualità Cluniacense,* pp. 83-99.

50. L. Delisle, *Inventaire des manuscrits de la Bibliothèque Nationale, Fonds de Cluni,* (Paris, 1884), p. 228.

51. Cf. infra, p. 79.

3.   Saecula Tenebrarum

Any deeper appraisal of Cluny and the *Renovatio* of
the Roman Empire in the West must be ever mindful that both
the Burgundian monastery and the renovated *imperium* came to
birth, grew and flourished on historical terrain forbidding
in the extreme. The works of numerous authorities[1] confirm
the truth that more than irony is contained in Baronius'
famous epigram on the century of iron, lead and obscurity.[2]
Both Schnürer and Dawson remind us that it is hardly possible
to exaggerate the confusion and horror which almost smothered
the Church in the late ninth and tenth centuries.[3] As a result of invasion from without all abbeys and towns of the
West from Bordeaux to Hamburg "had been put to the sack and
great tracts of country, especially in the Netherlands and
in northwestern France were converted into desert".[4] All
areas of life were affected in the spiritual breakdown: law,
authority, trade, husbandry in a situation approaching
bellum omnium contra omnes.[5] In many areas monasticism had
died out or disintegrated.[6] Odo of Cluny could find no
cloister where the Benedictine rule was being observed.[7]
Dom J. Leclercq has invoked for us the memory of this "brutal
tormented society" in his commentary on the collection of
tales, deeds and stories contained in the Miracles of St.
Benedict.[8] The chronicle of this name was kept for over
two and a half centuries from the middle of the ninth to the
beginnings of the twelfth centuries by six successive chroni-
clers of the monastery of St. Benoît-sur-Loire. Here a whole
period of Christendom is mirrored as one of crime, violence,
famine, social turbulence, invasion, force.

The most vivid memories of this period remaining in men's minds, perhaps, are those connected with the scandals of the Papacy, particularly in the tenth century. Duchesne's warning that the disastrous state of affairs in Rome only reflected a more widespread evil should be noted.[9] However, it is undeniable that the scandal given by this period of papal rule was also a consequence of their high office. Beginning with John VIII (872-882), the first pope to be assassinated, Duchesne's pages tell the story of papal profligacy which in the long history of the papacy admit of no comparison.[10] The papal office was demeaned for all practical purposes to that of a small territorial bishopric, its dignity the sinecure of various families of the Roman nobility.[11] In the hopeless situation of the Church preceding the advent of Otto I, bishops and abbots, as holders of feudal benefices, came to make hereditary claims on church property and possessions.[12] Inevitably, bishops and metropolitans, horror-struck at the news from Rome, became practically independent to the point of disclaiming obedience to the disgraceful occupants of the Holy See, so unlike their celebrated predecessors were they.[13] At the council of Saint-Basle of Verzy in 991 Arnulf of Orléans expressed the depth of the inner revolt of the French bishops against the disgrace in Rome in a long outcry that begins, *O lugenda Roma*, and which ends *Antichristus est in templo Dei sedens, et se ostendens tamquam sit Deus.*[14] When we compare this pronouncement of 991 with that of the synod of Trosly in 909,[15] we become cogently aware how enormous was the task of Christianization having to include the papacy itself.

We may summarize this aspect of the foregoing by saying that the Roman Church and monastic orders as we conceive of them today did not exist in the tenth century. Even the

oples of the southern Italian peninsula did not seek
idance from Rome: "When the Normans entered Sicily the
pulation was about one third Byzantine, the rest Saracen-
."[16] In language, religion, civilization, the inhabitants
oked either to Byzantium or Cairo.[17] In theory Byzantium
ill considered itself master of the central part of the
ninsula.[18]

Furthermore, it needs to be stressed that Cluny's
pearance on the historical scene took place in a period
d a context of marked political decentralization. At the
ginning of the tenth century there were three Burgundies:[19]
o were the Carolingian successor states known as upper and
wer Burgundy, which formed the kingdom of Burgundy, the
her, the west Frankish dukedom where the mother abbey was
cated. The very name of "Kingdom of Burgundy"--wherein
uny was active--designated a whole series of territories
cking unity or mutual ties over which royal control was
lusory.[20] Its approximate overall area extended from the
stern alps to the Saone and Rhone rivers and from the foot
the Vosges to the Mediterranean gulf of Lyons.[21] At the
ossroads of European life, by nature of the routes crossing
s territories and also the locus of the general language
undary of French and German, Burgundy's distance from Rome
d the power bases of the German emperors was to lend a
rticular stamp to its history.[22] Its composite character,
cking any real cohesion, is a consequence of the disintegra-
ion of the Carolingian inheritance and the competing claims
f its various descendants almost continuously at war.[23]
ring the same period that Burgundy was prey to Saracenic
vasions for eight decades,[24] no royal power was sovereign
ough to supply necessary protection, indeed Thietmar of
rseburg was amazed to find that the king's sustenance was

provided for by bishops elected by nobles, so all-powerful were the latter.[25] The entrance into this "power vacuum" over the succeeding centuries by the Saxon heirs of the Carolingian imperial tradition is clarified by Boehm's analysis and description of imperial interest in Burgundy.[26] The change in epoch was first signalled by the importance of the union linking Italy, Burgundy and Lorraine[27] before Germany, Italy and Burgundy became united under the Salian emperors Conrad II and Henry III.[28]

The most profound and lasting responses to this crisis of a society plagued with disunity on the social, political and religious fronts found near simultaneous expression in the monastery of Cluny and what has come to be called the Holy Roman Empire. The majestic figure of the Holy and Christian Emperor, the embodiment of Right and Justice on earth, as Dante still viewed him some centuries later, joined in a common effort of life's renewal with the monastic cells of sanctity inside the cloister of Cluny where the widespread despair of the times was channeled into a means for the redemption of souls. As is well known, other movements of monastic reform made their influence felt during the same period of Cluny's fame. Less well-known and emphasized is the existence of emperors other than the German.[29] However, it is Cluny and the Empire brought back to life by Otto the Great in 962 which force themselves to the forefront of the historian's consciousness by virtue of their influence and importance.

It is during this varied age of some one and a half centuries, which both monastery and empire helped to form and in whose high dramas they participated fully, that the acme of their power and fame was reached. The first of three extraordinary abbots to rule the destinies of the abbey during

these years, Majolus, was a witness to the reappearance of
the Roman Empire in the West. In 1109 the eighty-five year
old Hugh, the last of the three, had outlived by three years
his godson Henry IV, struck by tragedy and subjected to betrayal by his own son into the loss of the Empire.[30] With
the death of Hugh, too, scandal in the form of his successor,
the abbot Pontius, entered the annals of the abbey indicating
the end of an age.[31] The final nature of the almost simultaneous catastrophes in the destinies of both the monastery
and the imperial house were perhaps not merely coincidental
and indicate that some form of parallel historical evolution
took place. Certain it is, too, that the origins of the
regnum Theotonicum in 911 belied in similar fashion the
future before it, as did the modest beginnings of Cluny two
years previously. The extent to which their destinies were
intertwined is a large subject to which the present study
hopes to contribute.

NOTES

1. General introductions in C. W. Previté-Orton, *The Shorter Cambridge Medieval History*, vol. 1, (Cambridge, 1962), pp. 334f., and C. Dawson, *The Making of Europe*, (Cleveland, 1964) and *The Formation of Christendom*, (New York, 1967). An excellent summary with additional references, L. Zoepf, *Das Heiligen-Leben im 10 Jahrhundert*, (Leipzig and Berlin, 1908), pp. 3ff. A partial bibliography of specific aspects might include: F. Chalandon, *Histoire de la Domination Normande en Italie et en Sicile*, 2 vols., (1907; reprinted New York, 1960), L. White, *Latin Monasticism in Norman Sicily*, (Cambridge, 1938) and *I Normanni e la loro Espansione in Europe nell' Alto Medioevo*, (Centro Italiano di Studi Sull' Alto Medioevo, XVI, Spoleto, 1969). For the crisis in the Church: L. Duchesne, *Les Premiers Temps de l'Etat Pontifical*, (Paris, 1904); A. Poeschl, *Bischofsgut und Mensa Episcopalis*, 3 vols., (Bonn, 1908); J. Leclercq, "Violence and the Devotion to St. Benedict in the Middle Ages," *Downside Review*, vol. 88, (1970), pp. 344-360 and "La crise du monachisme aux XIe et XIIe siècles," *Bulletino dell Istituto storico Italiano per il medioevo a Archivio Muratoriano*, n. 70 (Rome, 1958), pp. 19-41; Dom G. Sitwell, (translator and editor) *St. Odo of Cluny*, (New York, 1958); P. Schmitz, *op. cit.*, I, passim; E. Sackur, *op. cit.*, I, 314f., II, 29, 441f.; A. Hauck, *Kirchengeschichte Deutschlands*, vol. III, 443f.; G. Schnürer, *L'église et la civilisation au moyen âge*, (translated by M. T. Burgard, 3 vols., Paris, 1933-1938). For introductory literature on the End of the World, P. E. Schramm, "Zur Geschichte der Buchmalerei in der Zeit der sächsischen Kaiser," *Jahrbuch für Kunstgeschichte*, vol. I, (1923), p. 77, n. 6.

2. L. Zoepf, *op. cit.*, p. 4.

3. G. Schnürer, *Kirche und Kultur im Mittelalter*, (Paderborn, 1929^2), II, 178f. C. Dawson, *The Making of Europe*, pp. 225-226.

4. C. Dawson, *The Making of Europe*, p. 207.

5. A. Pöschl, *Bischofsgut* etc., III, pp. 1-6.

6. Sackur I, 95ff.

7. J. Evans, *Monastic Life at Cluny*, (London, 1931), 1f. Also G. Sitwell, *op. cit.*

8. "Violence and the Devotion" etc., p. 349.

9. "La même cause produisit un peu partout les mêmes 'fets." "Il n'est que juste....de ne pas se représenter le lieu romain comme plus mauvais que les autres." *Les 'emiers Temps* etc., p. 413, n. 1.

10. Duchesne, *ibid.*, p. 282f.

11. Sackur II, p. 441.

12. Sackur I, p. 314.

13. Sackur II, pp. 442, 29.

14. *MGH*, SS, III, 672. C. Hefele, *Histoire des Con- 'les*, IV, pt. 1, p. 856, n. 2.

15. For Trosly, A. d'Haenens, *Les invasions normandes a Belgique au IXe siècle: Le phenomène et sa repercussion ms l'historiographie médiévale*, (Louvain, 1967), p. 211; efele-Leclercq, IV, pt. 2, p. 722f.; A. Dumas, "L'église de eims au temps des luttes entre Carolingiens et Robertiens 388-1027)," *RHEF*, 30 (1944), pp. 12-13. For St. Basle-de- erzy, *idem*, pp. 32-34. The work of d'Haenens, although onscientious, is not convincing. He seeks to minimize the mportance of the psychological shock of the invasions while t the same time agreeing with the generally accepted view p. 83) that the Normands were dominated by "le goût du sang t de la destruction, avec par moments, de grand déchaîne- ents, un peu fous, où la violence ne connaissait pas de reins" (M. Bloch). He also misunderstands the "rhetoric f lamentations" taken from the Bible as indicating the lack f "un souci d'écrire exactement la réalité", leaving out f account that medieval "reality" was part of a history of alvation. Cf. infra, pp. 47-48, n. 14, n. 16.

16. L. White, *Latin Monasticism*, p. 58.

17. *Ibid.*, p. 38. As late as 1866 there were still 24 asilian monasteries in southern Italy, *ibid.*, p. 46.

18. F. Chalandon, *op. cit.*, I, p. 1f.

19. L. Boehm, *Geschichte Burgunds*, (Stuttgart, 1971), p. 103f. For the links between the Duchy of Burgundy and the Crown and the "Burgundische Heiratspolitik" from 911-1056, see pp. 121-122. Further on the Duchy and its relations with Cluny, J. Richard, *Les ducs de Bourgogne et la formation du duché du XIᵉ siècle*, (Publications de l'Université de Dijon, XII, Paris, 1954).

20. L. Halphen, "The Kingdom of Burgundy" etc., p. 145.

21. F. Baethgen, "Das Köngreich Burgund", p. 25.

22. *Ibid.*, p. 26.

23. *Ibid.*, p. 28f. Also R. Poupardin, *Le Royaume de Bourgogne*, p. ix.

24. Baethgen, *ibid.*, p. 32.

25. R. Poupardin, *op. cit.*, p. 177 and p. xiii.

26. L. Boehm, *ibid.* For the key role of the kingdom of Italy in imperial politics cf. pp. 107-108. Otto I's marriage in 951 to Adelaide, daughter of Rudolph II of Burgundy and Bertha of Swabia, sister of King Conrad of Burgundy, belongs in this context.

27. Boehm, pp. 103-104.

28. Boehm, p. 119f. and Baethgen, *op. cit.*, pp. 32-39, who also stress the importance of Burgundy for imperial policy, culminating in the marriage of Agnes of Aquitaine to Henry III and the difficulty of maintaining it during the struggle around investiture.

29. C. Erdmann, *Forschungen zur politischen Ideenwelt des Frühmittelalters*, (Berlin, 1951).

30. *Epistolae Henrici IV*, p. 122f. and *Vita Heinrici IV imperatoris*, 446f. in *Ausgewählte Quellen zur deutschen Geschichte des Mittelalters*, ed. R. Buchner, vol. 12, (Berlin, 1963).

31. L. Smith, *Cluny in the Eleventh Century* etc., pp. 237f. and L. H. Champly, *Histoire de l'Abbaye de Cluny*, (reprint of edition of 1878, Paris, 1930), pp. 89f. However the circumstances of Pontius' replacement have to be reviewed in the light of the following monographs viz., H. White, "Pontius

of Cluny, The Curia Romana, and The End of Gregorianism in Rome," *Church History*, vol. 27, (1928), pp. 197-219; G. Tellenbach, "La chute de l'abbé Pons de Cluny et sa signification historique," *Annales du Midi*, 76, (1964), pp. 355-362; *idem*, *QFIAB*, vol. 42, (1964), pp. 13-55; Dom A. Wilmart, "Deux pièces relatives à l'abdication de Pons abbé de Cluny en 1122," *RB*, vol. 44, (1932), pp. 351-353. More recently: A. H. Bredero, "Cluny et Cîteaux au XIIe siècle: les origines de la controverse," *Studi Medievali*, (Centro Italiano di Studi sull' Alto Medioevo, Spoleto) III s., XII, Fasc. 1, (1971), pp. 135-175; P. Zerbi, "Intorno allo scisma di Ponzio, abate de Cluny," *Studi storicii in onore di O. Bertolini*, vol. II, Pisa, (1972), pp. 835-891; J. Leclercq, A. H. Bredero, P. Zerbi, "Encore sur Pons de Cluny et Pierre le Vénérable," *Aevum* XLVIII, Fasc. 1-2, (1974), pp. 134-149. The essence of the conflict does not concern so much the abbots but Cluny's independence vis-à-vis the Papacy. In 1173 Cluny turned away again from papal partiality to Frederick I who in 1178 was crowned King of Burgundy in Arles.

CHAPTER I

CLUNY AND THE EMPERORS
IN THE SERVICE OF THE CHURCH

1. Cluny's View of History

When we interrogate the Cluniac sources as to the
response of Monastery and Empire to the despairing circumstances of the tenth and early eleventh centuries, we find
the answer to be irreovocably clear. The deepest concern
of both Cluniac abbots and Roman emperors during the period
964-1109 was to seek models for their conduct in the history
of Christianity.

Odilo introduces his *Vita Maioli* with an extended passage
which presents nothing less than a brief digest of Church history.[1] After a short preface dedicated to his fellow monks
Hugh and Alamanus,[2] Odilo begins his biography by invoking the
early ages of the Church.[3] This beginning is a prelude to a
description of the progress and advance of the Church through
time. For thanks to apostolic priests and illustrious men and
their divine wisdom, knowledge of spiritual things and Holy
Scripture, continuity is maintained with the first martyrs.[4]
Following the completion of their mission and their attainment
of heavenly reward, the divine will called forth the spread of
monastic orders so that the grace previously diffused by the
strong and the illustrious should now be transmitted by the

humble, the innocent and the simple, by which he means of
course the monks.[5] Through them the word of the Lord is
fully realized in answer to the question of the young man
who asked what was necessary for eternal life and was told
to sell all that he had, give it to the poor and he would
have a treasure in heaven. *Et veni sequere me* (Matthew 19,
21).[6] Among the monks the names of the founder Benedict,
his disciple St. Maur, and the monk-pope, Gregory I, bishop
of the apostolic see and author of the patriarch Benedict's
life, are extolled for having so diligently taken this precept to heart and enacted it. Through many spaces of time[7]
this monastic religion reached the height of perfection until
negligence and laxness toward the Rule were to develop in the
course of time and cause decay of monastic life. It is within this historical context of a Christian history that is
placed the actual founding of Cluny itself by the favor of
the most Christian prince William of Aquitaine.[8] A short
commentary on the first three abbots, Berno, Odo, Aymard
follows in the same vein until, at the end of this long introduction, Odilo comes to the subject of his book, Majolus, who
appears as a link in a chain, as one distilling "all that is
good in these just and holy men".[9] Cluny, in brief, viewed its
own history as a part of a continuous ongoing process of the
history of salvation. From this passage of Odilo we acquire
an essential starting point in our appraisal of Cluny and the
Cluniac movement: Cluny through its abbot saw its own role
in a very special sense, as participants in and continuators
of the Christian era. Just as the "illustrious men" of later
centuries established a continuity in time with the apostolic
age, the martyrs and Christ, so is Majolus represented as an
heir whose acts, deeds and words are to be understood as a
continuance of that same story of the progress of the Gospel

nd its precepts through time. Simply expressed, Cluny saw
ts own history as one chapter in the furtherance and con-
inuance of the life of the Church. We are even told by
yrus that Cluny was fulfilling what had existed from the
eginning of the budding Church.[10] This historical orienta-
ion of the monastery imparting to it the sense of its own
niqueness is consistently overlooked. However it is fully
upported by the evidence. Moreover, that Cluny undeviat-
ngly viewed her role within the context of a Christian his-
ory of salvation fulfilling its destiny by assuming differ-
nt forms to surmount the crises of "several spaces of time"
stablishes itself as a first principle for all investiga-
ion of Cluny's role and development. We must remember that
n the year 1000 there was no "history of the world", no
"history of the West", nor of Europe, nor of the nations,
o segmented "religious history" or Church history conceived
n compartmentalized fashion.[11] However, the firm continuity
eveloped within the Christian era and within the Church pro-
ided the only possible historical unity then available to
an. Although the tradition of Rome presented a special
ase, it, too, as we shall see, was rendered potent only by
ssociation with the Church.

Let us now turn to the *vitae* and writings of those three
bbots who together during a century and a half wrote the most
mportant chapter in the monastery's history and seek therein
he answers to two questions. The first asks what these docu-
ents tell us about these men as regards their relationship to
he Church and their life, service and commitment to its teach-
ngs. Our second question inquires as to the relationship of
luny with the Roman emperors as revealed in these same Cluniac
ources.

There exists as yet no acceptable study devoted entirely
to Majolus (964-994). The sources available on his life are
few in number,[12] and we possess little from his own pen.[13]
Also these *vitae* are animated by an underlying motif, ever
present as well in the documents relating to the lives of
Odilo and Hugh. This motif is the *Imitatio Christi* which
cannot be ignored, not only if we are to penetrate to the
center of Cluniac life but to that of the Roman emperors as
well.[14]

As Heer has pointed out, "If we look for the heart of
the Church in the days before it was transformed by the impact of heresy, Islam, and its own reforming movements, we
shall find it in the cloister."[15] Indeed true monks themselves were regarded as living a *vita angelica* in the form
of celestial beings who had taken on flesh.[16] Odo of Cluny
was characterized by an epithet due to Christ, that of a
cornerstone in whom were conjoined for the monk, the two
"walls" of man and angel, *angelicus videlicet et humanus.*[17]

Our three abbots also stand firmly within this tradition.
For Odilo Majolus is a *devotus imitator sanctorum*,[18] a man
through whose signs and miracles in his life it has pleased
God to operate in the world,[19] one who has made paralyzed
and crippled walk, the blind to see, those possessed by
demons to be cleansed.[20] His tomb at Souvigny is the scene
of further miracles and benefits to the human kind too numerous to recount.[21] If Majolus did not raise bodies from the
dead, says Odilo,[22] he did more famous things by which God
achieved miracles. For the soul being more than the body,
rather than to bring the body back to re-encounter dangers
and to submit to the hardships of life, *excellentior est ani-
morum ad vitam aeternam reparatio.* "He brought many men into the ways of life by his example and aroused many from the

death of their souls, the number of which is known to God
alone."[23] Majolus was further described by Odilo as one
who, though very erudite and learned in the Church Fathers,
had preferred to dialectical syllogisms and rhetorical arguments and all the genius of all the philosophers, the example
of apostolic simplicity in accordance with the words of Paul
contained in Phil. 4, 11-13.[24]

The death of this most eminent and truly catholic of
men, *praestantissimo viro et vere catholico*,[25] coming on May
11, the day following the feast of the Ascension, allows
Christ, the conqueror of death, to show him the way.[26] In the
hymns composed by Odilo in his predecessor's memory he is
lamented by both clergy and people alike as Majolus the
Great,[27] he lives in paradise, a messenger of celestial life,
rightly called an angel.[28]

Far more scholarly attention has been given to Odilo and
the remaining Cluniac sources of his life, writings and activity[29] are markedly more extensive than those of Majolus.
While the epithets used to describe him may vary from those
applied to his predecessor, the charismatic character of the
saint is repeatedly stressed by his biographer[30] and those who
comment on his life. Significant in the descriptions of Odilo, as for his fellow abbots, are the repeated references to
the life of Christ which they evoke and, in Odilo's case particularly, his sense of justice. The lengthy comments indicate the standard by which these men were measured, one which
needs to be taken into account in making our own historical
appraisals. Hence we find Peter Damian describing Odilo as
belonging to those of whom it is said: "You are the light of
the world" (Matthew 5, 14).[31] For Jotsald he was the very
embodiment of justice and he went to great pains to illustrate
how Odilo was the prototype of a whole society in the exercise

of this virtue.[32] By Fulbert of Chartres, to whom he addressed
a letter quoting the prophet Daniel's moving words that those
who taught justice to others were like stars in perpetual
eternities,[33] he was called the *archangelus monachorum*.[34]
Like Majolus he is characterized as an angel: *non aliter
quam angelus*.[35] A telling insight into his character is expressed in his own words: *Ego, inquit, magis volo de misericordia misericorditer judicari, quam de crudelitate crudeliter
damnari*.[36] Certain tales of his life such as the story of
his forgiveness towards a thief who stole his horse illustrate
his firm adherence to this precept.[37] Odilo's death is de-
plored by his biographer, in terms that indicate the depth of
the loss not only for the monastery but for society at large.[38]
Jotsald devotes well over half of his *Vita Odilonis* to a re-
counting of the miracles of the saint and his generosity to the
poor which together transmit the overwhelming imprint of a
noble man, both forceful and saintly.[39] The Cluniac abbots
were monks indeed but they were not merely "otherworldly"
types.

The Cluniac sources for the life of St. Hugh[40] cover a
period when the Cluniac congregation reached the pinnacle of
its influence, fame and respect. During the sixty years of
Hugh's leadership of the abbey (1049-1109) the historical
perspective of Church, Empire and society opened to new horizons making it necessary for him to deal with a starkly changed
situation. That the sources are largely reticent about events
external to the monasteries has disappointed many historians.
However, despite the changed historical context which begins to
appear in 1049, the year of Hugh's assumption of office, there
remains no doubt that the parts of Hugh's existence are viewed
in accordance with the same Christian standards established for
the lives of his predecessors. Change on this score is not in

vidence. By Raynald he is called: *O, fidelem Christi
ispensatorem.*[41] The same author also reports that the
pope-to-be, Gregory VII, monk and subdeacon of the Roman
Church, saw Christ the Lord Jesus beside Hugh in chapter.[42]
He was an abbot who caused numbers of young people to enter
the monastery and they considered themselves fortunate to
have such a father.[43] He was referred to as a *medicus
sapiens animarum*, a "wise doctor of souls".[44] His miracu-
lous power to cure various illnesses, to control a storm by
making a sign of the cross, to heal the sick is recounted
by Hildebert.[45] In verse he was praised as *vas templumque
Dei, libamen et hostia Christi.*[46]

The number of these examples in the lives of all three
abbots could be multiplied. However, the principal concern
of the writers of the various *vitae* and related documents
of the Cluniac order was not merely edification, but a re-
affirmation of Odilo's sincere and classic formulation
Salus nostra est Christus,[47] spoken within a history of
salvation unfolding inside the Christian era.

Such a conclusion runs counter to the prevailing view
which dismisses this aspect of the *vitae* as mere hagiography.
However to accept this latter view is to be greatly limited
in one's approach to an understanding of Cluny's role. It
would seem obvious that our starting point should not originate either in a preemptory rejection of nor a casual in-
difference to the *primary* allegiance of the leading representatives of the monastery while ignoring Cluny's own view
of history and place within it. Historians rightly feel that
the validity of miracles reported in the sources goes beyond
the scope of historical inquiry. However, here once again,
Odilo's brief historical sketch stands us in good stead.
We find no mention of miracles there as a basis of faith.

Indeed the abbots were very outspoken on this score. It is
made clear by Hugh that whatever extraordinary powers he
possessed did not come from himself, and his monks discovered
that it was well not to insist on them because of his revul-
sion for superstitious beliefs.[48] Jotsald makes the same
point: "Our virtues demonstrate our degree of perfection,
not our power to work signs and miracles."[49] And the words
of Christ himself are quoted: Do not rejoice that demons are
subjected to you but that your names are written in heaven
(Luke 10, 20).[50] Historians all too often ignore that it is
within this strongly rooted Christian context that Cluny acts
and reacts on the age, not only in a religious sense, but so as
to affect the political, social and economic dimension as well.

Our sources also make it clear that their abbots' faith
was not isolated from the sufferings of the time and environ-
ment. Cluny was surrounded, so to speak, by an atmosphere of
widespread fear, terror and despair. Fear of death, fear of
judgement, fear of demons was widespread.[51] The uncertainty
of life after death was then a frightening experience for
living souls.[52] The abbots of Cluny became justly famous
for their power to respond to these deep fears expressed by
profound concern for the salvation of souls. They showed
"the right way".[53] A story is told of Odilo's being a guest
in a man's house when the host became seized with fear during
the night.[54] By invocation of Odilo's name his prayer was
answered with the onset of happiness and well-being. The
legend of All Souls, of which we shall have more to say later,
represents souls suffering unutterable agonies for their sins
in the midst of flames shooting from the depths of the earth.
The monks of Cluny and their abbots are the enemies of the
demons who hold the souls in their thrall.[55] We are even told
that the Roman popes themselves were prey to these widespread

ears. Benedict VIII found himself to be under judgement after his death, *pro commissis poenale judicium luebat*, and appealed to Odilo's intervention.[56] Stephen IX was so frightened by an evil spirit that he sent for Hugh in order to die *inter sacras abbatis manus*.[57] The sanctity of the abbots, their power to still fear and terror in men's souls is emphasized repeatedly by illustrations of the force of their prayers.[58] Hence Cluny as represented in the unique office of its abbots made manifest a spiritual force of the highest order in society reaching laymen of different ages and sexes, clergy and even popes as the most integral embodiment of Christianity in its time.

NOTES

1. *Vita beati Maioli abbatis, P.L.* 142, 943-947.

2. *P.L.* 142, 943-944. The Hugh referred to is his successor. Alemanus, the claustral prior, belonged to the group who elected him after Odilo's death. See Udal. c. 1, *P.L.* 149, 732.

3. *Post apostolorum et evangelistarum sacrosancta divina et salutaria documenta, ac victoriosissima et invictissima beatorum martyrum gloriosa certamina....praestit divina dignatio Ecclesiae suae nova solatia, luminaria videlicet amore ardentia sermone lucentia, P.L.* 142, 943.

4. *Ibid.,* 945.

5. *Ibid.*

6. The use of Biblical quotation may be easily misunderstood as nothing more than a monastic expression of piety. Nothing is further from the truth and with regard to Cluny especially such an assumption can only lead to misinterpretation. For the following commentary see G. Schreiber, *Kurie und Klöster im 12 Jahrhundert,* (Stuttgart, 1910), I, p. 215f.; W. Jorden, *Das cluniazensische Totengedächtniswesen,* (Münsterische Beiträge zur Theologie, Heft 15, Münster in Westfalen, 1930), p. 48-49, and especially W. Ullmann, "The Bible and Principles of Government" in *La Bibbia Nell' Alto Medioevo,* (Centro Italiano di Studi Sull' Alto Medioevo, Spoleto, 1963), pp. 181-227.

The frequent quotation of Holy Scripture in Cluniac sources, as Schreiber and Jorden rightly tell us (*loc. cit.*), supplies a legal justification of the monastery's actions and commitments. The numerous Biblical references were chosen and applied with great astuteness and should not be interpreted, as is customary, as mere religiosity. Rather in the absence of any universal, objective system of law the Bible provided needed historical continuity and justification for decisions and interpretations of events. A grasp of this point is necessary, not only for reading the Cluniac sources, but

for dealing with all aspects of medieval government and
social order as well. However, the entire area is virgin
territory, yet to be explored, a situation which has called
forth a vigorous cry of dismay from W. Ullmann who protests
the irrelevancy of much medievalistic scholarship which
blithely goes its own aimless way as though such an important lacuna did not exist.

7. *Per plurima spatia temporum*, P.L. 142, 946.

8. *Favente Willelmo Christianissimo Aquitanorum
principe, ibid.*

9. *Ibid.*, 947.

10. *Partibus namque ex diversis ad ejus coenobium
multitudo confluxit innumerabilis: sed nationibus licet
diversi, mente tamen ita erant uniti, ut illud ad litteram
in eis impletum videretur, quod de initio nascentis Ecclesiae
in apostolorum Actibus legitur: Erat illis cor unum et anima
una* (Acts IV, 32). Syrus, *Vita S. Maioli*, P.L., 137, 757.

11. Nineteenth and twentieth century rationalism has
made us forget that, hence it is not surprising that Odilo's
prefatory remarks to his life of St. Majolus have been passed
over. However, the Cluniac view of history is obviously central to understanding the totally different view of the history of the Church contained in the letters of Gregory VII,
e.g. to the Bishop of Metz, E. Caspar, *Das Register Gregors
VII, MGH*, VIII, 547. Gregory also justifies his excommunication of Henry IV by reference to Holy Scripture.

12. Cf. infra p. 46, n. 1, p. 47, n. 10 and p. 26, n.
n. 46.

13. The *Electio S. Odilonis vivente sancto Maiolo*, P.L.
137, 777-780 which indicates the irregular circumstances
surrounding Odilo's election, at least as they pertain to
the Benedictine rule, is signed and assented to by Majolus.
The reason for the unusual proceedings witnessed by King
Rudolph III, high ranking prelates, three counts and two
other abbots is given by Majolus: *ne insolentia nostrae in-
firmitatis ordo deterescat, ibid.*, 778. Majolus was following Aymard's example. See *P.L.* 137, 754-755.

14. The usual criticism of these *vitae* that they were
written for purposes of edification to show that the abbots
were saints, hence lack the solidity of "historical facts",

is short-sided. The lives of the abbots are presented, like
the monastery itself, in terms of their participation in
Church history, a fact of which the historian first needs
to be quite sure in order to evaluate Cluny's history in
other terms. To discount this aspect is to deprive oneself
of an essential element needed for understanding what Cluny
is about. Cf. n. 16 below.

15. F. Heer, *The Medieval World, 1050, 1300*, translated
by Janet Sonderheimer, (New York, 1963), p. 61.

16. K. Hallinger, "Le climat spirituel des premiers
temps de Cluny," *RM*, 46, (1956), p. 127. Indispensable for
dealing with the vocabulary and *vitae* of saints, particularly
as regards great saints, is W. v. d. Steinen, "Heilige als
Hagiographen," *HZ*, 143, (1930), pp. 229-256: Causality does
not interest the hagiographer, only the phenomenon through
which the saint asserts himself. The *causae primae*, which
are the "ursprüngliche" workings of God, are what the saintly
writer is interested in describing about the saint. Unlike
the modern view,which assumes that man lives from birth to
death, the great saint is shown always as being drawn forward from the end by the higher will of God. The assumption
is that his only possible calling must have been working within him long before he knew of it himself. Hence conditionali-
ty ("Bedingtheit") and evolutionary development are lacking
while inner struggles and "historical circumstances" are mentioned only to show that the saint has been chosen by God to
conquer. Further J. Leclercq, "L'Ecriture sainte dans
l'hagiographie monastique du moyen âge," (*La Bibbia*), pp.
103-128. "Lorsqu'il s'agit des saints, la narration devient
une épopée chrétienne...pour les comprendre...on applique à
l'histoire sainte qui se continue en eux la méthode typolo-
gique valable pour l'Ecriture Sainte," p. 111f. This way of
thinking about a man's life makes sense for a redeemed
Christian,as contrasted with those who are only converted,
viz., by one who knew the difference, "Jedermann ist ur-
sprünglich Christ," E. Rosenstock-Huessy, *Soziologie, II,
Die Vollzahl der Zeiten*, (Stuttgart, 1958), pp. 571-572.

17. E. Kantorowicz, *The King's Two Bodies*, (Princeton,
1957), p. 43. Odilo himself said that *duas ad intelligendum
et laudandum se creaturas, angelicam videlicet et humanam,
in primordio Deum fecisse cognoscimus, Sermo de Nativitate
Domini Salvatoris*, P.L. 142, 991.

18. *P.L.* 142, 954. P. Lamma, *Momenti di storiografio
cluniacense*, (Rome, 1961) emphasizes Cluny's pride in the
monastic and spiritual vocation of the *societas*, p. 12f.

19. *P.L.* 142, 955.

20. *P.L.* 142, 959.

21. *P.L.* 142, 959.

22. *P.L.* 142, 956.

23. *P.L.* 142, 956.

24. *P.L.* 142, 954.

25. *P.L.* 142, 951.

26. *P.L.* 142, 958.

27. *In Vigilia Beati Maioli, P.L.* 142, 961, 963.

28. *Coelestis vitae nuntius, recte vocatur angelus, P.L.* 142, 963.

29. The main biography is Jotsald's *Vita Odilonis, P.L.* 142, 897f. Peter Damian's version based on Jotsald is found in *P.L.* 144, 925f. Odilo's Life of Majolus is referred to in n. 1. The best edition of his *Epitaphium* of Adelaide is that by H. Paulhart, *Die Lebensbeschreibung der Kaiserin Adelheid von Abt Odilo von Cluny, (Cluniacensis abbatis Epitaphium domine Adelheide auguste), MIÖG,* (Ergänzungsband XX, Heft 2, 1962), hereafter Paulhart. We also possess some *Epistolae, P.L.* 142, 939f. and his invaluable *Sermones, P.L.* 142, 991-1036. Other source documents of a somewhat disparate character are referred to in appropriate contexts. A detailed list of Odilo's writings is found in J. Hourlier, *Saint Odilon,* pp. 205-210.

30. *P.L.* 142, 900-901.

31. *P.L.* 144, 930. See p. 10, n. 1.

32. *P.L.* 142, 902-903. The contrast with the life of the *saeculum* is unmistakable, all the more so in view of Odilo's social and political activity.

33. *Qui ad justitiam erudiunt multos, sicut stellae in perpetuas aeternitates. P.L.* 142, 939.

34. *P.L.* 142, 906.

35. *P.L.* 142, 902.

36. *P.L.* 142, 903.

37. *P.L.* 142, 918-919.

38. *P.L.* 142, 897. Cf. infra p. 100.

39. *P.L.* 142, 915-940.

40. *Vitae* in *P.L.* 159, 858-927 include *auctore Hildeberto Cenomanensi Episcopo, auctore Raynaldo Abbate Vezeliacensi, auctore Hugone Monacho,* a *Synopsis Vitae Metrica* by Raynald. For Gilo, the longest account, see *Epistola Gilonis de Vita Hugonis Cluniacensis Abbatis* edited in A. L'Huillier *Vie de Saint Hugues,* (Solesmes, 1888), pp. 574-618. An incomplete anonymous excerpt is found in *Bibl. Clun.,* 447-62, part of which is reproduced in *P.L.* 159, 923-928. We also possess a few *epistolae* written by St. Hugh, probably only a portion of the total number actually once in existence, others written to him by various dignitaries, *statutae,* an *Exhortatio* to the nuns of Marcigny, a *Commonitorum* to his successors, again regarding the nuns, an *Imprecatio B. Hugonis.* In addition there is Peter the Venerable's *Quid beatus Hugo narraverit in capitulo vigilia Natalis Domini,* taken from his *Liber Miraculis* I, cap. 15, all in *P.L.* 159, 927-956. Also, the group of anecdotes told by Hugh to Anselm of Canterbury which centers on Hugh and Hildebrand provide sources edited and made available by the Anselmian scholar Dom P. S. Schmitt; see p. 14, n. 46, and the previous reference, English translation and the comments of Dom A. Stacpoole, "Hugh of Cluny and the Hildebrandine Miracle Tradition," *RB,* 77, (1967), pp. 341-363. For studies on St. Hugh himself, see the works of Pignot, p. 10, n. 7, and L'Huillier, *op. cit.,* R. Lehmann, *Forschungen zur Geschichte des Abtes Hugo I von Cluny,* (Phil. Dissertation, Göttingen, 1869) and R. Neumann, *Hugo der heilige Abt von Cluny,* (Frankfort, 1879). On the *vitae* themselves T. Schieffer, "Notice sur les Vies de S. Hugues, Abbé de Cluny," *Le Moyen Age,* VII, (1936), pp. 81-103.

41. *P.L.* 159, 895.

42. *Ibid.*

43. *Ibid.*

44. *Synopsis Vitae Metrica Auctore Raynaldo, P.L.* 159, 907.

45. *P.L.* 159, 873f. See also Gilo's accounts, L'Huillier, *op. cit.*, pp. 371-390.

46. *P.L.* 159, 906.

47. *Sermo de Epiphania, P.L.* 142, 999. *Salus nostra* seems preferable to the *Salus nos* of the text.

48. *Sane tutum minime erat ut ille qui nullam pestem plus perhorrebat quam superstitionem vanamque laudem, de lavacro suarum manuum tale quid deprehenderet. Epistola Gilonis,* L'Huillier, *op. cit.*, p. 595.

49. *Neque enim miracula vel signa nos Deo commendant, sed virtutes operum perfectos esse demonstrant. P.L.* 142, 913.

50. *P.L.* 142, 914.

51. "Die Herzen zerriss nicht nur der Kummer um die Existenz, sondern vornehmlich die Sorge um die ewige Rettung." Sackur II, p. 223.

52. "Ein banges Todeserwarten ist auch in den festen Charaktern." B. Barbetti, "Adalbert von Prag und der Glaube an den Weltuntergang im Jahre 1000," *Archiv für Kulturgeschichte,* vol. 35, (1953), p. 138. Indeed Peter Damian noted that he found Cluny's refectory *nulla superstitione depictim* which Sackur took to mean the absence of ancient fables such as those of Aesop painted on the walls of the other monasteries,such as Fleury. See F. Dressler, *Petrus Damiani, Leben und Werk (Studia Anselmiana,* XXXIV, Rome, 1954) and Sackur II, p. 375-385. However,it would be probably rewarding to investigate this pagan symbolism further.

53. *P.L.* 137, 759.

54. *P.L.* 142, 919.

55. *P.L.* 142, 926-927.

56. *P.L.* 142, 928.

57. *P.L.* 159, 865. Raynald's description is even more explicit: *cum ecce humani generis inimicus, horis quibus vir Dei aberat, obtutibus morientis pontificis se ingerere et horrore sui mentem ejus terrere atque turbare, sed ad viri*

Dei ingressum, fugere, ei quandiu cum eo erat non ultra ap-
parere. P.L. 159, 896.

58. *P.L.* 137, 759; *P.L.* 142, 902, 907, 928; *P.L.* 159,
866.

2. Empire and Monastery *in vinculo pacis*

The next question to be posed is an outgrowth of the
onclusion reached in the first part of this chapter. What
o the Cluniac sources--the same sources which emphasize so
ttentively the Christlike lives of the three saintly abbots
-tell us of the relationships between the Burgundian congre-
ation and the Roman emperors? And secondly, are the conclu-
ions at which we arrive corroborated from the imperial side?
n the interests of clarity a discussion of these questions
s they pertain to the rule of St. Hugh shall best be post-
oned until we are in a position to deal with the changing
istorical situation that appears during his reign.[1] However
f we restrict ourselves to the years 964-1049 we find that
he Cluniac sources remove all doubts as to the close bonds
orged between the monastic movement and the Roman emperors.

We have it on no less an authority than Odilo himself,
nd his complimentary tone is not to be denied, that by
mperors, kings and princes of the world Majolus was called
senior et dominus.[2] He was also honored by popes and truly
vas in his time the leader of monastic religion.[3] Otto I
loved him with his whole heart as did his imperial spouse
Adelaide whose feeling for him was expressed with the most
sincere charity and the most esteemed devotion.[4] The same
is said of their son Otto II, her brother Conrad and his
vife Mathilda. The more often they saw his face the more
lid they grow in their love for him.[5]

Majolus' biographer Syrus tells us that the reputation
of his sanctity having spread far and wide, Otto the Great

(962-973) ardently desired his presence.[6] Then follows a
rather lengthy and significant appraisal of the emperor.
Although he was master of the empire, his devotion to monasteries was great since only by pleasing the highest king could
he hope to hold his empire.[7] Indeed he often lamented the
fact that he had to travel on the precipitous paths of the
world while the monks devoted themselves to God, man's first
and highest duty. Indeed we are told: *verum quidquid incipi-
ebat, efficacia nullo modo Deo auctore carebat* a faith which
his spouse Adelaide shared with him fully.[8] The Christian
tenor of his acts is made fully evident by his attitude towards the poor, the ill and the weak.[9] He is then spoken of
by the Cluniac author in terms similar to those employed to
describe the abbots themselves, all of whom are of noble
birth,[10] all of whom are characterized as men of sanctity.
The emperor Otto, too, is shown to fuse the same qualities
of birth and sanctity. The language used in speaking of him
indicates that he, too, assumes a place inside the Church
which is a special one in view of its Christlike character:
*Gaudebat cum gaudentibus, flebat cum flentibus, spes misero-
rum, solamen lugentium: quo regali nobilis stemmate, eo per
omnia pollebat nobilior sanctitate.*[11] Although both abbot
and emperor are set apart from other fearful and unredeemed
men, including popes, by their sanctity, it is through the
prayers of Majolus, we are told, that the emperor hoped to
be visited by the grace of the divine presence;[12] for not
only did all princes love this abbot, but so trusted was he
that anyone who dealt with the emperor sought him, the most
trusted of councillors, as a mediator.[13] He had already refused a high clerical post in the world, the archbishopric
of Besançon, before entering the Cluniac order.[14] From
Otto II (973-983), scandalized like his father at the con-

dition of the Papacy, he now refused the gift of the papal office though beseeched to do so by the Emperor and his mother.[15]

It should be apparent that during the reign of Majolus, and the evidence for that of his successor Odilo is also telling in this regard, Cluny owed its allegiance to neither pope nor emperor. Majolus' intercessory role in the quarrel between Otto II and his mother Adelaide supplies weighty support for such a conclusion.[16] The Empress Adelaide had been falsely accused at the imperial court, leading to strife with her son and causing her to flee. No one dared to defend her at the court, although some were aware she had been unjustly accused. Yet Majolus not only visited the emperor himself, but he accused him publicly before his court, reminding him of his transitory dignity and the quickness with which he could be reduced to nothing, asking why the emperor had spurned the precepts of truth by not honoring his parents. The humbled caesar deeply moved by the abbot's accusation made peace with his mother which Majolus alone was capable of achieving: *ad matris concordiam convenire nullus audebat.*[17] It should be pointed out that to address the emperor in this fashion was possible only for the highest representative of the living Church both in spirit and in fact. It is because of that kind of spiritual eminence emphasized in Odilo's introduction to the Life of Majolus,[18] which was *recognized* as Christlike by the highest dignitaries in the land that Cluny's abbots came to make such an overwhelming impression on society overall, including the emperor himself. Once this recognition was challenged and lost Cluny's star was sure to wane. But that was still far off. Following his death Majolus could be compared with Moses himself as one glorifying God before kings, expressing in part Cluny's atti-

tude towards kings in Ecclesiasticus 45, 3 and in the passages
taken from the New Testament which follow: "Give to Caesar
what is Caesar's and to God what is God's" (Matthew 22, 21),
as well as St. Peter's precept, "Fear God, honor the king"
(I Peter 2, 17).[19] Hence the links between Cluny and the
Emperors were firmly forged within the Church, but it was the
former who embodied and even spelled out, as we shall see
further, the spiritual ideal for the latter. Majolus' deep
sorrow at the deaths of Otto I and Otto II which he prophesied[20] is also indicative of the spiritual ties between them.

As for Odilo, he was spoken of as being loved and solemn-
ly respected by all, among whom were Pope Benedict VIII,
Robert, king of France, Adelaide, the two imperial Henrys,
Conrad II and the nobility.[21] Indeed we are told that he
was one heart and soul with them.[22] He was completely at
one with the first reform pope Clement II,[23] placed on the
papal throne by Henry III at Sutri, and paid a visit to him
just before his death despite the acute state of his own
health. He certainly welcomed the change of which the Papacy
was so much in need for, like the Emperor, Cluny relied in
great measure on a strong link with apostolic tradition. By
the same token the city of Rome expressed its pleasure that
Odilo visited there so frequently.[24] We are told that all
Italy rejoiced at his presence when through his intercession
with Henry II and Conrad II Pavia was saved from destruction.[25]
The praise of his acts was fulsome for "who would not desire
to have Odilo as a friend and father, like another Solomon,
intercessor with God?"[26] He was the recipient of many precious gifts from emperors, including ecclesiastical vessels,
the regalia of office and the imperial crown itself from
Henry II, all of which he had melted down for the use of the
poor during the many years of misery which weighed on the

land, judging it unworthy to deny such things to the poor of Christ for whom his blood was shed.[27] With the same Henry he celebrated the Feast of the Nativity at Pavia and also in all likelihood the Feast of Easter in the same city following the former's coronation.[28]

In his own writings Odilo's strong spiritual tie with the Holy Roman Emperors is expressed even more forcefully. His funeral orations for Otto I,[29] and Henry II,[30] and the Empress Adelaide,[31] the first two in the form of poems, are revealing. He compares Otto I with David, "that wise Solomon, *amicus pacis*",[32] and Josue, who took the name of Jesus to lead his people into the promised land. It has been Otto's glory to drive out demons and to make conspicuous the triumph of the cross.[33] With the death of him who was lord of Rome, peace vanishes and, the text continues, he is taken up to heaven as a redeemed soul. Yet his pedigree, the stable link with tradition, protects the world which rejoiced when Otto II was born just as there is joy in heaven at the rule of Otto III.[34]

At the death of Henry II he pours out his grief beseeching the prayers of the monks in the lament which begins *Omne quod est plangat, quod posse plangere constat.*[35] It is a lament for one surrounded by the aura of sanctity, an emperor, conquered and unconquered, radiating with the glory of God who goes to his final end so that with the saints he may receive the rewards of life. Like the beloved in the Song of Songs he is commended to Christ.

However, it is in the life of the Empress Adelaide, queen of Otto I, mother of Otto II, the *mater regnorum*[36] that Odilo presented a model of the ideal ruler.[37] Adelaide's life, her pious works, her many sufferings, the miracles associated with her name both in life and death, the frequent referrals

to Holy Scripture to illustrate her virtues, all are meant to
indicate the true embodiment of the Christian life in the
midst of imperial affairs: *Cum igitur summis rei publice
fascibus implicata teneretur, variis miserorum et inopum
anxietatibus subsidia prebere non dedignabatur.*[38]

Hence this life is specifically written, despite Odilo's
feeling that he cannot adequately commemorate her memory by
the written word,[39] so that it may nonetheless resound in the
ears of emperors and queens, and by the example of Adelaide
the *res publica* may benefit. And what is this example and
how is it expressed? The answer is unequivocal: *pauperibus
largienda decernebat aut Dominice crucis vexilla et Christi
evangelia exinde adornari parabat, sedula imitatrix sui exis-
tens Redemptoris, qui cum omnium esset altissimus, humanitatis
abiecta perpeti non est dedignatus.*[40] The empress in fact refers to herself as *Adalheida, servorum Dei ancilla, ex se peccatrix dono Dei imperatrix.*[41] The blend between the monastic
and imperial forms of the *Imitatio Redemptoris* is clearly
marked here. For Odilo Adelaide represents the highest fulfillment of the needs of the Church and the commands of its
founder. So that the reader will not misunderstand his motives, he freely admits that he writes *ad laudem tante virtu-
tis atque nobilitatis*[42] out of love,[43] based on personal experience.[44] The Christian virtues extolled are those of
justice, which we have already encountered in Jotsald's
characterization of Odilo himself, and concern for the poor,[45]
which together repose on faith which, as Paul, who is quoted
often in the text, says, is the foundation of all virtues.
And again in accordance with the virtue in which Odilo saw the
source of monasticism,[46] generosity and magnanimity towards
the poor, he finds in her the embodiment of a faith which like
that of his predecessor Majolus, does not belong to the world.

delaide is at the head of a spiritual army gathered around
er wherever she goes and to them she makes a spiritual gift
n the form of alms to the poor of Christ on the days when
nniversary masses were sung for her dead friends and spiri-
ual associates (*familiares*).[47] Odilo finds in her the
aithful follower of Christ, one who, when the monastery of
t. Martin burned down, gave towards its restoration not
nly a generous amount of money but also, to the honor of
he altar, a part of the imperial cloak of Otto II, recall-
ng the act of St. Martin himself.[48] Accompanying the
aintly gift is a request to pray for her son to him whose
lothes having been appropriated by others, clothed himself
n the poor, namely Christ himself. In view of the strong
piritual bonds uniting them it is possible that the Empress
isited Cluny.[49] Adelaide's gift of the mantle to the poor
ay be considered as the counterpart to Odilo's disposal of
he imperial crown for the same purpose.[50] Monkish renun-
iation and asceticism are seen as the highest form of free-
om from the world, the *saeculum*, both for monastery and em-
ire together, who not only share a common goal in terms of
ustice, but also a single past within the unity of the Church.
delaide's splendor is an expression of her unity with Christ
ossessed only by the saints, as the text makes clear.[51]

Cluny was also united to the Empire during the reign of
Odilo in a common effort to establish peace. The goal of
Odilo's activity was not only peace for his monks but the
penetration of the peace of the monastery into the world.
Already anticipated by his admiration of the empress Adelaide,
the underlying purpose of the abbot's labors is summed up in
the term *tranquillitas universorum*.[52] Odilo himself is characterized by Jotsald as a *fraternae pacis amicus*.[53] The
abbey, too, was an asylum of peace.[54] Odilo, responsible[55]

for introduction of the *Treuga Dei*,[56] ("that heavenly gift of
God's compassion", as Sackur[57] refers to it), restored by his
presence at the councils "the calm of public peace".[58] We
have already noted that Otto the Great had been glorified
as an *amicus pacis* as had Adelaide.[59] We also have a letter
from Odilo written to Henry III informing him of his complete
support of imperial policy regarding spiritual matters. It
is the emperor's obligation, he says, *sicut cum militibus
ordinare militiam, ita cum spiritualibus ecclesiasticum
tractare negotium.*[60] Here, and the abbot's letter refers
in all likelihood to the deposition of three popes at Sutri
in 1046, we find worldly and spiritual duties considered as
one, in accordance with the imperial view that the interests
of the Church and the interests of the Empire together formed
an indissoluble unity.[61]

This unity is reflected in Odilo's sermons, almost totally ignored in Cluniac research, as well as in his other writings. Christ's majesty as King and King of Kings is stressed
by reference to his descent from the seed and house of King
David. Just as the Emperors are compared with the kings of
the Old Testament by use of terms such as *magnitudo, maiesta-
tis* and *gloria* so is Christ's kingship emphasized, especially
in the glory of his resurrection, as the *rex coelorum.*[62] As
Fechter rightly says: "The resurrected Christ was obviously
even more important for him than the son of God become man.
Never does Odilo refer to Christ's becoming man without at
the same time emphasizing that his divine and kingly nature
is not thereby infringed upon."[63] Odilo's conception of the
peacebringer, Christ the king, ruling in heaven, extending his
power to kings (*per me reges regnant*[64]), corresponds to the
earthly image of the Christlike king on earth incarnate in
the peacemaking mission of the imperial leader of a Christian
Empire.

A single vivid illustration from the imperial side[65] shall have to suffice as an example of how these two strands of world and spirit, law and grace, Empire and Church were welded together for the first time in the prototype of an imperial bishop possessing worldly power resulting from his royal birth.[66] In a monograph filled with telling quotes Bruno, Otto I's brother, imperial archbishop *and* archduke, is presented to us as a *filius pacis* in which *pax* is the leitmotif of the entire narration.[67] Only through Bruno is *pacis bonum longe lateque propagatum*[68] and his deeds following his assumption of worldly and spiritual duties have as their goal *pro pace ecclesiarum Dei se ipse impenderit.*[69] We are also told that, drawing on I Peter 2, 9, the unity of *regnum* and *sacerdotium* for the imperial bishops found its clearest expression in the term *regale sacerdotium* spoken by Otto I who saw Bruno's work as his own. Ruotger wishes that one supports the other not only before God but before men: *Opto et cumulate desidero, ut ea nobis sit votorum et oblectamenti summa non tantum coram Deo, sed etiam coram hominibus provideri bona alter utrum ea quae sunt.*[70] Here we discover the conception common to Cluny and the Empire so erroneously presented in the texts as "Church" and "State", as though the Empire were the state relative to the Church. The biblical image of Paul, *coram Deo* ("Church") *coram hominibus* ("State"), however, represents the true situation in which the political and moral goals are fused. Paul's authority was also invoked by Bruno to support the *pax ecclesiae*, which brings about the *salus populi*[71] in such a way that opponents of his Church policy became political enemies.[72] His subordinates are directed to maintain the *unitas spiritus in vinculo pacis* (Letter to the Ephesians 4, 3)[73] so that the maintenance of peace was considered as based on the unity of imperial policy and Church policy.[74]

Hence we may conclude that the common goal of both the Cluniac abbots and the Roman emperors, although differently expressed and manifested, points towards an overall renewal of society concomitant with a renewal of the Church and its peacemaking mission. Peace in Cluniac terms took a spiritual form, concentrated within the cloister walls but effective also by propagation of the spirit of monasticism and its precepts in the world, thanks largely to the esteem and reverence felt for its abbots as leaders of the spiritual army.[75] Peace in terms of the Empire was of course associated with a victorious army whose triumphs in the field had led to the *Renovatio Romani Imperium* in 962 and the firm establishment of the king's household as its basic social unit. On all of this and related aspects there is an extensive literature.[76]

It goes beyond the framework of this study to make more than passing reference to the characteristics of this renewed Empire. It was founded by the Saxon house and its renewal did not relate to the Roman but to the Carolingian epoch.[77] The leading idea of Saxon politics was to restore the imperial dignity of Charlemagne. Since Charlemagne, however, was at the head of an *imperium Christianum*, he, as king and emperor, had a claim over the Church and the most intimate concerns of the Church.[78] He was responsible for calling councils and synods where questions of liturgy, monastic reform, heresy, founding of bishoprics, and similar matters, were dependent on his decision. All we wish to point out here is that the assumption of this Carolingian imperial inheritance by the Saxon kings carried with it as well a responsibility for the renewal of the Church variously expressed as *restitutio, reformatio, reparatio*.[79] Consequently, we find that the Ottonians have unquestioned rights over the Church and Papacy,[80] imperial missionary and synodal activities of Henry II are in succes-

ion to those of Otto III,[81] Conrad's policy is in a direct
line with that of Henry II,[82] while by virtue of his spiri-
ual authority Henry III's power over the Church is well-
nown.[83] The whole task of *renovatio*, renewal, amidst the
arbaric and disintegrating forces of the tenth and early
leventh centuries was therefore viewed by contemporaries
s a part of Church history, that is, animated by a faith
n opposition to its own time.[84]

The additional link with the universal appeal of the
ame Roman helped to serve this purpose. The word by being
dded to the imperial title lifted the church of Rome out
rom its parochialism by welding it to the fortunes of the
eborn Roman Empire embodied in the Roman emperor at its
ead.[85] All Roman emperors therefore are referred to and
ppraised in Christian terms which unite them to the history
f salvation and further the life of the Church. A brief
ummary of some of these imperial names and titles by which
Roman emperors are characterized may serve to illustrate the
oint. Otto I is called *defensor sancti Dei ecclesiae*,[86]
ilator imperii christiani,[87] and *sanctus imperator*[88] whose
rown is the *signum sanctitatis* and the *signum gloriae*,[89]
tto II as *pater pauperum*.[90] Otto III assumes the title
ervus Jesu Christi[91] and *servus apostolorum*,[92] Henry II is
nown as *Apostolus*[93] and becomes a saint of the Church. The
mperor Conrad II asserts his role as *vicarius Christi*,[94]
enry III is addressed as *caput ecclesiae*.[95] Henry IV as
well was similarly addressed, although only by his partisans,
in like manner as "vicar of the Creator", "Your Blessedness",
or, like Christ himself, "my hope".[96]

NOTES

1. See Chapter III.

2. *P.L.* 142, 956.

3. *Ibid.*

4. *Ibid.*

5. *Ibid.*

6. *P.L.* 137, 763.

7. *Ibid.*

8. *Ibid.*

9. *Ibid.* The tradition still applied to the Emperor Henry IV. Cf. L. Bornscheuer, *Miseriae Regum. Untersuchungen zum Krisen- und Todesgedanken in den herrschaftstheologischen Vorstellungen der ottonisch-salischen Zeit,* (Arbeiten zur Frühmittelalterforschung 4), Berlin, (1968), p. 157f.

10. For Majolus' lineage: *P.L.* 137, 745 and *P.L.* 142, 947. Odilo's: *P.L.* 142, 899, and Hugh's: *P.L.* 159, 860. There are also other references to their noble stock which occur.

11. *P.L.* 137, 763.

12. *P.L.* 137, 764.

13. *P.L.* 137, 764. "Diese warme Aufnahme hat Cluny dem deutschen Hofe nicht vergessen", (when later troubles beset the Empire), Tomek, *Studien*, p. 42.

14. *P.L.* 137, 750.

15. *P.L.* 137, 769-770. The manner of his rejection of this offer represents Cluny's attitude at this time toward the Papacy. Quoting St. Paul, Coloss. 2, 8, he expresses his apprehension of being deceived "according to the tradition of

men, according to the elements of the world and not according
to Christ". For Cluny the Papacy belonged to the *mundus* and
for Majolus to become Pope was to make a choice that would
keep him from Christ. He also confessed that he would not
be able to get along with the Romans. Also see Tomek, *op.
cit.*, p. 41f. for Cluny's appearance in Germany via Bertha,
the Burgundian mother of Adelaide, who built Payerne and
staffed it with Cluniac monks. Hence, Cluniac privileges
had to be confirmed by the emperor. Thanks to the bonds
created within the newly founded Empire, as Tomek indicates,
Majolus had become the most respected power of the Church in
the West, a fact not to be overlooked in writing the history
of Cluny.

16. *P.L.* 137, 770-771.

17. *P.L.* 137, 771.

18. *P.L.* 142, 944-945.

19. *P.L.* 142, 957-958. See also Odilo's hymn to Majolus
whom it pleased Christ, *Regibus coram hominumque turmis glori-
ficare.* *P.L.* 142, 964.

20. *P.L.* 137, 771. P. Lamma, *op. cit.*, notes the harmoni-
ous relationships of the imperial house with the monastery,
particularly during the lives of Majolus and Odilo, while view-
ing emperors as laymen.

21. *Quorum omnium amicitus, officus et imperialibus muner-
ibus ita magnificatus est.* *P.L.* 142, 902.

22. *Ibid.* Cf. infra n. 10, p. 47 meaning that the unity
of the early Church in the days of the apostles was restored
in their friendship. Hence Odilo is complimented as one who
did not resist princes or Christian rulers in any way. It is
a typical misunderstanding to consider this relationship as
outside of Church history. Note the latest expression of it,
H. E. Cowdrey, *The Cluniacs and the Gregorian Reform Movement*,
esp. p. 158 for his comments on this passage and emperors.
However, the emperors at this time were not "secular".

23. *Ibid.*, and Sackur II, p. 286f.

24. *P.L.* 142, 902.

25. *Ibid.*

26. *Ibid.*

27. *P.L.* 142, 904.

28. *P.L.* 142, 917f.

29. *P.L.* 142, 967-968.

30. *Ibid.*

31. Paulhart, *op. cit.*

32. *P.L.* 142, 967. Cf. n. 26 above describing Odilo as another Solomon. The Saxon kings are thereby seen as the heirs of the Old Testament *rex-sacerdos* tradition glorified by the Franks who acclaimed Charlemagne as its incarnate representative at the Council of Frankfort in 794. On the disastrous consequences for the Church see my article, "The Western Schism of the Franks and the Filioque," *Journal of Ecclesiastical History*, vol. XXIII, no. 2 (April, 1972), pp. 97-113.

33. *P.L.* 142, 967. Cf. Odilo's *Sermo* VI, *De Resurrectione Domini: Cum ipso igitur mortis auctore hodie mors subacta detruditur, hodie per Christum vita mortalibus redditur. Servitus hodie daemoniaca pellitur, libertas Dominica hodie Christianis conceditur,* P.L. 142, 1007.

34. *P.L.* 142, 968.

35. *P.L.* 142, 967-968.

36. Paulhart, p. 7.

37. L. Bornscheuer, *op. cit.*, pp. 41-59. Also J. Fechter, *Cluny, Adel und Volk*, (dissertation, Tübingen, 1966), p. 7.

38. Paulhart, p. 38.

39. Odilo says that in order to describe the virtues of this woman properly it would be necessary either to recall Cicero the rhetorician from hell or to have Jerome the priest sent down from heaven! Paulhart, p. 28.

40. Paulhart, p. 38.

41. *Ibid.*, p. 42.

42. *Ibid.*, p. 27.

43. *Ibid.*, p. 28.

44. *Ibid.*, pp. 33, 42.

45. Fechter, *op. cit.*, p. 73.

46. *Ibid.*, p. 77.

47. Paulhart, p. 43.

48. *Ibid.*, p. 42.

49. J. Wollasch, "Das Grabkloster der Kaiserin Adelheid in Selz am Rhein," *FM*, 2, (1968), p. 138f. The effect of the miracles occurring at her grave creating a special free status for the monastery, becoming in turn an important center of intercessory prayer acquired by the Cluniacs, is well brought out. During Hugh's abbacy Adelaide was canonized in 1097 by Pope Urban II. Doubt is cast on her visit to Cluny by K. J. Benz, "A propos du dernier voyage de l'impératrice Adélaïde en 999," *RHE*, 67, (1972), pp. 81-91, while the strong links of the Empress with the *societas* are reaffirmed.

50. Cf. infra n. 27, pp. 56-57.

51. Paulhart, p. 44.

52. Fechter, *op. cit.*, p. 73: *Multiplices etiam et diversos labores sustinuit pro pace Ecclesiarum, pro statu locorum, pro utilitate proximorum et propriis periculis quaesivit tranquillitatem universorum.* P.L. 142, 907.

53. *P.L.* 142, 1043.

54. U. Berlière, *L'ordre monastique des origines au XIIe siècle*, (Lille, 1924), p. 256.

55. This political program took as a model the liturgical order of Holy Week. Rosenstock-Huessy, *Die e. Revolutionen*, p. 127.

56. Cf. infra p. 14, n. 43, 44.

57. E. Sackur II, pp. 267-268.

58. H. Hartmann, *Gottesfrieden* etc., pp. 41, 45. Cluny's activity was political, but not in Brackmann's sense, *op. cit.*

59. Cf. infra p. 66, n. 32 and Paulhart, pp. 38-39.

60. E. Sackur, "Ein Schreiben Odilos von Cluni an Heinrich III vom Oktober 1046," *Neues Archiv*, vol. 24, (1899), pp. 734f. There is some disagreement as to whether this letter was addressed to Henry II or Henry III. The adversary positions are listed in H. G. Krause, "Das Papstwahldekret von 1059 und seine Rolle im Investiturstreit," *SG*, 7, (1960), p. 47, n. 60. Tellenbach's reinstatement of the older view, *Church, State* etc., p. 174, seems more persuasive. However, there is no question about Odilo's view of Henry's exalted place in the Church and his action at Sutri in 1046, v.p. 212, n. 1.

61. P. E. Schramm, *Kaiser, Rom, Renovatio*, (Leipzig, Berlin, 1929), I, p. 273 and passim.

62. *P.L.* 142, 993, 994, 998, 999, 1000. Also Fechter, *op. cit.*, p. 78.

63. Fechter, *ibid.*

64. This Biblical verse (Prov. 8, 15) is of course to be found on the imperial crown. The whole passage deserves to be quoted: *Quomodo Christum regum esse credamus, divina auctoritate approbavimus. Ipse enim de se dicit in psalmo: Ego autem constitutus sum rex ab eo,* (Ps. 2, 6), *id est a Deo Patre; et David patriarcha: Deus, judicium tuum regi da* (Ps. 71, 2). *Et quod sit Rex regnum, ipse dicit per Sapientiam: Per me reges regnant, et principes legum jura decernunt.* Psalm 71, seen as a prefiguration of the coming Christ, should be read in its entirety. The high hopes held out for the ruler--justice, peace, eternal life, world-wide rule by a king given the divine gift of justice--are noted in the *Jerome Biblical Commentary* (Englewood Cliffs, N.J., 1968), p. 588. *P.L.* 142, 998.

65. F. Lotter, *Die Vita Bruonis des Ruotger*, (Bonner Historische Forschungen, vol. 9, Bonn, 1958).

66. *Ibid.*, p. 23.

67. *Ibid.*, p. 29f.

68. *Ibid.*, p. 120ff. See Paulhart, p. 27.

69. Lotter, *op. cit.*, p. 57.

70. *Ibid.*, p. 122. The image was taken from St. Paul, (Romans, 12, 17).

71. *Ibid.*, p. 125.

72. *Ibid.*, p. 121.

73. *Ibid.* In a monastic community subject to Cluniac influence the monks within the same confraternity were supposed to find a charitable reception *in vinculo pacis.* Cf. infra p. 82, n. 2.

74. The example of Bruno in no way implies of course that Cluny was at the origin of the imperial peace policy or was unique in her approval of them. Imperial monasteries were naturally identified with the emperor's policy while Bruno seems to have had special ties to Gorze, see Lotter, *op. cit.*, p. 41 and Hallinger, I, p. 180ff.

75. Peter Damian refers to Hugh as *spiritualis militiae lux, P.L.* 144, 925.

76. A very partial list relevant to the present study might include several works already referred to, among them: E. Kantorowicz, C. Erdmann, G. Tellenbach, A. Sprengler. To these one might add: E. Rosenstock-Huessy, *Königshaus und Stämme in Deutschland zwischen 911 und 1250,* (Leipzig, 1914; reprint, Aalen, 1965); R. Holtzmann, *Geschichte der sächsischen Kaiserzeit,* (Munich, 1931, 3rd edition 1955); A. Hauck, *op. cit.*, p. 410ff.; M. Boye, "Die Synoden Deutschlands und Reichsitalien von 922-1059," *ZRG, KA,* vol. 18, (1929), p. 131-284; H. Beumann and H. Büttner, *Das Kaisertum Ottos des Grossen,* (Munich, 1963); H. Bresslau, *Jahrbücher des deutschen Reiches unter Konrad II,* vol. 1, (1879), *Die Werke Wipos,* (3rd edition, Hannover, 1915); H. Mikoletzsky, *Heinrich II und die Kirche,* (Vienna, 1946); T. Schieffer, "Heinrich II und Konrad II," *DA,* vol. 8, (1950), 384-437; E. Steindorff, *Jahrbücher des deutschen Reiches unter Heinrich III,* (Leipzig, 1874-1881); G. Meyer von Knonau, *Jahrbücher des deutschen Reiches unter Heinrich IV und V,* 7 vols., (Leipzig, 1890-1903). Also K. Strecker, *Die Cambridger Lieder,* (*MGH* Carmina cantabrigiensia, Berlin, 1926).

77. Schramm, *op. cit.*, I, pp. 68f.

78. Cf. infra p. 66, n. 32.

79. Schramm, *op. cit.*, I, p. 85.

80. *Ibid.*, p. 273.

81. R. Holtzmann, *op. cit.*, p. 427ff. and E. Tomek, *op. cit.*, pp. 7, 15.

82. T. Schieffer, *op. cit.*

83. Hauck, *loc. cit.*

84. The cynicism of R. S. Lopez, *The Tenth Century, How Dark the Dark Ages?* (New York, 1959) is indicative of what results by lumping everything together in historistic fashion: mere categories of "Gloom", "Bloom", "World", "Work", "Love", "Lore".

85. E. Rosenstock-Huessy, *Out of Revolution*, p. 492f. Also P. E. Schramm, *Kaiser, Rom* etc., I, p. 78f.

86. H. Beumann, *op. cit.*, p. 31.

87. *Ibid.*, p. 43.

88. H. Büttner, *ibid.*, p. 76.

89. *Ibid.*, p. 71.

90. K. Strecker, *op. cit.*, no. 11 the *Modus Ottinc*, p. 35. The entire poem represents the blend between the imperial and Christian traditions, as do many of the others.

91. P. E. Schramm, *ibid.*, I, p. 135f.

92. *Ibid.*, p. 147f.

93. E. Rosenstock-Huessy, *Die europäischen Revolutionen*, pp. 565-566, who points out that the elevation of the emperor to apostolic status goes hand in hand with the uninhibited self-criticism and declarations of guilt in the so-called "apologies" which disappear once the emperor is accused by the Pope Gregory VII of counting for less than the lowest exorcist in the Roman church. Also to be noted is the fact that under Henry II the Frankish creed containing the controversial addition of the "Filioque" was introduced into the Roman mass, ending papal resistance to the obstacle to unity with the Greek church. The special relationship of this emperor to Cluny shall be discussed in the next chapter.

94. T. Schieffer, *op. cit.*, p. 421; also A. Sprengler, *op. cit.*, pp. 121f.

95. Ecbertus abbas, *Ad Heinricum III*, (*MGH, Ep. Sel.*, III, 142).

96. K. Morrison, *Imperial Lives and Letters of the Eleventh Century*, p. 24.

CHAPTER II

THE SANCTUS IMPERATOR
AND THE CLUNIAC CONFRATERNITAS

1. The Uniqueness of the
Cluniac Confraternitas

Two questions seldom posed in the extensive literature need to be faced. What was the experiential driving force of the Cluniac movement which allowed it to penetrate in historical fashion the minds, hearts, actions of its contemporaries from all walks of life? And of equal importance, as a corollary to this question, we want to know what form, or forms, this inspiration took so that we may evaluate them historically in terms of the monastery's importance, influence, relationships, and effectiveness in the world. Some knowledge of the inner workings of the confraternity, to the extent that we are capable of uncovering them and illustrating them for a specific case, may be of assistance here.

Ulrich has described for us the great appeal of the Cluniac *societas* or *confraternitas* to those outside the monastery. In the very last passage in his book he tells us that not only congregations of monks but of clerics desired to become members of the Cluniac fraternity.[1] In addition, we are told, many Christians rich and poor came to the chapter to seek entrance into this community. Their request accepted, they then took part in all the good works accomplished either by prayers or alms, not only at Cluny but in all the monasteries subject to her jurisdiction.[2] Then follows mention of the psalms and prayers said for the living and the dead as part of the liturgical day. Also four times a year there was a special commemoration of the dead with ceremonies equivalent to those for an absent monk dying away from Cluny.[3] In what then, did this confraternity consist which made such an overwhelming appeal? What was its overall significance and the source of its success? What are the origins of such an association[4] and how was its Cluniac expression distinct from others, if at all?

The terms *confraternitas* or *fraternitas*, the latter having more common usage at Cluny, are etymologically rooted in the word *frater*, brother, and hence carry with them connotations of a spiritual union in evidence since antiquity.[5] Christianity from the beginning extended the meaning of this word by the command of its founder to treat all men as brothers (Matt. 23, 8) which was followed not only in an individualistic sense but as part of the like-minded community formed by the mystical body of Christ. Within this community of the faithful brotherhood came to be expressed in the profound conception of spiritual aid or assistance (*suffragium*) offered in the forms of prayers and good works during life and after death. Herein lie the origins of what came to be called confraternities, communities of both the living and the dead united by sacrificial acts and prayers of intercession allowing all members to share in their spiritual benefits. It is above all in monastic communities that formal spiritual bonds between monks and lay benefactors came into existence by the ceremony of acceptance into a confraternity.[6] By entrance into such a society laymen and clerics were given the opportunity to share the life of the monastic community in

a particular way. Thanks to their commitment they were remembered in the prayers of the monks and in their good works,
primary among which was almsgiving, hence in a position to
receive spiritual benefits which the monks hoped to obtain
for them.[7] By becoming a member of the spiritual family,
the members became known as *familiares* by which term they
are referred to in the documents.

It is to designate members of this spiritual family
uniting the living and the dead that memorial books[8] and
necrologies[9] come into existence. Molinier's historical
survey which we briefly summarize here shows that both of
these have a common source and inspiration in the desire
of the Church to retain the memory of those who had served
her faithfully.[10] Of central importance in this connection
during the early history of the Church are the diptychs con-
sisting of various kinds and used for various purposes.[11]
Ecclesiastical diptychs are of particular interest to us
because of their use in the first centuries as official tablets from which one read during the mass. They listed the
names of those both living and dead, including the names of
martyrs, saints and those who had died in the orthodox faith,
certifying in this manner the close bonds uniting the faithful, living and dead, while extending particular reverence to
the dead.[12] Since the honor of being placed on these lists
was reserved to the orthodox alone, the inscription of one's
name on the diptychs was an affirmation of orthodoxy.[13]

These ecclesiastical diptychs lent themselves to a tri-
partite division: diptychs of bishops, diptychs of the living,
diptychs of the dead.[14] Diptychs of the living listed the
names of the Pope, the emperor, the patriarch, members of the
imperial family, the *offerentes*, those who brought bread and
wine (oblations) to the priest, and anyone whom the celebrant

might deem appropriate. Another category of diptychs was confined solely to bishops. Originally, only the names of bishops
whose faithful lives had shown them to be exemplary in the
service of the Church were inscribed on these sacred tablets.
It should be noted that their remembrance did not consist in
having prayers said for them by the Church since having reached
the beatific state they no longer had need of prayers by the
living. On the contrary they were asked to serve as inter-
cessors with God by those whom they had served so well as
pastors, asking Him to accept the prayers and offerings of
the faithful still living. Thus did they enter the canon of
the mass, whence the derivation of the word canonize.[15] It
is not difficult to understand why it is from these early
episcopal diptychs, unlike those later lists which contain
the names of all bishops indiscriminately, that martyrologies
originate. Martyrologies which supply the calendar feast days
of martyrs for the practical use of individual churches also
provide witness to the perpetuity of orthodox faith.

Memorial books and necrologies are in turn an outgrowth
of the spiritual community, created by prayer and expressed
liturgically, although the differences between them are significant.[16] Thanks to the evidence contained in these largely
unexploited sources[17] we are able to obtain a penetrating
cross-sectional view of particular monastic social structures
and organization specifically as they relate to the orientation
of the monastery in its relationship with friends and relatives
as well as prelates, kings and emperors.

Memorial books, *libri memoriales*, or *libri vitae*, contain
the names of those to be remembered in life and in death and
were therefore placed on the altar so that the names could be
read out during the liturgical services.[18] By the inscription
of his name in such a book the fraternal associate was certain

of remembrance during hourly prayers and during the mass, which is prayer, in the hope that by means of this inter- cession in his behalf he would be entered in the book of life as described in Phillipians 4, 3.[19] Not only was the person remembered in that particular monastery where he had entered his name,but also in all monasteries united with it in a bond of confraternity. Consequently,by means of these memorial books one's name was assured of widespread dissemin- ation in the prayers of monks. This form of remembrance reached its height during the Carolingian period where the monastery of Reichenau stands out as the prime example. Some 40,000 names of those for whom the monks prayed have been counted in its memorial books.[20] At first these lists were recited individually during the daily liturgical ser- vices; however once the names to be remembered had reached unmanageable proportions, the shortcomings of this method of remembrance became obvious and a general summary refer- ence had to suffice.[21] Necrologies were to offer a remedy.[22] It is this form of remembrance contained in the obituary notice which was to attain its highest development at Cluny.

Necrologies, *liber obituum, liber defunctorum, necrolo- gium, obituarius,* and often, *martyrologium,*[23] (the last most likely because lists of the faithful dead were read along with lists of the martyrs) are lists of the dead presented in calendrical form which contain the names of the deceased on given days of the month. On this day masses were said in their memory. The Christian having replaced the pagan birth- day with the day of death, as the Pseudo-Ambrosius reports,[24] this day on which the names of the dead were inscribed in the calendar was their *dies natalis,* their day of birth into eternal life. Unlike the lists contained in the ancient ec- clesiastical diptychs and *libri memoriales,* obituaries offered

the advantage of having the members' names appear but once
during the liturgical year, marking the day he died. At the
same time it became possible once again to name each of the
dead individually since in a necrology containing 10,000
entries no calendar day would contain more than 50 or 60
names.[25]   As a consequence the names of the spiritual associates formed by members of a confraternity (*societas*) and
its principal benefactors, as listed in the necrological
calendar by day and month, became subject to precise determination.   In addition to the name of the deceased we are
informed by a brief designation as to his role or office in
life.   It deserves to be pointed out that there were really
no necrologies before the Carolingian period, that is, lists
of the dead in the form of a calendar.[26]   The introduction of
such lists coincides with the increase of spiritual associations in the form of confraternities between different monasteries as well as between abbeys and lay people with the result that the number of people benefiting from prayers came
to increase significantly.   In the ninth century the utility
of obituary lists came to be recognized: the most ancient
one in France (858-869) is joined, along with the monastic
rule, by Usuard to his famous martyrology.[27]

Since the obituary lists contain the names not only of
the actual members of the congregation, but the names of members of associated congregations, it was essential to establish some means of communication between the separated monasteries, hence the need for the "rouleaux des morts".[28]   These
circular letters were known as *breve mortuorum, encyclica,
brevia*, and were transmitted to monastic affiliates by a monk
especially appointed for this purpose, known as a *rotuliger*
or *brevetarius*.[29]   The recipients of these announcements transcribed the contents in turn in their necrologies, that is, the

name and the deceased's office or rank under the appropriate
day and month. Often a reply (*titulus*) was added to the
rotuli sometimes in verse, promising prayers and asking others
in return for their own dead. In this manner the cult for the
dead found extension outside the individual monastery. Most
of these *rotuli* are lost, yet we may be confident that the information contained on those we have is correct. The unique
character and quantity of such obituary lists for measuring
Cluny's effectiveness and influence in its prayers for the
dead with its resulting social and economic consequences has
been insisted upon.[30] One major hindrance towards proceeding
in that direction has been the loss of the necrology of the
mother abbey. That some such list had been compiled seems to
be indicated by a reference in 1876 contained in Abbé L. J.
Ogerdias' *Histoire de Saint Mayol.*[31] There we find an extract
from the *Necrologium historicum Cluniacense* by Georges de
Buren (Buyrin) in the form of a certified copy signed and
countersigned by a librarian of the library of Cluny and the
mayor of the town. However the brilliant suggestion of A.
Molinier, made decades ago, has led to a line of thinking
which allows a partial reconstruction of the original Cluniac
obituary list.[32] In view of the filiation principle so
strongly emphasized by Cluny, Molinier proposed that the
various Cluniac necrologies which we possess must refer to
an original source at Cluny itself. Since the names and dates
contained in the Cluniac necrologies of S. Martin-des-Champs,[33]
Notre-Dame de Longpont,[34] and S. Martial de Limoges[35] so frequently coincide it would be possible by means of a comparative
study, he thought, to arrive at a partial reconstruction of the
original and more comprehensive model retained at the mother
abbey. Two other Cluniac necrologies may now be added to the
three listed above. The lesser of these in length comes from

the Cluniac dependency of Moissac and is still in manuscript form.[36] Of greatest importance of all these, however, at least as far as completeness is concerned, is the necrological source published at the beginning of the century and thought to be the necrology of a small Swiss priory.[37] Recent research however has shown that this huge necrology--it contains some 10,000 names and is the largest that we possess from the entire medieval period--was composed at Marcigny-sur-Loire, the Cluniac nunnery with which Cluny was intimately bound in spiritual association.[38] The necrology was composed near the beginning of the twelfth century[39] and it is this list which provides the most complete single reference we have as to what the original necrology of Cluny was like, since the latter provided the model. It is these five French necrologies, only that of Marcigny having been fully edited and published, which comprehend the totality of available Cluniac obituary lists.[40] None have been found within the limits of the medieval German empire while the monastic libraries of England, Spain and Italy still have to be searched to see if they contain such Cluniac registers of the dead.[41] Partial though these sources may be, Wollasch has shown that the Cluniac confraternity was unique.[42]

A consequence of the proper use and understanding of these sources is the possibility now present of obtaining an answer to the question: Who were the Cluniacs?[43] Questions regarding number and family background of the Cluniac monks themselves as well as the identification of outstanding personages including popes, abbots, archbishops whose names are synonymous with medieval history can often find their answers in these lists. They obviously form an essential part of our basic understanding of who belonged to the Cluniac confraternity either as monks or *familiares*. Certainly they provide

the evidence that in extent and intensity the Cluniac confraternity had no equal. It represented a single unity flood-
ing the areas of its influence with its prayers and remem-
brances and masses for the dead. The essential monastic and
spiritual character of the Cluniac movement is revealed in
these sources, a conclusion reinforced by other documents of
the abbey. They also reveal a consciousness of oneness and
community independent of papal and imperial control, whose
social and economic effects on a society basically disunited
are incalculable.[44] It should not be forgotten that every
mention of a name in the necrology was accompanied by feeding one of the poor with portions of bread and wine daily
available to monks known as *praebenda*.[45] Hence, the Cluniac
confraternity played a unique economic and social role as an
aspect of its communion with the dead, growing with steadily
increasing strength throughout the entire eleventh century.

However, before utilizing the obituary notices for our
own study we wish to add to our knowledge of the *societas*
and identify its liturgical aspects, so powerful in uniting
the living and the dead, the poor and the rich, the high and
the low. A closing remark for the moment on obituaries may
assist us in our attempt. As has been pointed out, the
raison d'être of the obituary notice postulates and presupposes the efficacy of prayers for the dead and the living.
This faith has as its corollary a belief in the existence of
purgatory, the intermediate state between heaven and hell.
In order for prayers to benefit the souls of the dead they
must have neither reached the beatific state nor at the same
time be condemned to the eternal pains of hell.[46] The feast
of All Souls was to invoke the state of purgatory as never
before.

NOTES

1. *Udal.* III, c. 33, *P.L.* 149, 777-778.

2. *Ibid.,* 777. U. Berlière, "Les fraternités monastiques," p. 18, says that a member "prend place dans la communauté, oú il trouve porte ouverte, logis, nourriture, toute charité *in vinculo pacis*".

3. *Ibid.,* 778.

4. One pioneering work is still a basic text: A. Ebner, *Die klösterlichen Gebetsverbrüderungen bis zum Ausgang des karolingischen Zeitalters,* (Regensburg, 1890). Also on the general topic from an earlier period, U. Berlière, "Les fraternités monastiques et leur rôle juridique," *Mémoires de l'Académie Royale de Belgique,* (Classe des Lettres et des Sciences Morales et Politiques, sér. 2, v. 11, fasc. 3), pp. 1-26, and "Les confraternités monastiques au Moyen-Âge," *Revue liturgique et monastique,* vol. 11, (1925/1926), pp. 134-142. E. Bishop, *Liturgica Historica,* (Oxford, 1918), pp. 349ff. and "Some Ancient Benedictine Confraternity Books," *Downside Review,* vol. 4, (1885), pp. 2-14. G. Zappert, "Ueber sogenannte Verbrüderungsbücher und Nekrologien im Mittelalter," *SBdAkW,* Phil-Hist Classe, X, (1853). More recently, the invaluable monographs, K. Schmid and J. Wollasch, "Die Gemeinschaft der Lebenden und Verstorbenen in Zeugnissen des Mittelalters," *FS,* 1, (1967), pp. 365-405 and *"Societas et Fraternitas:* Begründung eines kommentierten Quellenwerkes zur Erforschung der Personen und Personengruppen des Mittelalters," *FS,* 9, (1975), pp. 1-48. Also J. Wollasch, "Gemeinschaftsbewusstsein und soziale Leistung," *idem,* pp. 268-286. G. Tellenbach, "Liturgische Gedenkbucher als historische Quellen," (Mélanges Eugène Tisserant, 5, *Studi e Testi,* vol. 235, 1964), pp. 389-399. O. Mitis, "Bermerkungen zu den Verbrüderungsbüchern und über deren Wert," *Zeitschrift für schweizerische Kirchengeschichte,* vol. 43, (1949), pp. 28-42. E. Hlawitschka, "Gebetsverbrüderung," (*LTK,* 4, 1960). R. H. Connolly, "Liturgical Prayers of Intercession," *Journal of Theological Studies,* vol. 21, (1920). G. Schreiber, "Kirchliches Abgabenwesen an französischen Eigenkirchen aus Anlass von Ordalien," *ZRG, KA,* 5, (1915), p. 435f. M. Heimbucher, *Die Orden und Kongregationen*

der katholischen Kirche, vol. I, (Paderborn, 1927), pp. 236ff.
D. Knowles, *The Monastic Order in England,* pp. 472-479. J.
Duhr, "La confrérie dans la vie de l'Eglise," *RHE,* 35, pt. 1,
(1939), pp. 437-478.

5. A. Ebner, *op. cit.,* pp. 5-7f. for the origins. The
terms *societas* or *societas fraterna* were also frequently employed to express the same idea and often *societas et fraternitas* reinforce one another. Cf. Wollasch and Schmid,
"Societas et Fraternitas," *loc. cit.,* p. 2f. and Duhr, *loc.
cit.,* p. 440.

6. An example of the form this took is given in a document printed by B. Egger, *op. cit.,* p. 251.

7. Udal., *loc. cit.* The Orient was not favorable to the
development of this Western phenomenon which sought spiritual
sustenance for the living and remembrance of them after death.
J. Duhr, *loc. cit.,* p. 440.

8. See n. 4.

9. The classic work is A. Molinier, *Les obituaires
français au moyen-âge,* (Paris, 1890), although there exist
many special studies. Thanks to K. Hallinger the entire field
of research in obituaries was given new life, *Gorze-Cluny,* I,
p. 26f. With respect to Cluniac necrologies the works of J.
Wollasch are indispensable, including *art. cit.,* n. 4 above,
"Ein cluniacensisches Totenbuch aus der Zeit Abt Hugos von
Cluny," *FS,* 1, (1967), pp. 406-443; "Qu'a signifié Cluny pour
l'abbaye de Moissac?", *Annales du Midi,* vol. 75, (1963), pp.
345-352; "Gerard von Brogne im Reformmönchtum," *RB,* 70, (1960),
pp. 224-231; "Die Wahl des Papstes Nicholas II," *Adel und
Kirche* (ed. K. Schmid and J. Fleckenstein), (Freiburg, 1968),
pp. 205-218. Also W. Jorden, *op. cit.,* and H. E. J. Cowdrey,
"Unions and Confraternity with Cluny," *Journal of Ecclesiastical History,* vol. 16, (1965), pp. 152-162, which does not
utilize Cluniac necrological sources. These references are
of course complementary to those contained in n. 4. Recently
announced for publication in *FM,* vol. 10, (1976) and vol. 11,
(1977), J. Mehne, "Eine Totenliste aus S. Martin-des-Champs"
and "Cluniacenserbischöfe".

10. A. Molinier, *op. cit.,* p. 1ff.

11. Molinier's reference for diptychs, Gori's *Thesaurus,*
is the source of his analysis.

12. Molinier, *op. cit.*, p. 4f.

13. *Ibid.*

14. *Ibid.*, p. 7.

15. *Ibid.*

16. K. Schmid and J. Wollasch, *op. cit.*, p. 365f.

17. "Only a very few scholars have been conscious that the endless lists of benefactors in the memorial books are comparable in their importance to thousands of source documents." O. Mitis, *op. cit.*, p. 29.

18. K. Schmid, "Probleme der Erforschung Frühmittelalterliche Gedenkbücher," p. 366 in "Die Gemeinschaft" etc., *loc. cit.*, which contains the best study of confraternities during the Carolingian period.

19. G. Zappert, *op. cit.*, pp. 440-441. Also K. Schmid, *ibid.*, p. 367.

20. K. Schmid, *ibid.*, p. 373.

21. *Ibid.*, p. 368.

22. *Ibid.*

23. *New Catholic Encyclopedia*, vol. 10, p. 296, and articles "Obituaire," vol. 12, (1935), 1834-1857, and "Mort," vol. 12, (1935), 44-49, in *DACL*.

24. E. Freistedt, *Altchristliche Totengedächtnistage und ihre Beziehung zum Jenseitsglauben und Totenkultus der Antike*, (Münster i.W., 1928), p. 38. Freistedt, having seen that the term *dies depositio* was called *dies natalis* for the reason indicated, asks further what the derivation of the word *depositio* might be. The earliest text that he quotes is taken from Albers, *CF*, 193, which describes the procedure followed for a dying Cluniac monk. He is laid out *in cinere et cilicio* because only in this manner is the son of a Christian allowed to die following the example of many saints, pp. 39-40. This insistence on a form of Christian burial based on a sure, unquestioned faith in the resurrected soul was probably necessary to counteract the tribal cults and widespread superstitions regarding death so prevalent in the tenth century. See infra, n. 48, p. 51. The twentieth century also has its difficulties in

this area with a different form of superstition, J. Mitford, *The American Way of Death*, (New York, 1963).

25. J. Wollasch, "Die Überlieferung cluniacensischen Totengedächtnisses," pt. 2 of "Die Gemeinschaft" etc., *loc. cit.*, p. 400.

26. A. Molinier, *op. cit.*, p. 21f.

27. *Ibid.*

28. On this subject, L. Delisle, *Rouleaux des morts du IXe au XVe siècle*, (Société de l'Histoire de France, Paris, 1866), *idem, Rouleau mortuaire du b. Vital*, (Paris, 1909) and "Des monuments paléographiques concernant l'usage de prier pour les morts," *Bibliothèque de l'Ecole des Chartes*, 2e série, vol. 3, (1846).

29. L. Delisle, "Des monuments paléographiques" etc., p. 371 and A. Molinier, *op. cit.*, pp. 42-43. Also L. Delisle, *Rouleaux des Morts du IXe au XVe siècle*, p. 1.

30. W. Jorden, *op. cit.*

31. *Op. cit.*, pp. 355-356.

32. A. Molinier, *op. cit.*, p. 233f.

33. A. Molinier, *Obituaires de la Province de Sens*, (Recueil des Historiens de la France, vol. 1, Paris, 1902), pp. 419f.

34. *Ibid.*, pp. 519ff.

35. E. Molinier, *Documents historiques bas-latins, provençaux et francais concernant principalement la Marche et le Limousin*, vol. 1, (Limoges, 1883), pp. 1f.

36. See n. 9, *Annales du Midi, loc. cit.*

37. G. Schnürer, *Das Necrologium des Clunicenser-Priorates Münchenwiler*, (Collectanea Friburgensia, NF, X, 1909).

38. J. Wollasch, "Ein cluniacensische Totenbuch" etc., *op. cit.*, n. 9, hereafter Wollasch, *MN (Marcigny Necrology)*.

39. G. Schnürer, *Das Necrologium* etc., p. xxv.

40. The necrological fragment published in Sackur I, pp. 383-386 is an excerpt from the Marcigny list. It is also incorrectly entitled. See Schnürer's comments, *Das Necrologium*, Vorwort. Cf. now Mehne's forthcoming "Eine Totenliste" etc.

41. Wollasch, *MN*, p. 397.

42. In brief: in spite of the loss of Cluny's necrology the coincidence of names in those of its dependencies brings us far closer to a reconstitution of the source than is possible for any other monastic movement, viz. Hirsau or Gorze, *ibid.*, p. 399.

43. *Ibid.*, p. 397.

44. W. Jorden, "Das Totengedächtniswesen," pp. 20-69.

45. J. Wollasch, *MN*, p. 399. According to his best estimate, "Gemeinschaftsbewusstsein" etc., p. 281, n. 4, Cluny, with 300 monks before the middle of the twelfth century, fed 10,000 poor in memory of the 10,000 Cluniac dead, i.e. the monastery was the metropolis of the West. Kindly refer to pp. 88, n. 7, 94, n. 16.

46. A. Molinier, *Les obituaires français*, p. 1.

2. Cluny's Response to the
Saecula Tenebrarum

(a) Liturgical Economics at Cluny

It is at Cluny that the historical currents distilled
in necrologies, customals, *rotuli mortuorum,* and the prayers
of affiliated monasteries concentrate themselves as "ein
gewaltiger Drang....die Seelenpflege nach dem Tode einem
Mönchtum anzuvertrauen das mit Cluny in der Liturgie und be-
sonders in der Totenliturgie einen Höhepunkt erstiegen hatte,
wie ihn die Laienwelt zuvor nie erlebte."[1]   Cluny was more
closely allied with the dead than the living and indeed in
and with Cluny the dead obtained an amazing power over the
living.[2]   Jorden has stressed in a study based on careful
analysis of the charters down to 942 that Cluny's primary
concern was with the salvation of souls.[3]   Yet the recurrent
theme of donations made to the abbey, *donatio pro remedio
animae,* or *pro salute, pro anima, pro peccatis redimentis,
pro liberatione, pro redemptione, pro commendacione, pro re-
missione meorum peccatorum,* to obtain salvation had reper-
cussions of such scope as to determine, unlike any other in-
stitution, the economic order of the Middle Ages.[4]   The inter-
twining of the liturgy with the economic aspects of life deserves full emphasis and attention: the exchange between
monks and laymen turned on this double motif, property of
considerable value entrusted to the monastery as trustees
for Sts. Peter and Paul[5] in return for one's becoming a member of the Cluniac *societas* and being remembered in its liturgical prayers.[6]   Not less important was the participation

in the spiritual benefits derived from feeding the poor which reached staggering proportions. A new class of inhabitants known as *burgensis* (bourgeois) appeared around the year 1,000 to supply the services called for in the emerging Cluniac "city"; Ulrich claims that 17,000 poor were fed each year.[7] Whatever the exact number may be, this report makes it obvious that Cluny acquired its full resonance and depth by becoming a popular movement,[8] while, conversely, its liturgical prayers would not have attained their widespread effect without the participation of its *familiares*. As a consequence of this dovetailing process Cluny became an economic center of striking magnitude where property was administrated by the abbot while the sacrifice of perishable things and goods of this world was liturgically sanctified by the perennial hope of man to outlive his death. The predominant motive underlying the gifts, *Date et dabitur vobis*, far from being idealistic, stemmed from the conviction that what we do in this world shall one day be judged.[9] For Cluny the Last Judgment was a *present* reality that made man conscious of his earthly mortality by confronting him with a yardstick against which to measure the meaning of his life lived on earth.[10]

Another aspect of prayers and gifts to monasteries which has received far too little attention is one not directly rooted in Christianity itself but in the encounter of Christian faith with tribal memories and obligations towards ancestors.[11] A monograph showing that during the Carolingian period founders of monasteries extended their family relationships to monasteries by making their own sons and daughters abbots and abbesses, not only to retain the foundations as private property, but to remain spiritually related to their kin in life and death,[12] calls for further aboration. For Cluny itself studies are in their infancy.[13]

t it is in the sociological context of a multiplicity of

nily and tribal units haunted by clannish fears, memories

d cults of the dead that the purifying effects of the Cluni-

liturgy deserve a detailed investigation.[14]

However,before our return to the sources and a dis-

ssion of some specific elements of Cluniac liturgy which

parted to it a particular form and stamp, a last word is

order. All those who wish to make a closer study of the

uniac liturgy, seeing that its importance is constantly

phasized, and rightly so, make the striking discovery that

yet there exists no specialized study of the liturgy of

uny.[15] The reason is the absence of liturgical manuscripts

ming from the main abbey itself.[16] That there was a litur-

cal directory there is confirmed by a passage in Bernard.[17]

wever, as with the main necrology, its loss causes a lacuna

ich might well be partially compensated for by the use of

turgical manuscripts which indicate a Cluniac source.[18]

wever the fact remains that no sacramentary, missal or an-

phonary of the eleventh or twelfth centuries has come down

us. A handful of breviaries has survived.[19] Our main

urces of information thus far have been contained in the

stomals discussed previously and this is a use to which

ey do not readily lend themselves.

We may nonetheless declare with confidence that these

tter sources make it clear that the command of St. Benedict

allow nothing to take precedence over the divine service

God, *nihil operi Dei praeponatur*, was followed at Cluny.[20]

. Peter Damian observed during his week-long stay that monks

ent so much time in choir that they hardly had half an hour

themselves during the day.[21] The strains of the long hours

ent praying are evident in Ulrich's comments.[22] Some 215

Psalms were sung every day, both Old and New Testaments were read in their entirety throughout the year, long patristic readings were part of the liturgical cycle:[23] those few examples are witness to the preponderance of liturgical prayer at Cluny. Other characteristics of Cluny's liturgy include the special reverence tendered to saints,[24] the part played by processions and, of overriding emphasis, the constant care and concern for the dead.[25] References in the customals to this last aspect, the most important element of all, are too numerous to specify here. In the Farfa customal we find frequent high masses being said for the dead,[26] masses being offered during 30 days for the same purpose,[27] the distribution of the *justitia*, portions of bread and wine, to the poor which accompany them, for 30 days,[28] the 30 psalms said before Nocturnes; one may say that the liturgy of Cluny is saturated with the thoughts of the dead and prayers for their souls.[29] The concern with masses for the dead became so developed that it was proposed that they be said every day, even on Sundays.[30] Although the latter proposal was rejected in order to show particular reverence to Him alone who conquered death fully, week-day masses for the dead became a feature of Cluniac liturgy. Ulrich writes of these daily masses for the dead and adds that from November to Septuagesima Sunday the office of the dead was recited only at night with the exception of Sunday.[31] Offices for the dead are to be found in the earliest Cluniac customals and were of course celebrated in other monasteries.[32]

(b) *Ista nostra fidelis inventio*

However, it is by its addition of a new feast day to the
calendar of the Church as their own faithful discovery, *ista
nostra fidelis inventio*,[1] that the monks of Cluny sublimated
the widespread fear of death and judgment contained in a purgatorial mentality to a higher plane of consciousness. All
Souls Day was the profoundest of replies given to the despair
of fear-striken, terrorized souls neither sure of heaven, nor
resigned to hell. The legend of its introduction by Odilo
related by both Rudolphus Glaber and Jotsald defines the role
fulfilled in unique fashion by Cluny. Jotsald's version reads
as follows: "A monk from the south of France on his return
from a pilgrimage to Jerusalem became shipwrecked on an island
near Sicily inhabited by a pious hermit. While there, he was
asked if he had heard of the monastery of Cluny and its abbot
Odilo. Replying in the affirmative, he asked his questioner
as to the reason for his query. Near here, he was told, I
have often seen by God's judgment angry flames shooting out
from the depths of the earth and in the midst of them souls
are suffering for their sins. Indeed, their torments are constantly renewed by a multitude of demons who increase their
punishments in intolerable fashion day by day, while ever preparing new torments for them. Often I have heard these demons
lament that many of these souls of the damned were liberated
from their punishments by the prayers and alms of monks. But
they complained especially of the monks of Cluny and their
abbot because it is they who caused them the greatest losses.
For that reason I urge you in God's name on your return to
your country to tell these things you have heard from me to
this congregation of religious men at Cluny and to beg of
them for me to increase their sacrifices and their prayers

for the salvation of souls in torment. In this way the number
of souls taken from the devil shall be even greater and the
elect in paradise shall be filled with joy. On his return
the pilgrim went directly to Cluny and discharged himself of
his commission to Odilo. Immediately thereupon, Odilo decreed
that, just as all monasteries celebrated the Feast of All Saints
on November 1, so on the following day all the faithful souls
would be commemorated, that masses would be sung for this purpose, prayers multiplied, alms for the poor increased, so that
our enemy shall augment his groans because of his losses and
the suffering Christian can rejoice in hope of compassion."[2]

R. Glaber's account is similar. However, he adds that
Cluny is preeminent in liberating souls from the devil's domination within the Roman world, indicating thereby that part of
the earth ruled by the emperor in the West. We see here that
Cluny complemented the *Renovatio Romani Imperii* by its *liber-
atio animarum a daemonica dominatione*.[3]

All Souls follows directly on All Saints. From the foregoing passages we can see why. The communion of saints who
individually have conquered death by the strength of their
faith are remembered by a jubilant joyous Church, triumphant
in its memory of redeemed souls. The feast of All Souls is
introduced at a moment in history[4] when the individual soul
feels himself too weak to rise to the demands of Christianity
by the sole example of saints. Even the popes themselves are
filled with the fears and torments of the age, despite being
baptized.[5] The souls of a clannish, tribal society caught between the demands of ancestor cults and a Christianity which
has only scratched the surface of their lives finds itself
literally crucified by demons. These are the words of Peter
Damian himself in speaking of the creation of All Souls: *ut
de manibus daemonum eos qui ab illis cruciantur educant.*[6]

y attempt to slight this terminology as mere allegory will
cessarily miss the significance of Odilo's desire to intro-
ce a new feast-day to act as a profound spiritual counter-
ight to a despairing historical situation. The souls of
e unredeemed, wailing in purgatory, neither in heaven nor
 hell, are pushed to the forefront by solemn and dramatic
sses for the dead. Odilo himself was seen as the leader of
ose by whose intercession the devil felt himself most
reatened since the suffering souls in purgatory were freed
om his law. *Inter caetera de Cluniacensium coetu permaxi-*
m et eorum abbate querimoniam faciunt, quia quam saepe per
s sui juris vernaculo perdunt.[7] The feast of All Saints is
ereby circumscribed and limited to a single day, although
rich is careful to point out that its importance is in no
y diminished![8] However, the shadows and laments of purga-
ry quickly darken the lights and sober the mood of the in-
cations of saints in paradise by the juxtaposition. Al-
ady during the celebration of All Saints prayers and masses
r the dead were introduced in anticipation of the following
y.[9]

The recurrent Cluniac themes of judgment, souls suffer-
g in purgatory, man's ghostly fears and hope of compassion,
e emphasis on, one might even say obsession with, the souls
 the dead, the search for redemption by the sacrifice of
operty transmitted to the monastery: all have been known
 contribute either singly or together to an intensification
 religious life and piety at Cluny, while their presence is
marked at other monasteries. However, it is the feast of All
uls alone which introduces a consciousness, peculiarly West-
n, of a *totality in time* complemented by the claim of the
perial household[10] to represent the *totality of space* com-
ehended by the term Roman Empire. Previously, every monastery

had prayed for the souls of its own community or those relate
to it by confraternal ties based on benefactions, family rela
tionships and the like.[11] It was Odilo's gift to history to
introduce a festive commemoration of all faithful souls who
lived from the beginning of time to its end; *ita agatur apud
nos festivo more commemoratio omnium fidelium defunctorum qui
ab initio mundi fuerunt usque in finem.*[12] The totality of
sinful mankind is included in Odilo's conception. It is
thanks to this universal vision contained in All Souls that
Cluny acquires a special significance for world history, ele-
vating it above other monastic reform movements of the tenth
and eleventh centuries. Furthermore *because of the feast of
All Souls the very kernel of a belief in a world history
taking place on this side of the grave on the middle ground
between saints and pagans is planted for the first time.*[13]
Odilo did not hesitate to extend his discovery to all promising that anyone partaking in its celebration would participat
in all works of intercession.[14]

It was this comprehensive quality imparted by All Souls
that gave Cluny its unique stamp, infusing the growing number
of monasteries under its influence with a unifying inspiration. By the same token the realization of the federal or
corporative principle in Cluny's organization gave scope and
amplitude to the new feast day. All authority over the
various monasteries within the Cluniac orbit culminated in
the one abbot of the mother abbey who dictated the *consuetudines* for them all.[15] The abbots of dependent monasteries
under the jurisdiction of the Cluniac order became priors.
Under the new corporative principle Cluny alone had about 100
monks at the time of Odilo's death while under his successor
there were about 300,[16] themselves enormous concentrations of
men in eleventh century Europe. The architectural scope of

Cluny also gave evidence of the grandeur of the new appeal to
"all".[17] Odilo jocosely remarked that, like Augustus, he had
found Cluny built of wood and left it built of marble.[18]
Cluny III, whose architectural plans have been so painstaking-
ly reconstructed by Conant, was a church of grandiose proportion carefully designed "to enrich and reinforce the acousti-
cal qualities of liturgical chants".[19] Not only did the
chants resound throughout the largest and most influential
church in Christendom, but throughout the houses of the order
itself. Hugh in a farewell address to the community had
spoken of the extension of the order into Italy, Lorraine,
England, Normandy, France, Aquitaine, Gascony, Provence and
Spain.[20] Hence the triumph over men's hearts offered a
counterweight to the daily economic, social and political
fragmentation by a new experience offering the possibility
of uniting these spheres of life by a conception and practice
available to all sinners.

  We are particularly fortunate in having three manuscript
texts available which permit us to have some precise idea of
the dramatic liturgical celebration introduced by the non-
Roman mass of All Souls Day.[21] The most complete and significant of these comes to us in an eleventh century document from
the monastery of Saint-Vaast, located in the northern French
town of Arras.[22] Since the originality and importance of this
source have been neither recognized nor evaluated within the
larger context of Cluniac research, its special character deserves attention.[23]

  Let us briefly summarize its main features and elements
following the expert analysis of L. Brou: The mass is of
monastic origin which in itself makes it original, since monasteries, having no reason to compose a special office of the
dead, utilized the Roman office. This mass contains a number

of liturgical texts found nowhere else including a long series
of Collects, hymns for different Hours, these being of special
interest since hymns have never been accepted in the Roman
office for the dead, long Scriptural passages, soon to be com-
mented on, a series of special Responsaries, an imposing type
of ceremonial whose festive character is accentuated by a noc-
turnal procession with lights, candles and a litany unique of
its kind, a procession during the day to the cemetery followed
by another litany for the dead, the whole ending by a Mass for
the Dead substantially different from that used today.

More specifically, the constituent elements of this mass
are formed by twelve Responsories, three hymns, of which this
manuscript is the oldest source, which were probably composed
for the occasion, and multiple readings which deserve particular mention. All of them, and there are twelve,[24] emphasize
the same theme, the end of the world with its frightening cata-
clysms, the second coming of the Son of Man and the Last Judgment. These selections from Holy Scripture make it clear that
more than the idea of resurrection alone was intended here,
although it too was represented. There is also a large number of Orations which originate with this mass, chosen in all
likelihood in attention to the remembrance of all the faithful
dead. More than ten of them end in a manner characteristic of
this early version of the All Souls' office: Through our Lord
Jesus Christ who has come to judge the living and the *saeculum
per ignem* by fire.[25] That this ending has especial interest
for Cluniac research is indicated by the discovery of the same
close in Odilo's confession of faith which ends likewise *inde
venturum ad judicandum vivos et mortuos et saeculum per ignem.*[26] There would also seem to be a connection between this
emphasis on the End by fire and a Cluniac text, of which there
must be other examples, which runs: *Sicut acqua extinguit*

nem, helemosina extinguit peccatum,[27] which appears to be
e practical implementation of this eschatological faith
nce generosity and compassion for the poor were part of the
rvice.[28] The last essential component of this mass which
shall mention are the four processions. There was one at
spers, one at Nocturnes, another at the end of Lauds. The
adings again at every occasion refer to the last days. The
ird and fourth processions are of particular interest. The
rmer, taking place after Lauds, leaves the chapel, or altar,
the Holy Cross in order to go *ad sanctum Michahelem,* there-
paying especial reverence to this saint. After Nones a
urth procession takes its departure for the cemetery carry-
g an ikon of the Lord. On their significance we shall elab-
ate later. With Brou's conclusion there can be no disagree-
nt that this office creates "une atmosphère savamment évoca-
ice de la fin du monde et du jugement universel, et qui
emporte sur les plus étudiées des paraliturgies modernes".[29]

The constant references in the text to *omnium fidelium*
functorum leave no doubt that this mass for November 2 was
spired by Odilo's statute. Indeed the elements of his de-
ee are present in all the three offices which include mul-
ple masses said by priests, psalms sung by monks apart, alms
the poor and the dramatic festive element, *in festive*
re.[30] Although Dom Brou does not conceive that the prin-
ple of filiation is operative here, that assumption must be
allenged. It is of course impossible as yet to conclude
at we possess a Mass of All Souls as it was sung at Cluny.
wever, it is certain that those we do possess are Cluniac in
eir very essence and as such were adopted, and possibly
apted, but not invented, by either dependent Cluniac houses
those subject to Cluniac influence. Otherwise we would
ve to assume that the discovery of earthshaking proportions

made by Odilo was to find liturgical implementation only outside of Cluny.[31]

(c) Planctus de Transitu Domni Odilonis

The penitential fears of souls awaiting judgment expresse
most dramatically in All Souls lent somber tones to the liturg
at Cluny by numerous masses for the dead. It was Hugh who in-
stituted a special mass for all those buried in the cemetery a
Cluny.[1] There were also masses for the dead that had no speci
feast for themselves.[2] However, perhaps the most extraordinary
indication of Cluny's concern with guilt, judgment, penitence
and the intermediary, undetermined state of the sinful souls
in purgatory was another liturgical change, not an addition,
but a repression. In the early days of Cluny the monks had
prayed faithfully with the Church: *O felix culpa, O neces-
sarium Adae peccatum*.[3] "O happy guilt, how necessary was
Adam's sin." As Cardinal Schuster says well, it is in the
simple certainty of mankind's salvation through Christ that
this exclamatory prayer offers no obstacle in understanding
to the believer, Adam's sin being seen quite intelligibly as
a source which can be used to reveal the wisdom of God. Only
one who limits himself to considering the sinful aspect of the
prayer implying that God in his majesty is thereby slighted,
who does not grasp that God creates good from evil, becomes
offended by the expression.[4] The newly oriented piety of
the Cluniacs setting the West off from the "other-worldly"
holiness and adoration of the Church in the East led to just
this result. We are told by Ulrich that the abbot Hugh apparently found this prayer, proclaimed during Easter week on
Holy Saturday to express the joy and exultation of the Resur-

ection, intolerable and prohibited further reading of it.[5]

ot serene joy at the certainty of salvation as in the Ortho-
ox communion, but a mood of tears and compunction expressed
n a purgatorial spirit for the sinful, unredeemed side of
an's nature: that is the spiritual direction taken at Cluny.

Yet this repression of the *O felix culpa*, however sig-
ificant, is but evidence of a deeper current flowing through-
ut the Cluniac sources. Odilo's *Epitaphium* for the Empress
delaide, his *Planctus* for Otto the Great, his lament on the
eath of Henry II: all emphasize *triumphant* souls facing the
ast Judge.[6] The most impressive popular example we have to-
ay of this dread moment is contained in the sequence of the
ass for the Dead found in the Roman liturgy, the famous *Dies
rae*.[7] No other hymn of the Church has received such a
ariety of translations so telling is its appeal to the human
pirit. It is generally accepted that Thomas of Celano (fl.
220-1249) was the author. However, that claim is disputed by
he discovery of a codex said to date from the end of the
welfth century.[8] The published version of this text by an
nidentified author presents in fact but few variations with
hat from the thirteenth century now in use. The eleventh
trophe of the present *Dies Irae* is lacking, while the sixth
nd last strophes differ entirely. Otherwise the texts are
emarkably identical.[9]

However, well before the appearance of the *Dies Irae*,
he themes of Last Judgment and Resurrection reached their
ighest pitch of expression at a moment of crisis in the
bbey's history. This moment was the death of the great ab-
ot who had led them to the forefront of spiritual life, Od-
lo himself. Jotsald's *Planctus de Transitu Domni Odilonis*
ould well be called Cluny's first *Dies Irae*, as Rosenstock-
uessy alone has observed, since it plants in germinal form

the characteristics and associations later to be found in the celebrated sequence.[10]

Usually this lament, if not ignored, has been considered merely a pious cry of grief following the death of a friend.[11] However the death of Odilo, creator of the celebration of All Souls, the peacemaker par excellence in a society rent by war, the fullest and highest embodiment of man's hopes amidst the forces of evil and disintegration assaulting his own soul, had to represent far more than the mournful passing of a beloved monk, or individual saint. For it is in him that the dreams, wishes, desires of his contemporaries had to be realized to the full.[12] And of their deepest yearning, as believing Christians, there can be little doubt, the triumph over death, the union with Christ the Last Judge beyond all fear and torment, beyond, one might say, all reason. In Odilo the resurrection had to become reality not solely to indicate the salvation of a saintly individual, but it was Odilo's destiny to represent the prototype of an entire society seeking a model by which to channel its deepest aspirations by seeing them fulfilled.

Hence his death, says his biographer,[13] occasions groans of desolation, not of one man or two or three but of a multitude composed of people of different sex, of diverse standing, age and rank. He laments the vast numbers of noble monks, the large family made destitute by the death of its father Odilo on whose teaching and virtues they were dependent and to whom they were indissolubly bound in bonds of love. The loss of him who has excited so many tears, denounced so much wrong, is cause to cry out asking: How did he depart, the helper of the miserable? How did he become silent, the consoler of the afflicted? Where did he go, the leader of so many monks and the leader of untold multitudes?[14] However, it is in the *Planctus* that this expression of grief reaches its highest

point. And to it is added the promise of judgment and redemption.

The lament takes the form of a dialogue beginning with
a dramatic outburst of grief: Wail peoples and you the stars,
the tongues of heaven, Let the burning sun sink into darkness,
Let the radiant crescent of the moon lose its light, Let the
whole world grieve on its face.[15] Then the thrice-repeated
cry:

> *Odilo, dulce decus, venturi gloria secli*
> *Odilo, dulce decus fraternae pacis amicus*
> *Odilo, dulce decus, meritorum lampade clarus*

is followed by the response of reason, *ratio,* which describes
the law of life which leads to death:

> Our bodies in succession are enclosed in the
>   funereal tomb
> In everlasting compact, such is the law for
>   mortals.
> The begettor of nature, author and creator
>   of all things
> Has decreed that all the dead depart into
>   darkness.
> Learned and unlearned meet the same fate.
> The shadow of death envelopes rich and poor
>   alike,
> Everything turns to dust when life departs:
> And what cannot be changed, should be borne
>   patiently.[16]

The first cry is then answered[17] by a three-fold response of
the triumph over death:

> *Odilo non moritur, sed mortis funera spernit*
> *Odilo non moritur sed vitam duxit honestam*
> *Odilo non moritur sed vitam morte recepit*

He reigns joyfully in eternity perceiving Christ whom he cultivated, taught, sought and glorified, whose glory was the cross and Christ crucified. After a passage on Odilo's devotion to the virgin, Odilo's resurrection and union with him who has judged him is announced: He suffered with Christ, now he already lives gloriously in him (*radians jam vivit in illo*). He died with Christ, hence he rises with him.

William of Volpiano, his friend, who died on the same day, is commemorated as another father of monks preceding Odilo's mystical marriage with his bride as in the Song of Songs. He is described as a bridegroom filled with joy, compared with a tower protected by heavenly weapons. Solomon brings him the heavenly throne from which he sings out his joy. The poet then asks the daughters of Jerusalem to be at rest until the shadow of death passes and he rises into the day which knows no night.[18] The moment comes: *Odilo supremum spectat de morte triumphum*. The first palm of victory is bestowed on him. Thereupon follows a description of that dreaded day: When the heavens shall be opened and the arbiter of the universe shall come to judge men's acts and motives. Then shall judgment by the cross appear in the heights of heaven which the crucified Lord made sacred by his death. The throngs of angels shall tremble and all the powers of heaven now resounding shall be reduced to trembling silence. The shining sun shall take flight, the moon shall turn pale and disappear and from the opened tombs of the dead the bodies of the dead shall arise. The glory of the redeemed shall then be separated from the fate of the evil doers, the good shall enter the light of paradise the depraved given over to the flames.[19] Then comes the climax of the entire lament: *Odilo tuncque novus coelesti lumine clarus, sanctorum medius incedet, et obvius ibit, Agmine multorum vallatus commilitonum, Quos*

Domino verbis, exemplis consociavit. Odilo triumphant over death meets the Lord accompanied by the multitude of those companions won over for the Lord by his word and example.[20] The *Planctus* represents for the living the culminating point of the entire Cluniac *confraternitas*, the victory (in the person of its saintly leader) over the fears and terrors of the Last Judgment from which one sought to free himself by prayer and alms in the Mass for All Souls. Cluny's main concern therefore was not only with the dead, that aspect has been often pointed out, but with the state of the soul before judgment. As we have seen,[21] the theme of the Last Judgment led the development of the Cluniac liturgy to a point far beyond the usual masses for the dead. Yet in the source documents of Cluny that we possess there is no more telling and forceful emphasis on the soul triumphantly facing the Last Judge than in the rhythmic hexameters of Odilo's biographer.

The intensity of the dialogue between the grieved outpourings of the heart and the cool, analytical *ratio* vividly demonstrates that the Cluniac *societas* was not only a community invoking fear of judgment, but one living in hope of judgment as well. The privilege of being judged brought with it the opportunity for salvation. Hence, by obliging the individual soul to be exposed to lines of force emanating from the end of time and stretching back into his present life and then extending this experience to all souls that had ever lived or would live, a Christian democracy applying to all souls facing death came into being.[22] Cluny's confraternity made man conscious of death in an unheard-of way as the unremitting equalizer between men. It may be now clear that anyone marked out for special eminence in the Cluniac liturgy must have held a significant meaning for the *confraternitas*.

NOTES

Liturgical Economics at Cluny

1. G. Schreiber, *Gemeinschaften des Mittelalters,* (Münster, 1948), pp. 172-173. (Reprint of "Kirchliches Abgabenwesen," *loc. cit.*)

2. *Idem, Gemeinschaften,* pp. 99-125.

3. W. Jorden, *op. cit.,* p. 47.

4. *Ibid.* The greatest concentration of gifts took place between 970-1020, G. Duby, *L'économie rurale et la vie des campagnes dans l'Occident médiévale,* (Paris, 1962), vol. II, p. 385.

5. "Man liess den Schutzheiligen der Kirche oder des Klosters als juristische Person und eigentlichen Besitzer des Vermögens auftreten," *ibid.,* p. 17f. This point, like that of Ullmann, cf. infra, p. 46, n. 6, is almost always ignored.

6. G. Schreiber, *Gemeinschaften,* pp. 177f.

7. G. Duby, *La société aux XIe et XIIe siècles dans la region mâconnaise,* (Paris, 1953), p. 341f. Udal., III, 11, *P.L.* 149, 753. No city of the time had that many inhabitants, viz. Wollasch, "Gemeinschaftsbewusstsein," p. 281, n. 4.

8. F. Heer, *Aufgang Europas,* (Vienna, 1948), pp. 386f.

9. Jorden, *op. cit.,* pp. 47f. and Hallinger, *Gorze-Kluny,* II, p. 746, n. 746 for numerous references.

10. Jorden, *ibid.,* pp. 50-51.

11. G. Schreiber, *Gemeinschaften,* pp. 364-365.

12. K. Schmid, "Religiöses und sippengebundenes Gemeinschaftsbewusstsein in frühmittelalterlichen Gedenkbucheinträgen," *DA,* 21, (1965), pp. 18-81. Here we see already the

.mportance of the *libri vitae* in coming to grips with these
family and tribal units. Also Heer, *op. cit.*, p. 398f.

13. See some of the general source material in M. H.
Mengstl, *Totenklage und Nachruf in der mittelalterlichen
Literatur seit dem Ausgang der Antike*, (Dissertation, Würzburg, Munich, 1936). Now K. Schmid and J. Wollasch, "*Societas et Fraternitas*," *loc. cit.*

14. Jorden, *ibid.*, p. 63.

15. P. Schmitz, "La Liturgie de Cluny," *Spiritualità
Cluniacense*, pp. 85-99; G. de Valous, *Le Monachisme Clunisien*, I, pp. 327-372; N. Hunt, *op. cit.*, pp. 99-123 are
helpful.

16. N. Hunt, *op. cit.*, p. 109.

17. Ber. II, 17; *Herrgott*, p. 317. Also Hunt, *ibid.*,
pp. 17-18.

18. J. Hourlier, "Le Breviare de Saint-Turin," *Etudes
Grégoriennes*, III, 1959, pp. 163-173. This procedure will
be followed for a specific instance in the next section on
All Souls, infra, p. 91f.

19. P. Schmitz, "La Liturgie," p. 87.

20. *Ibid.*, p. 86f. However the liturgy at Cluny was
not the Roman liturgy imposed by Charlemagne within his
empire during the eighth century. Not only did it differ
in basic elements such as the Creed, the *Quicumque vult*
being chanted at Cluny, Udal., 1. I. c. 3, *P.L.* 149, 646,
but Cluny followed the more solemn and complicated forms of
worship connected with the Gallican rite. This rite is intertwined with expressive dramatic and symbolic elements
lacking Roman sobriety in its appeal to the feelings, *ibid.*,
p. 86. "There is no evidence that Cluny herself ever received any liturgical directives from Rome or anywhere,"
N. Hunt, *op. cit.*, p. 113. This statement alone should
make it quite clear that the evidence of papal privileges
with respect to Cluny's independence is greatly overrated,
viz. the works of Letonnelier, Lemarignier and Cowdrey, *op.
cit.*, especially before 1075.

21. N. Hunt, *op. cit.*, p. 103.

22. *Ibid.*

23. Udal., I., 1, *P.L.* 149, 643f. and P. Schmitz, *ibid.*, p. 89.

24. Udal., I., 5, *P.L.* 149, 650.

25. P. Schmitz, *art. cit.*, pp. 92, 97.

26. Albers, *CF*, pp. 34, 36, 88.

27. *Ibid.*, pp. 126, 196.

28. *Ibid.*, pp. 126, 197, 204.

29. "Cluny pensait à eux tout le long du jour," P. Schmitz, *art. cit.*, p. 92.

30. *CF*, p. 202.

31. Udal., I, 4, *P.L.* 149, 648 and Ber. I, Herrgott, p. 278.

32. Albers, II, BB[1], pp. 3-4, C, pp. 33-34.

Ista nostra fidelis inventio

1. *Statutum S. Odilonis de Defunctis*, *P.L.*, 142, 1037.

2. *Vita S. Odilonis*, *P.L.* 142, 926-927. (Cf. P. Lamma, *op. cit.*, pp. 53f., 107f.)

3. *Ibid.*, 692. Without this complementary effort spiritually oriented towards calming the fears of men's hearts and unified by its organizational principle around a stable base, the *renovatio* would have been far too circumscribed, being dependent as it was on an army trying to enforce peace through the sacred authority of an emperor constantly on the move. Those who defend the "Holy Emperor" against his opponents forget too easily the shortcomings of his position. Both Cluny and the Emperor's policy are responses to an emergency. Extended indefinitely, one would have retained the feudal order, the other would have led to a caliphate.

4. For dating see Sackur II, pp. 475-476 who deduces the 1030's opposing Ringholz, *op. cit.*, p. 63f. Jardet,

op. cit., is not inclined to agree with Sackur,who insists
that an earlier date than 1024, the year of Henry II's
death, is untenable because of mention of the emperor's
name in the statute. However,it is not inconceivable that
All Souls was decreed in the monastery before the statute
in its present form was composed. J. Hourlier's case for
dating the feast day between 1024-1033 is, nonetheless,
persuasive in "Saint Odilon et la fête des morts," *Revue
Grégorienne*, 28, (1949), pp. 209-212 and *Saint Odilon,
Abbé de Cluny*, pp. 102, 126ff.

5. Benedict VIII cannot leave purgatory by himself.
He needs Odilo's intercession. *P.L.* 142, 927-929. Cf.
infra, pp. 44-45.

6. *P.L.* 144, 936. "The Age of Anxiety", too, it may
be recalled, is one which has lost its spiritual props.

7. *Ibid.* and *P.L.* 142, 928, *ipsius enim suffragiis
destinavit superna censura illum eripi a tormentis.*

8. Udal., I., 1., c. 42, *P.L.* 149, 689.

9. *Ibid.*

10. The King's Household was the basis of his Empire.
The essential study is E. Rosenstock-Huessy's *Königshaus und
Stämme.*

11. See Mabillon, *Elogium S. Odilonis*, *P.L.* 142, 878.

12. *P.L.* 142, 1037-1038 and Ringholz, *op. cit.*, pp.
xxx-xxxiv, who also emphasizes the unique character of the
feast.

13. E. Rosenstock-Huessy, *Die europäischen Revolutionen*,
p. 122, who rightfully stresses the important point that
Odilo's action breaks off the West from the East. "Die Welt-
geschichte ist das Weltgericht" is foreign to Greek or Orthodox thought, as is Cluny.

14. *P.L.* 142, 1037-1038.

15. See D. Knowles, *The Monastic Order in England*, pp.
145f.; Guy de Valous, *op. cit.*, II, pp. 27f. Also Ber. I,
1, 137. N. Bulst, *Untersuchungen zu den Klosterreformen
Wilhelms von Dijon, 962-1031*, (Pariser Historische Studien,
11, Bonn, 1973) points up the differences of organizational

structure between Odilo's Cluny and all other cloisters, p. 207. With respect to the reforms of the Cluniac William of Dijon, whose preceptor was Majolus: St. Bénigne was not a centralized reform center to which all other abbeys were subjected. Abbeys did not lose their independence to "priors" under a centralized federalism, even though they had a common *consuetudo* and bonds of confraternity, p. 209f. Cf. p. 153, n. 36.

16. N. Hunt, *op. cit.*, pp. 82-83, also p. 169f. U. Berlière, "Le nombre des moines dans les anciens monastères," *RB*, 41, (1932), p. 253, following Baluze, *Miscellanea*, V, p. 443, states that Cluny had 300 monks when Peter the Venerable became abbot. Cf. infra, p. 150, n. 8.

17. F. Heer, *Aufgang Europas*, pp. 415f.

18. *P.L.* 142, 908.

19. K. J. Conant, "Medieval Academy Excavations at Cluny," *Speculum*, vol. 29, (1954), p. 6. Cluny III "was the largest monastic church, the largest French church and the largest Romanesque church," *ibid.*, p. 10. See F. Mercier, *Les Primitifs français. La Peinture Clunysienne en Bourgogne à l'Epoque Romane*, (Paris, 1931), p. 21, for the liturgical orientation of Cluniac art.

20. *Imprecatio B. Hugonis Abbatis*, *P.L.* 159, 951.

21. A. Wilmart and L. Brou, "Un office monastique pour le 2 novembre," *Sacris Erudiri*, vol. 5, (1953), pp. 247-330, hereafter WB, and R. J. Hesbert, "L'Office de la Commemoraison des Défunts à Saint-Benoît-sur-Loire au XIIIe siècle," *Miscellanea Liturgica in honorem L. Cuniberti Mohlberg*, II, (1949), pp. 392-421.

22. WB. Dom Brou who became co-editor responsible for the publication of this manuscript after the death of Dom Wilmart, who discovered it, was able to uncover a small fragment of another office of this kind, also originating in the eleventh century, this time from the abbey of St. Amand, also in northern France. Although we shall concentrate on WB, the presence of multiple masses of this kind indicates a diffusion outside of Cluny's jurisdiction.

23. My thanks is herewith expressed to Dr. Gerhart Ladner for having called this source to my attention, albeit in another connection.

24. These include:
1. Jonas, II, 3-19
2. Joel, II, 1-11
3. Ezechiel, XXXVII, 1-14
4. Isaiah, XIII, 2-13
5. II Peter, III, 8-14
6. I Corinthians, XV, 12-26
7. *Ibid.*, 25-45
8. *Ibid.*, 46-47
9. Matthew, XIII, 36-43
10. Mark, XIII, 19-32
11. Luke, XX, 27-38
12. John, V, 19-30

The editor rightly calls attention to the reading from Peter (no. 5), "That one day is with the Lord as a thousand years and a thousand years as one day", which is an obvious selection to counteract the fears of the millenium, WB, pp. 300-301. It should also be noted in the passage that the expectation of the millenium offers man time to come to repentance (v. 9), a particular Cluniac theme (cf. infra, p. 187, n. 48). Also the final destruction by fire, *Adveniet autem dies Domini....elementa vero calore solventur* (v. 10) and *in adventum diei Domini, per quem caeli ardentes solventur et elementa ignis ardore tabescent* (v. 12) is central to the impression which the mass wants to impart.

25. This expression occurs in previous texts of the eighth and ninth centuries, but very infrequently and never with such emphasis. *Ibid.*, pp. 303, 322.

26. *Sancti Odilonis Credulitas, P.L.* 142, 1036.

27. Bruel, I, no. 564, p. 545. See W. Jorden, *op. cit.*, p. 49 and Ecclesiasticus 3, 30.

28. *Dumque aguntur ista fiat pro posse loci pauperibus larga misericordia* which occurred during the daytime procession. WB, p. 279.

29. *Ibid.*, p. 323.

30. *P.L.* 142, 1037.

31. Dom Brou's position that Cluny retained the old Roman rite for the deceased is untenable. And it leads him to the contorted conclusion that any monastery having a special mass for All Souls must in principle not have belonged to the Cluniac order! For the monastery of St. Vaast

and its abbots Poppo, Leduin and Richard of St. Vannes, "der in seinen klösterlichen Bestrebungen an Cluni anknüpfte," see Sackur II, 133f., 290f. and passim. Also,that the Cambrai manuscript in question was transcribed before 1067, the year of Odilo's canonization, seems likely since Majolus is listed among the saints of the calendar while Odilo is not.

Planctus de Transitu Domni Odilonis

1. Udal., I, 26, *P.L.* 149, 673.

2. *Ibid.*, I, 6, 651, and I, 7, 653.

3. I. Schuster, *Liber Sacramentorum*, (translated by P. R. Bauersfeld, Regensburg, 10 vols., 1929-32), IV, p. 56.

4. *Ibid.*

5. Udal., l. c., *P.L.* 149, 663.

6. See infra, pp. 57f.

7. Introduced by Pope Pius V in 1570.

8. D. M. Inguanez, "Dies Irae in un codice del sec. XII," *Miscellanea Cassinese*, (Monte Cassino, 1931). See further J. Szövérffy, "Dies Irae," *New Catholic Encyclopedia*, IV, (1967), pp. 863-864.

9. *Ibid.* Further research, although uncovering verses of similar content where the theme of the Last Judgment is preeminent, has not found any earlier version of the *Dies Irae* text. Previous references to Zephaniah I, 14-18 apply to other historical contexts, viz. K. Strecker, "Dies irae," *Zeitschrift für deutsches Altertum und deutsche Literatur*, vol. 54, (1909), pp. 227-255.

10. E. Rosenstock-Huessy, *Die europäischen Revolutionen*, p. 124. See the edition and commentary of F. Ermini, "Il Pianto di Zotsaldo per la morte di Odilone" in *Medio Evo latino*, Modena, (1938), pp. 199-213.

11. O. Ringholz, *op. cit.*, p. LIIIf. and P. Jardet, *S. Odilon*, p. 654f., have translated all or part of these verses into their respective languages.

12. Odilo's renown was so widespread and the grief at his death so profound that his name is found in the chronicles and necrologies of Germany as well as in France. O. Ringholz, *op. cit.*, p. 116.

13. *P.L.* 142, 897.

14. *Ibid.* Jotsald also refers to Odilo as *caecorum baculus, esurientium cibus, spes miserorum, solamen lugentium, P.L.* 142, 903.

15. F. Ermini, *op. cit.*, p. 209.

16. *Ordine funereo clauduntur membra sepulcro*
    Foedere perpetuo, lex est mortalibus ista:
    Naturae genitor, rerum plasmator et auctor
    Jussit in occiduas morientes ire tenebras.
    Tendit ad occasum quidquid lucis capit ortum,
    Doctus et indoctus aequali sorte recedunt.
    Divitis et modici similem mors suscipit umbra,
    Vertitur in cinerem cineris compago soluta:
    Quod nequit absolvi, debet patienter haberi.
    Ibid.

17. Cf. M. H. Hengstl, *op. cit.*, p. 39.

18. F. Ermini, *op. cit.*, p. 212.

19. *Ibid.* Also kindly refer infra to pp. 96-97, notes 25, 26, 27, p. 164, n. 20, (Pl. 48, p. 32 in Wolflin, *The Last Judgment*).

20. *Ibid.*

21. Cf. infra, p. 91f.

22. The marked contrast between Odilo's innovative discovery and the essential preparatory groundwork of Majolus and William of Volpiano may be stressed here. Cf. infra, p. 107, n. 15. As Hesbert, *op. cit.*, p. 398, points out: All Souls was not simply a prayer of intercession for the faithful departed but more, "un avant-goût de la grande fête de la resurrection générale". F. Neiske, "Cluniacs in Italy and the Connections between William of Dijon's Reform of Monasteries" is now being prepared for forthcoming publication in *FS* (1976).

3. The Imperial Name in
the Cluniac Liturgy

Having seen that the Cluniac brotherhood was based on
liturgical and eschatological foundations, we now ask about
the relationship of the German emperors to this community.
For example did the emperor have a special or particular place
in Cluny's liturgy and life of prayer? Did this liturgical
relationship remain constant or did it vary during the period
under consideration?

Attention expended on the monastery as a *confraternitas*
or community of intercessory prayer has been slight. References to this aspect of Cluny are for the most part lacking
in the works of pragmatic historians, products of an era concerned more with questions of Church and government than those
of Church and Society. A remark of an outstanding scholar is
illustrative. In rejecting the position that Cluny was a participant in the holy war waged against the Muslims in Spain,
Erdmann states that the only proof we find of Cluniac support
of the warring Christian knights is Odilo's statement that
"he will pray to heaven for them!"[1] The implication here of
course is that the only measurable result of such activity is
total and meaningless historical ineffectiveness. From this
position prayers for popes, prayers for kings, emperors or
laymen by the Cluniac congregation have received little attention. Liturgical studies themselves have all too often tended
to confirm this view based, as the majority of them have been,
on an arid division between the sacred and the profane. Part
of the reason for this state of affairs lies in the refusal to
consider the role of religious rites and ceremonies in Chris-

tian civilization with a respect at least equal to that accorded to the cults of antiquity. The cause here is not far
distant; it lies in the emotional associations still strongly
connected with all aspects of Church history viewed in compe-
tition with the various national states, the obvious consequence of centuries-old polemical attitudes long since rejected for the pre-Christian world.[2] However, the growth of
liturgical studies as a branch of historical science during
this century has done much to bridge the gap brought about
by the rigid compartmentalization into religious and secular
studies still all too prevalent in an age obsessed with
specialization.

Any investigation of the place of the German emperors
in the Cluniac liturgy might well begin with Odilo's statute
for the celebration of All Souls Day, the first Cluniac
statute which we possess. All the poor who attended were
fed with bread and wine, in itself a festive occasion, but
rendered more so by the reliving of the Last Supper of Holy
Thursday in Easter Week: *sicut mos est agi in Coena Domini*.[3]
All the church bells were sounded, several masses were sung,
the early morning mass being celebrated, we are told, *festivo
more* for the souls of all faithful Christians and those of
the monks. In this context the name and memory of the emperor
Henry II (1002-1024) are cited with telling affection and
gratitude as one to be particularly singled out above all
others by his place within the spiritual community in view
of his frequent generosity: We also decree that the memory
of our dear emperor Henry, as is fitting, be celebrated above
all others with the members of the congregation, since we have
been enriched by his many favors, says the text.[4] Then follow
the psalms to be added to the office of the dead for the souls
of the dead monks and the emperor. The unique position of the

emperor in this army of the dead, and his intimate union with them, confirms a previous reference that he even more than others was "one heart and soul" with the community.[5]

The degree of honor and respect accorded to a feast day was indicated, as today, by the type of mass which was sung. Significant in this respect was the celebration of anniversaries, special offices created for the great dignitaries of the earth, kings, prelates, nobles. On such occasions a *plenarium officium* was ordered, requiring a mass to be said by each one of the priests belonging to the community, while other unordained members recited a certain number of psalms and other prayers including the *Pater noster* and the *Ave Maria*.[6] The *anniversarium* was a unique office, repeated the third, the seventh and the thirtieth day for important personages.[7] There were also offices of three days, *triduanum*, and of thirty days, *tricenarium*, said consecutively to mark special occasions or to honor particular dignitaries.

The customals' references to the Emperor in the Cluniac liturgy are few. In the earliest customals we find none which directly designate him by name or title nor does one find any mention of the feast day of All Souls in the early sources.

In the Farfa Customal, however, composed during the abbacy of Odilo, we find a series of observances relating to imperial anniversaries. First to be mentioned is a partial rendering of Odilo's statute discussed above.[8] Further on in a section devoted to the full office we find the prayer of the mass and the office for the dead composed for the commemoration of the emperor as follows: *In Anniversaria Imperatorum officium, Ne tradas bestiis, Responsorium, Si ambulem in medio umbre mortis. Tractum, Commovisti, domine, Offertorium, Erue domine animas eorum. Communio, Ego sum resurrectio.*[9]

Still in the Farfa text, accompanying the description of full offices to be celebrated three times during the year, --July 13, Henry's anniversary, the feast of Sts. Peter and Paul and All Saints, --the name of Henry II is again particularly outstanding, the mass in his honor being identified as the model for all imperial masses.[10] His name is included in a list which comprises all the *familiares* whose full office is to be sung for seven days in accordance with the custom followed for recently deceased monks. Then for the emperor his *dies natalis* is that of "the most beloved member of our society and fraternity". Also among the names of monks or friends remembered in the necrological fragment excerpted in the customary are those of Conrad II and Henry II. The latter again receives fulsome notice as *Einrici ducis amicorum nostrorum et aliorum familiorum nostrorum.*[11] Although these are the only references to the offices said for emperors in the sole customal which we can be certain comes from the reign of Odilo, they suffice to make it clear without contradiction that Cluny's bond with the emperors during this period was firmly anchored in a spiritual union. Henry II particularly is seen as the most honored and revered of spiritual associates referred to as friends or *familiares*.

The later customals composed during the reign of Hugh confirm that the monastery continued the liturgical prayers for the emperor. Bernard's customal, written, as he tells us, at the command of the abbot[12] is the only one composed for the main abbey proper. Its more detailed description is instructive as to the intensity of general prayers said for members of the fraternity and the fervent desire of both rich and poor to become participants during their lifetime in all prayers, alms and other good works. For these and for all benefactors still alive special prayers are sung, the

responsory, *Deus in adjutorium meum intende* and the collect
Pretende Domine, in each hour of the daily office; they are
also remembered in the low and high masses as often as these
are said.[13] After their death they were specially remembered
by the insertion of the collect *Omnipotens sempiterne Deus,
cui,*[14] the first to be sung in masses or offices of the dead
where it was lacking throughout the year. This collect was
also added to the Matins of the dead from Septuagesima Sunday
to All Saints, on days when the full office required twelve
readings and at Vespers and Matins during the Lenten period
and Rogation days. Also, in accordance with the precedent of
the Farfa customary, a special commemoration was held for them
three times a year with *praebendae*, gifts of food to the poor,
just as for monks who died outside the monastery, excepting
private masses, a privilege retained for the latter.

More significant, however, are Bernard's references to
perpetual anniversary masses established by the abbots themselves.[15] These are differentiated in importance. One category is that of the *anniversarium mediocre* or *septenarium* of
which there were various kinds differing in importance as expressed in liturgical prayers, the number of candles burned
and poor fed. However, in contra-distinction to all of these
was the *magnum anniversarium* reserved for emperors, empresses,
and kings *qui magnum quid contulerunt ecclesiae*. Only five
dignitaries seem to have met this condition in the abbot's
judgment: the emperor Henry II, "the second Henry", obviously
Henry III, Fernando, the king of Spain, and the empresses
Adelaide and Agnes.[19] The obituary commemorations of these
royal personages were celebrated with all possible festivity
and reverence: all bells were rung daily at Vespers and
during the Mass and Office and while the Mass was being celebrated twelve poor were well fed with bread, wine and meat

while in the refectory the monks "feasted" on fish and wine
spiced with honey, *pigmentum*.[17] The tract was sung in copes,
the responsory in tunics, antiphons and psalms were said at
Vespers, the whole office and the responsory were intoned,
five candlesticks were set before the altar.[18] By means of
this liturgical honor the union between Cluny and the German
Emperors became part of the core of the monastery's life.
Also the Emperor Henry III received special recognition in
Bernard's day along with Abbot Odilo and King Fernando by the
daily remembrance in the three daily *prebendae* offered to the
poor.[19] It might also be noted that no popes were included
in this select group, nor are any mentioned in this connection
in Ulrich or the *Farfa Customal*.

Ulrich's customary adds confirmation to these passages
in Bernard as one might expect in view of the fact that he
utilized Bernard's text in writing his own. His references,
however, are more succinct. Of the German emperors and empresses only Henry II is referred to by name with regard to
his anniversary[20] and the *praebendae* of three monks given
for alms.[21] Of the prayers said before nocturnes the pertinent verses sung for kings and all members of the spiritual
family were: *Domine, salvos fac reges; salvos fac servos et
ancillas* preceding the collect, *Praetende Domine*. To these
verses discretionary choice could permit the addition of other
Collects followed by: *Et pacem tuam nostris concede tempori-
bus* and *Animae famulorum tuorum requiescant in pace*.[22] Daily
masses for kings and other princes are also noted by Ulrich
in a passage which indicates special attention shifting to the
reges Hispaniarum.[23]

We may summarize then the conclusion from this first
group of evidence: that the Roman emperors were united to
Cluny by close spiritual bonds, those of special mention in
the liturgy of the far-flung monastic confraternity.

The obituary sources show themselves to be even more
explicit as to the widespread commemoration of the imperial
name by the Cluniac *ecclesia*. If we accept the principle, in
the absence of any necrology still extant from the mother abbey, that in view of the corporative nature of the Cluniac
confraternity, the names of the emperors appearing in the necrologies of its dependencies must have also been celebrated
at Cluny, it follows that customal and necrological sources
complement one another. In the largest of the remaining
Cluniac necrologies, that of Marcigny,[24] there are not only
imperial names but also evidence of the communal aspect of
the Cluniac confraternity itself presented in a manner that
other documents cannot transmit. Names as varied in time and
space as Archbishop Burchard of Lyon,[25] Ademar of Monteil,
Bishop of Le Puy,[26] Anselm, Archbishop of Canterbury,[27] Anselm,
Bishop of Lucca,[28] are listed as professed Cluniacs, Bertha,[29]
queen of Burgundy, widow of Rudolph II, Henry I, King of England,[30] Henry, Bishop of Toul,[31] as spiritual associates,
familiares, of the *fraternitas*. Hence from this huge, although only partial, obituary list, conclusions may be drawn
as to who was a member of *nostrę congregationis monachi*, as
the necrology is entitled, and who was included among *alii
familiares nostri*.[32] In addition the recurrence of these
entries in other Cluniac obituary lists shows a highly developed sense of community, uniquely Cluniac, whose origin is
in the feast of All Souls.[33]

Here we can see how prayers for *all* the dead began to
realize themselves in the practical consequences tied to
membership in the expanding confraternity. *By its example
Cluny tried to bring about a state of affairs where all souls
could and would be remembered by name and date in the multiple
necrologies of the one confraternity.* Conversely, necrologies

f other monastic movements during the tenth and eleventh
enturies cannot be used in the same manner. The appearance
f the names of the Cluniac abbots in other non-Cluniac
oituaries indicates in no way their Cluniac source as do
he Cluniac necrologies we possess.[34] Hence, while being
indful of the fragmentary nature of our evidence, we can
onetheless feel ourselves to be on firm ground in identify-
ng the members of the Cluniac *societas* by following the com-
arative method suggested almost a century ago by Molinier
nd since advanced by the further research of Schnürer and
ollasch.

Some examples taken from the Marcigny lists of names
f emperors, popes and abbots are highly illustrative.
chnürer has indicated the presence of the names in the ex-
erpts of other necrologies available to him by use of the
ollowing code: St.-Martin-des-Champs = SMC, Longpont = L,
t. Martial de Limoges = SML, followed by the page number,
hich method we too shall employ. It may be recalled again
hat the Moissac necrology has been neither edited nor pub-
ished, and was not utilized. However, for our purposes, the
hree obituary lists which are available in addition to that
f Marcigny-sur-Loire prove to be of value in their present
orm, since the names excerpted from the manuscripts for pub-
ication are those of ranking dignitaries. As a consequence,
he lists of the deceased monks which were not published in
he three smaller necrologies do not detract from the com-
leteness of the comparison, at least within the limits im-
osed by the small number of available sources.

Beginning with the Marcigny necrology, the names of the
mperors are listed according to date and month with both
ames and title indicated in the margins, apart from the main
roup of names. As Wollasch has shown,[35] the list of names

contained in the margin forms a separate column composed of
the *familiares* differentiated from the larger and main list-
ing which, again by name, day and month, identifies the professed monks. Four German emperors are commemorated: Otto
II[36] on December 7 (†983), the Empress Adelaide[37] on December
17 (†999), Henry II[38] on July 13 (SMC, 446; L, 525), Agnes,[39]
(SMC, 473) the spouse of Henry III (1039-1056), on December
14 (†1077). From an analysis of the script Schnürer informs
us that the names of Otto II and Adelaide were inserted during
the tenth century, those of Henry II and Agnes during the first
and second half of the eleventh respectively.[40] Missing from
the list are the names of the emperors Otto I, Otto III, Conrad II, Henry III and, perhaps significantly, Henry IV. Alphonso VI of Castille-Leon (SMC, 453)[41] is also listed among
the *familiares*, on August 21 as an emperor.

However, on the basis of the customal texts and other
sources of the abbey, there should be little doubt that all
emperors since 962 were commemorated in the Cluniac necrology.
We already know from Bernard that Henry III was commemorated
in anniversary masses of signal solemnity. From an earlier
period we have a reference taken from a Cluniac necrology
which assures us that the full office of the dead was sung
for Conrad II. Despite the absence of the names of Otto I
and Otto III, it is hardly conceivable to the reader of Odilo's
Epitaphium that their passing did not call forth obituary remembrance particularly in view of Jotsald's description of
Otto I and of Otto III's links to Farfa. As to the relations
between Cluny and Henry IV, they merit a discussion in terms
of the reign of Saint Hugh.

Nonetheless, we may note the appearance of the reform
popes of the latter half of the eleventh century in the lists.
Victor II[42] is included with the *familiares* for July 28 (1057)

whereas Stephen IX[43] under March 29 (1058), Nicholas II[44] under July 25 (1061), Urban II[45] under July 29 (1099) (SMC, 449; L, 525; SML, 74), are all listed as professed monks. Our other three necrologies supplement this invaluable information. In the thirteenth century necrology of S. Martial de Limoges[46] we find the obituary notice of Alexander II[47] listed under April 20 (1073). Whereas in the necrology of the Cluniac priory St. Martin-des-Champs Gregory VII,[48] May 25 (1085), Pascal II,[49] January 22 (1119), and Gelasius II,[50] January 29 (1119), also have their names inscribed. The name of Leo IX on April 13 (1054) is reported to be in the unpublished manuscript of Moissac.[51] That all these popes mentioned were professed Cluniacs with the exception of Victor II, and possibly Alexander II, is of course a fact of major importance as is its corollary that papal names from earlier times do not appear in the obituary notices which we possess.

From this inquiry into Cluniac obituaries, supplemented by customal references, we may draw some brief conclusions. The first is based on the certitude that the emperor's name resounded on the most solemn occasions of the Cluniac confraternity. What better way for Cluny to express the bonds uniting monastery to empire? Such a conclusion is valid for the imperial period that ends with the death of Henry III in 1056. One may state with confidence that no other benefactors stood higher in Cluny's esteem during this time. Also beginning with the latter half of the eleventh century the marked appearance of the reform popes in the Cluniac obituary notices indicates that Cluny was a source of popes and that the bonds of confraternity were kept alive. However, our comments on this aspect of Cluniac involvement in the history of the eleventh and twelfth centuries[52] must await the further development of our central theme.

The highest dignity in Christendom was drawn into this spiritual orbit at a time in history when the liturgy was the paramount force which alone exerted a universal appeal beyond the widespread tribal and political divisiveness. As with all benefactors, prayers were granted only in recognition of some human act of renunciation of the goals of this world, made in the form of a gift, grant or donation. The magnanimity of imperial gifts to Cluny therefore received recognition in the daily and liturgical cycle of prayer. However, the monastery's relationship to the Saxon and early Salian emperors rested on other bases that supplemented the recognition of those *qui magnum quid contulerunt ecclesiae.*

NOTES

1. C. Erdmann, *Die Entstehung* etc., p. 61.

2. See E. Kantorowicz' introduction to his *Laudes egiae* on this point.

3. *P.L.* 142, 1038.

4. *Necnon ut memoria chari nostri imperatoris Heinrici um eisdem praecipue agatur, constituimus: ut merito debe-us, multis ab ipso ditati opibus. Ibid.*, 1039.

5. Cf. infra, p. 47, n. 10 and p. 56, n. 22.

6. A. Molinier, *Les obituaires français*, pp. 115-116.

7. *Ibid.*, and E. Freistedt, *op. cit.*, passim.

8. Albers, I, p. 134.

9. Albers, I, p. 201.

10. *Ibid.*, p. 204.

11. *Ibid.*, p. 205. Cf. infra, p. 84, n. 24.

12. Ber., *Prae.*, p. 134.

13. Ber., I, 26, Herrgott, p. 200 for what follows.

14. *Ibid.* Given in full by Udal., I, 7 as *cuius humana onditio.*

15. Ber., I, 27, Herrgott, p. 272 for the various kinds f anniversaries.

16. Ber., I, 13, Herrgott, p. 158.

17. Ber., I, 27, Herrgott, p. 272, also *ibid.*, 246.

18. Ber., I, 27, Herrgott, p. 272.

19. Ber., I, 19, Herrgott, p. 158.

20. Udal., III, 12, *P.L.* 149, 756.

21. Udal., III, 24, *P.L.* 149, 767.

22. Udal., I, 5, *P.L.* 149, 648-649.

23. Udal., I, 6, *P.L.* 149, 651.

24. G. Schnürer, *Das Necrologium* etc.

25. *Ibid.*, p. 48.

26. *Ibid.*, p. 58.

27. *Ibid.*, p. 32.

28. *Ibid.*, p. 22.

29. *Ibid.*, p. 19.

30. *Ibid.*, p. 90.

31. *Ibid.*, p. 44.

32. *Ibid.*, p. 1.

33. J. Wollasch, "Die Gemeinschaft der Lebenden" etc., p. 390.

34. *Ibid.*, p. 399.

35. J. Wollasch, "Ein cluniacenzisches Totenbuch," p. 416 n. 57.

36. G. Schnürer, *op. cit.*, p. 91.

37. *Ibid.*, p. 93.

38. *Ibid.*, p. 53.

39. *Ibid.*, p. 93.

40. *Ibid.*, p. xixf.

41. *Ibid.*, p. 71.

42. *Ibid.*, p. 57.

43. *Ibid.*, p. 25.

44. *Ibid.*, p. 56. Different days are listed in other non-Cluniac obituary lists. This source is the only one we have which certifies that Nicholas II was a professed monk, nor was Stephen IX considered to be a Cluniac, having been abbot of Monte Cassino. However, deathbed profession has to be taken into account in the latter case, if not others.

45. *Ibid.*, p. 57.

46. E. Molinier, *op. cit.*, p. 71.

47. E. Molinier, *op. cit.*, p. 71. Alexander II is listed under *peregrini*. Monks of S. Martial de Limoges were designated by l or le = *limovicensis*, and others, included with them in the list of *nostre congregationis monachi* were referred to by c or cl = *cluniacensis*. J. Wollasch, *Ein cluniacenzisches Totenbuch* etc., p. 433, also p. 426.

48. *Obituaires de la Province de Sens*, I, 1 (Recueil des Historiens de la France, 1902), p. 440.

49. *Ibid.*, p. 423.

50. *Ibid.*, p. 424.

51. J. Wollasch, "Die Wahl das Papstes Nicholas II," *Adel und Kirche*, p. 209.

52. Cluniac involvement with laymen is also of relevance here. It is the subject of a lengthy study by W. Teske, "Laienmönche und Laienbrüder in der Abtei Cluny" to appear as a two-part publication in *FS*, (1976 and 1977).

4. Crux Imperatorum Philosophia

The depth of the union between the monastery of Cluny and the renovated Roman Emperor was perhaps most vividly and unequivocally expressed in their common devotion to the life of the cross. Each in its own way became a model representative of a manner of making the cross effective in the renewal of life and institutions.

At Cluny itself and throughout the entire monastic confraternity that followed its *ordo* an increased veneration for the cross developed. Both the Exaltation of the Holy Cross and the Finding of the Holy Cross were celebrated at Cluny with especial reverence.[1] In view of the crowds that came to adore the cross at Cluny Odilo ordered the day to be one of fasting.[2] Both feast days, significantly, were associated with events occurring during the reign of the Byzantine emperor Heraclius. The *Inventio sanctae crucis* was celebrated May 3, the day on which a relic of the True Cross had been found by this emperor.[3] During the wars of the seventh century this cross was lost to the Sassanid Persians after the conquest of Jerusalem in 614. With the loss of the relic the old tradition of the *Adoratio sanctae crucis* disappeared from the liturgy of the Church only to reappear in renewed festivity as the *Exaltatio crucis* following its recovery through the imperial victory over the Persian army in 628.[4] The victor, Heraclius himself, bore this portion of the True Cross to Jerusalem in 692 where it was erected in the basilica on Mount Calvary. It was the material elevation of the cross that was celebrated.[5] This feast was celebrated on September 14.

Also, it was probably at Cluny that the three-fold sign of the cross on forehead, mouth and breast before the Gospel reading during the mass came into being.[6] In addition, as part of the increased attention for everything connected with the preparation and care of the Host,[7] whereas previously three signs of the cross were made over the chalice, two more were added by the pious monks to complete the representation of the five wounds.[8] Also at Cluny it was specified that the Cross in its intercessory power took precedence over the saints.[9] The increased use of the sign of the cross for one-self was doubtless linked to the desire to grasp the word of God in accordance with the words of Luke 8, 12: "The wicked enemy who is anxious to steal the word of God away from the hearts of the hearers."[10] Guests and pilgrims likewise who entered the church in order to pray were told to go first of all to adore the Holy Cross behind the main altar in the choir.[11] Especial care was shown in this respect to monks gravely ill or on the verge of death.[12] When a brother's last hour was seen to be approaching, he was given last rites by either the abbot or the prior, while a priest and other monks attended him.[13] Appropriate psalms were sung while the dying monk was anointed with the sign of the cross made over all his five senses: his eyes, ears, lips, nose, hands, as well as over his feet and genitals, and over whatever part of his body he might need the mercy of God.[14] During a monk's illness, a cross was affixed before his eyes. When death was seen to be certain, other monks exercized in such matters were summoned. They spread out his cloak, sprinkled ashes over it in the sign of the cross, lifted the dying brother from his bed, placed him on the vestment and enclosed him in it.[15] The death of Odilo is described by Jotsald in detail.[16] His description is one, we should realize, of that monk in-

voked in a hymn as *decus Ecclesiae*[17] and it is fair to assume
that not only is meant the leader of the Cluniac Church, but
the leading representative of the Church as a whole.[18]
Odilo's life is presented as one fulfilled and redeemed by
the glory of the cross and Christ crucified.[19] We are told,
too, of his own black thoughts and the illusions of evil
spirits warded off by the words, *crux Domini mei vita* before
he dies in peace.[20] We still possess a prayer of Odilo's[21]
to be said when adoring the cross, which indicates the deepest source of his own faith, intimately connected, it deserves
to be noted, with his unshakeable faith in resurrection.[22]

Among the fifteen remaining sermons of Odilo is one on
the Holy Cross, "the cross on which the author of our salvation hung".[23] He begins with historical commentary on this
theme by a review of feasts which commemorate the cross. The
celebration of the Finding of the Holy Cross cultivates anew
the resurrection of the crucified Lord, he says, while the
feast of the Exaltation of the same cross celebrates that by
which the crucified Saviour ascended to heaven.[24] Christ's
redeeming grace for women is invoked, along with the salvation
of Mary Magdalene and the image of the Virgin standing at the
foot of the cross, with references drawn from Ambrose and Sed-
ulius. In this context we are reminded of the Empress Helena's
discovery of the True Cross and, significantly, her influence
on her son Constantine "the first to concede favor and liberty
to the Roman Church".[25] It is thanks to Constantine that the
faith and victory of the crucified Lord extended throughout
the world as far as the imperial power reached.[26] And we are
told that St. Jerome in an eloquent discourse on the praise
of the cross described how its saving image of chastisement
decorated the military banners, the royal vestments and the
imperial crown.[27] The monks are then reminded by examples

drawn from the saints, particularly Peter and Paul, of the
need to accept the suffering and mystery of the cross without
which the highest knowledge and wisdom remain unaccessible.
The image of the cross in its height, depth, length and
breadth is made into the standard for life. Thanks to its
demands we are able to understand in its breadth, good works
of charity; in its length, perserverance to the end; in its
height, the hope of celestial rewards; in its depth, the in-
scrutable judgments of God.[28] Helena, ruling with Constantine and "the most Christian prince", Heraclius, are lauded
for the liturgical feasts associated with their names. At
this point Odilo finds himself at a loss for words to speak
of such a grand subject. Always self-depreciating as to his
own literary eloquence,[29] he turns to the Church Fathers.
After praising the celebrated Carolingian scholar Rabanus
Maurus,[30] he turns to St. John Chrysostom in order to distill
the savour and meaning of his words. Words from the Eastern
saint then bring his sermon to a close with a veritable hymn
of praise to the cross composed of fifty short ecstatic in-
vocations all beginning with the word *crux*, the first of
which read: "The cross is the hope of Christians, the cross
is the resurrection of the dead, the cross is the leader of
the blind," etc.[31] If we now turn to the customal of the old
imperial abbey of Farfa reformed by Odilo himself we find
twenty-seven of these same short rhythmical sentences invoking the glory of the cross and its central place as the source
of salvation there as well.[32] However this time they are recorded as being an inscription on the cross itself.[33] In view
of their unique place of honor[34] it may be assumed that Odilo's
intention was to imprint their language on the minds and
hearts of all who would adore the cross, which, as we are

told, included, apart from the monks, a considerable number of other celebrants and visitors.[35]

All of them taken together as a whole might be said to represent a Cluniac theology of the cross basic to the monastery's purpose of spiritual renewal. Indeed, if Cluny can be said to have a spiritual doctrine,[36] admittedly a debatable question, its source would seem to be found here in these verses so intimately connected with its liturgical devotion. One of them particularly deserves notice, not only because of its relationship to the historical commentary of Odilo's sermon, but, more significantly, because it succinctly formulates Cluny's crucial link to the emperors. The verse in question reads: *Crux imperatorum philosophia*; The Cross is the philosophy of emperors. These words of Chrysostom,[37] attributing the philosophical profundity contained in the cross to emperors and applied originally to the Christian rulers of the old Roman Empire, were no less applicable in the renovated Empire of Odilo's day. The Roman Emperor in the West, as previously under Constantine, bore responsibility for the liberty of the Roman Church. The Emperor's central place in God's plan of salvation, as Odilo makes clear in his sermon, has been present since the days of Constantine.[38] Emperors are seen by Odilo as unique embodiments of Church history, hence the single verse *Crux imperatorum philosophia* becomes extended in its meaning by those accompanying it. Like the musical variations in a fugue they compose a brief recital, so to speak, of the saving power of the cross in the history of salvation. The multi-faceted mystery of the reversal of values revealed by the cross,[39] that life becomes possible through death, strength through weakness, that God in his foolishness is wiser than man in his wisdom, is here expressed in pithy form by a variety of complementary themes

which serve to reinforce one another. That the cross is the
philosophy of emperors then is given added meaning by association with the other verses: "The cross is the guardian of
children." "The cross is the light fixed in the darkness."
"The cross is the wisdom of the foolish." "The cross is the
glorification of martyrs." "The cross is the foundation of
the Church." "The cross is the protection of the whole
earth."

At the same time by the choice of the term philosophy
a contrasting distinction is intended with the following
verses: "The cross is the magnificence of kings." "The
cross is the reunion of the apostles." "The cross is the
continence of monks." "The cross is the joy of priests."
Kings, apostles, monks and priests all are graced by particular relationships to the cross in their various Christian offices,[40] but none are characterized by an identification
of the cross with philosophy. Since the principle involved in
the choice of the somewhat ambiguous term *philosophia* introduces other associations, some further analysis of its usage
for the sake of clarity may be helpful.

Odilo himself in his *Vita Maioli* had spoken of philosophers in a depreciating, yet conventional, sense of the
word by stating that his predecessor had avoided their dialectical syllogisms and rhetorical arguments.[41] However, the
term acquired another historical usage with the advent of
Christianity.[42] In Eusebius philosophy is not only the Christian faith, but asceticism as well, hence philosophy later became identified with the monastic life.[43] Bruno of Querfurt
(†1009), the imperial archbishop,[44] writes that St. Adalbert
was fed with the philosophy of St. Benedict.[45] Cluniac usage
of the term was within this tradition. Ulrich refers to St.
Jerome as a philosopher of Christ[46] and St. Hugh as well is

called by his anonymous biographer *philosophus Christi*.[47]
The "cross as philosophy" lent monkish attributes to the
emperors,[48] one might even say it meant that emperors were
monks. However, such a meaning should be understood only as
indicative of their full acceptance and embodiment of Christianity. Also, the identification of the cross with the philosophy of emperors means that the emperors took monasticism as
their ideal. The saints with which Otto III surrounded himself confirm that the ideal became reality in the persons of
Sts. Adalbert, Romuald, Nilus and Sylvester. Henry II allowed
his line to die out by living as a monk with his queen Kuni-
gunde and had sainthood bestowed on him. The cross in its
triumph over all ancient wisdom by its power to redeem man
from the pangs of death had become for Augustine *nostra philo-*
sophia containing in itself the solution to the deepest contradictions and mysteries of life. Hence we are justified in
seeing the emperors with the cross as their philosophy strid-
ing through the world as the incarnation of the wisdom of
revelation.

We have already noted Odilo's description of the victorious wars of Otto I as a routing of demons and a triumph of the
cross and when he dies peace departs.[49] The same Otto is reported as having fasted when wearing the crown which was surmounted by a cross.[50] Hence it is by virtue of his Christian
authority that in his documents he speaks to *omnibus dei*
fidelibus et nostris or addresses the *universitas omnium*
fidelium sancte dei ecclesie nostrorumque.[51] A famous story
illustrates how this sovereign imperial power was cautioned
by the gift of a cross which served in turn as a recognition
by the emperor of Cluny's essence.[52] Pope Benedict VIII
(1012-1024) had presented Henry II (1002-1024) with a golden
apple covered with precious stones and surmounted by a cross.

The Emperor received it joyfully and praised the Pope for the discreet manner by which he indicated that the power of the monarchical function should be tempered. He then added that none were more fitted to receive the gift than those who pass over the pomps of the world to follow more readily the cross of the Saviour. And he thereupon sent the gift to Cluny.

There exists however perhaps no better illustration of the dictum quoted by Odilo and transcribed on the back of the cross at Cluny than its embodiment in the coronation ceremony of the Mainz *ordo*. Schramm tells us[53] that this *ordo*, composed about the year 980, add or subtract twenty years (the precedent for which was the crowning of Otto I in Aachen in 936), influenced in detail almost all royal coronations of Catholic Europe even outside of Germany.[54] Of the various steps in this royal ceremony which begins with the king being led to the church by two bishops holding the Gospel and two crosses, while singing *"Ecce mitto angelum meum"*,[55] there is one which recalls the procedure followed for professed monks. After the king lays down his weapons and his cloak, following his entrance into the church, he is then led to the altar. There he throws himself down in the form of a cross with his arms outstretched and remains in this position throughout the litany which follows according to Carolingian models.[56] Beside him lie bishops and priests who represent the "twelve apostles, martyrs, witnesses, virgins, etc."[57] The king in the form of the crucified Lord represents Christ the Saviour as Schramm emphasizes, *cuius typum geris in nomine, cuius nomen vicemque gestare crederis*.[58] *Crux imperatorum philosophia* was thus an expression of the Christian order of life given direction by the cross and stabilized by the person of the Holy Emperor.[59] The emperor, beginning with Otto I had spoken to the *universitas omnium fidelium*. Cluny in imitation of this imperial appeal to universality of all the faithful added its purgatorial *commemoratio omnium fidelium defunctorum*. It is in this appeal to "all" expressed in contrasting forms that the notions of unity and universality could enter Christian consciousness as never before.[60]

A passage in the Farfa customal deals with the extreme care devoted to liturgical vessels used for the sacrament of Communion: the chalice, containing the wine, and the paten on which the bread rests.[61] We are told particularly of the concern for cleanliness in preparation for the mass and, more importantly, of the verses ordered to be inscribed on them by order of the abbot, Odilo himself. Six possible inscriptions are listed. From among these two are to be chosen to be inscribed on each of the vessels along with a cross. The six versicles read as follows:

> From this source the mystical sacraments of the Lord are eaten.
>
> Oh children! that which you take from me embrace.
>
> This blood fused with the body of the Lord is eaten.
>
> You who drink this potion consume it with great trembling.
>
> The abbot having the name of Odilo had these vessels made.
>
> And by the gift of Henry the King he brought them to the altars.

The last word is followed by a cross.

The emperor's name then was inscribed on a portion of the liturgical vessels containing the very essence of the monastic community's union with our Creator, the Eucharist. Thereby through daily remembrance at mass and communion the emperor's name was prominent throughout the year.

Is the emperor referred to Henry II or Henry III? It is difficult to give a definitive answer to this question although the evidence seems heavily in favor of Henry II. Since it can be ascertained that the Farfa costumal was transcribed after the death of the emperor Conrad II in 1039, his successor Henry III (1039-1056) becomes a possibility as the originator of these gifts. We are informed of his munificence in sending presents to decorate the Cluniac house of the Lord and these could well include liturgical vessels.[62] However, the occasion on which these gifts were offered eliminate them as a possibility since they follow upon the date of Odilo's death, hence after the composition of the custumal in question.

The Emperor Henry II was regarded by Cluny under Odilo with marked affection. The statute for All Soul's Day, the gift of the golden apple of the Empire, the fact that the anniversary mass for Henry was taken as a model for all emperors, are indicative of reciprocity of regard. In addition Jotsald has recorded Henry's transmission to Cluny of the gifts of his royal crown and several ecclesiastical vessels,[63] a report described elsewhere in detail.[64] We are told by Ademar that Henry II presented Cluny with a scepter, a golden apple, a golden imperial vestment, a golden crown, a golden crucifix and many other things weighing together some 100 pounds.[65] In the Farfa custumal we find gifts of this kind referred to, not surprisingly, in a liturgical context, that of the Feast of the Ascension.[66] During this holy day at Cluny the imperial insignia in procession included a golden cross adorned with precious stones, the imperial apple and the royal scepter. These were accompanied by crosses,

banners, candelabra, reliquaries, holy water and a censer.[67]
On other high feast days of the year the imperial insignia
decorated the altar.[68] During the high feast days a tablet
portraying the image of Christ and the Virgin accompanied the
royal insignia in procession.[69] Hence there is no question
that Cluny's relationship to Henry II was of a special nature,
making it likely that it was his name which was inscribed on
the liturgical vessels.[70]

The emperor very likely paid a visit to the mother abbey,
although the date is still open to question.[71] Already before
Henry's visit to Cluny monasteries within the empire had encountered Cluniac influence through the monastic reform in
Lorraine. Impressed by the growth of the Cluniac order, he
resolved upon monastic renewal within the empire by the introduction of *consuetudines monasticae* which were, unlike
those of Cluny, subject to imperial control. The conclusion
appears therefore justified, coinciding as it does with the
evidence already presented, that for Henry II Cluny was considered as representing the model monastic community.[72]

NOTES

1. Udal., I, 38, *P.L.* 149, 684-685. This feast day is also found in the earliest Cluniac customaries: BB[1], C and EC in Albers, II, 28-29, 57-58, 114-115 respectively.

2. Udal., *loc. cit.*, 685.

3. G. Ellard, "Devotion to the Holy Cross and a Dislocated Mass-Text," *Theological Studies*, vol. 11, no. 3, (1950), pp. 333-355 for this aspect.

4. *Ibid.*, pp. 334f.

5. *Ibid.*

6. See J. Jungmann, *Missarum sollemnia*, I, p. 579-580. Ber., I, 72, Herrgott, p. 264 indicates the tendency: *singulas Cruces ad Sequentia sancti Evangelii, in fronte, in pectore, sibi depingit cum pollice, ac tertiam cum digitis duobus ante se.* The final form is in the *Constitutiones Hirsaugenses*, I, 86, Herrgott, p. 457 and *P.L.* 150, 1017: *singulas cruces facit cum pollice in fronte, ore et pectore.*

7. For reverence towards the Host at Cluny and the central place of crosses in its consecration see Ber., I, 35, Herrgott, p. 220-227. The first mention of the *ablutio oris*, the purification of the mouth with wine after communion is also found in the *Constitutiones* of Hirsau, I, 86, *P.L.* 150, 1019. Jungmann, *op. cit.*, II, 512. Also Udal., III, 13, 14, *P.L.* 149, 757, 758.

8. Ber., I, 72, Herrgott, 265. See Jungmann, *op. cit.*, II, p. 335, n. 4.

9. Udal., I, 5, *P.L.* 149, 650.

10. Jungmann, *op. cit.*, I, 580-581. It is, as he reminds us, a "blessing of oneself".

11. Udal., III, 12, *P.L.* 149, 764. Ber., II, 17, Herrgott, p. 317.

12. Udal., III, 28f., *P.L.* 149, 770 and Ber., I, 24, Herrgott, p. 190f.

13. Udal., *loc. cit.*, p. 770. Ber., *loc. cit.* The Cluniac abbots were identified with the saving power of the cross in the highest degree. A legend recounts Hugh's power to make a storm do his bidding by making the sign of the cross.

14. Udal., *loc. cit.*, p. 771. Ber., *ibid.*

15. Ber., *ibid.*, p. 192. Also Udal., *ibid.*, p. 772. The last five chapters of Ulrich's customary, *P.L.* 149, 771-778, are devoted to the death of monks, including special provisions for the death of a brother in another monastery, *ibid.*, p. 775, and the death of the abbot, *ibid.*, p. 776.

16. *P.L.* 142, 909f.

17. *Ibid.*, 1043.

18. Cf. infra, p. 100f. The term Cluniac Church in the sources refers to Cluny's independence and authority with regard to other churches, including the Roman.

19. *P.L.* 142, 910-912.

20. *Ibid.*, 910-911. He had once said: *Si Christus non crucifigeretur, homo non liberatetur. Sermo III, De Purificatione Sanctae Dei Genitricis Mariae, P.L.* 142, 1001.

21. *Ad Crucem adorandam Oratio, P.L.* 142, 1037-1038.

22. *Certissima fiducia est Christianorum divinitus promissa resurrectio mortuorum. De Resurrectione Domini, Sermo V, P.L.* 142, 1004.

23. *Sermo XV, De Sancta Cruce, P.L.* 142, 1031f.

24. *Ibid.*, 1031.

25. The connection between Roman Church and Roman Emperor is obvious. Here once again in this passage a Cluniac view of history is presented running parallel with that presented previously on p. 37f.

26. *Ibid.*, 1032.

27. *Ibid.*

28. Odilo probably drew on the Augustinian sources found in G. Ladner's "St. Gregory of Nyssa and St. Augustine on the Symbolism of the Cross" in *Late Classical and Medieval Studies in Honor of A. M. Friend*, (ed. K. Weitzmann, Princeton, N.J., 1955), p. 92f.

29. As in his preface to his *Vita Maioli*, *P.L.* 142, 944.

30. Whose *De laudibus sanctae crucis* was widely read in the ninth and tenth centuries.

31. *Op. cit.*, 1034.

32. Albers, I, p. 184.

33. *In posteriora crucis ista scribantur. Crux parvu-lorum custos. Crux virorum caput. Crux senum finis. Crux lumen in tenebris sedentium. Crux regum magnificentia. Crux scutum perpetuum. Crux insensatorum sapientia. Crux libertas servulorum. Crux imperatorum philosophia. Crux templorum destructio. Crux lex impiorum. Crux idolorum repulsio. Crux prophetarum praeconatio. Crux scandalum judaeorum. Crux adunatio apostolorum. Crux perditio impiorum. Crux martyrum gloriatio. Crux claudorum virtus. Crux monachorum abstinen-tia. Crux egrotantium medicus. Crux virginum castitas. Crux mundatio leprosorum. Crux gaudium sacerdotum. Crux paraliti-corum requies. Crux aecclesiae fundamentum. Crux orbis terrae cautela. Ibid.*

34. The cross referred to is in all likelihood the main cross behind the altar. The inscriptions were to be found therefore on the side facing away from the altar. On Good Friday *fertur crux retro majus altare, ut a popularibus adoretur*, Ber., II, 17, p. 317.

35. Cf. infra, p. 126.

36. J. Leclercq, "Pour une histoire de la vie à Cluny," *RHE*, 57, (1962), pp. 385-408, 783-812, K. Hallinger, "Le climat spirituel des premiers temps de Cluny" and the articles in *Spiritualità Cluniacense*, all emphasize the need for de-fining such a doctrine.

37. Who also said in the year 387, six years after the Second Ecumenical Council, "The emperor is without a peer

upon earth for he is the head and crown of everything in this world." *Homily on the Statues*, ii, 2, in W. H. C. Frend, *The Early Church*, (New York, 1966), p. 223. The saint also declared that "the Saviour did not leave his cross on earth but took it with him into heaven since he is to appear with his cross in his second and glorious coming of which he spoke (Matthew, 24-26) on account of false Christs, false prophets, the Antichrist....for the Antichrist is coming before Christ". *P.G.* 49, 403-404.

38. *P.L.* 142, 1032.

39. "Then, that through those things which you see fulfilled already you may know that all the other things also which are promised must indubitably be fulfilled, mark that the cross of Christ, His shame, His punishment—and the very mention of crucifixion was once abhorrent to the whole world—has now attained to so great glory that the cross is now worshipped by kings and has become to almost all men the object of love and veneration. Note that kings now glory in having their insignia adorned with that whereby, previously, punishment was meted out to sinners and to men utterly debauched." Otto, Bishop of Freising, *The Two Cities*, (translated by C. C. Mierow, New York, 1928), Book IV, 4, pp. 282-283.

40. It is not without significance that no reference is made here to popes.

41. Cf. infra, p. 41, n. 24. Odilo also refers to the "insanity of philosophers" rejected by the martyrs of the nascent Church, *P.L.* 142, 945.

42. The most informative survey is found in J. Leclercq, *Études sur le Vocabulaire Monastique du Moyen Âge*, (Studia Anselmiana, 48, Rome, 1961), who observes (p. 47) that the word philosophy becomes Christianized in the Latin translations of Chrysostom, as well as in the Greek text, after the word itself had been adopted early by Christian authors (p. 43). Augustine appears to be the first to suggest in Latin the expression "Christian philosophy" (p. 46, n. 61). Also E. R. Curtius, *Europaïsche Literatur und Lateinisches Mittelalter*, (Bern and Munich, 1963), p. 217f.

43. For the application of philosophy to the monastic life: I. Auf der Maur, *Mönchtum und Glaubensverkündigung in den Schriften des hl. Johannes Chrysostomus*, (Fribourg, Switzerland, 1959), pp. 87-92 and passim, G. J. M. Bartelink, "'Philosophie' et 'philosophes' dans quelques oeuvres de Jean

Chrysostom" in *RHS*, 36, (1960), pp. 487-492, who refers (p. 489f.) to Eusebian usage. Also as an illustration: "Das Mönchtum als 'Pneumatische Philosophie' in den Nilusbriefen" in *Vom christlichen Mysterium: zum Gedächtnis von O. Casel*, (Düsseldorf, 1951), pp. 135-151. Noteworthy is Auf der Maur's observation that monasticism as "gelebte Philosophie" (p. 88f.) requires not only self-domination and strength of soul but also that one philosophize about God and the future, death and resurrection, the Last Judgment, heaven and earth, that is, the philosopher reflects on the final truths and voices them in his daily life. Included in Chrysostom's definition are contemplation of the cross and prayer.

44. "Der ganz in in den Ideen Ottos III unde der christlichen Mission lebte,"...."trotz des erzbischöflichen Titels und Palliums ein Mönch," R. Holtzmann, *Geschichte der sächsischen Kaiserzeit*, pp. 428-430, 497-499. He died a martyr's death, as did his spiritual forebearer, St. Adalbert of Prague.

45. E. R. Curtius, *op. cit.*, p. 219. Also in this tradition Erasmus of Rotterdam calls Christianity *philosophia Christi. Ibid.*

46. Udal., III, Prae., *P.L.* 149, 731.

47. *P.L.* 159, 924.

48. Cf. infra, p. 219.

49. Cf. infra, p. 57f.

50. H. Dörries, "Der Glaube Ottos des Grossen" in *Jahrbuch der Gesellschaft für niedersächsische Kirchengeschichte*, vol. 47, (Separate printing, 1949), p. 15.

51. *Ibid.*, p. 22.

52. *P.L.* 142, 625-626.

53. P. E. Schramm, *Die Krönung in Deutschland bis zum Beginn des salischen Hauses (1028)*, *ZRG*, vol. 55, *KA*, 24, (1935), pp. 184-332.

54. *Ibid.*, p. 196f. and p. 304f.

55. *Ibid.*, p. 311f.

56. *Ibid.*, pp. 236, 311.

142

57. *Ibid*. Dr. Milton Anastos of the University of California at Los Angeles, who has specialized in Byzantine coronation rituals, assures me that there is no such ceremony for Byzantine emperors. Both Cluny and the Roman Emperors are a bridge between East and West.

58. *Ibid.*, p. 317. See also A. Sprengler, *op. cit.*, p. 91f. for the assimilation of the king to Christ.

59. Examples could be multiplied. On the Imperial Cross of Conrad II, P. E. Schramm, *Herrschaftszeichen und Staatssymbolik*, (3 vols., Stuttgart, 1954-1956), p. 511f.

60. Cf. infra, p. 188.

61. *De secretariis, seu versiculi qualiter sunt conscribendi in calice seu patena.*

> *Secretari namque lavent omni quarta feria callices et die sabbatorum valde mane, omnique tempore, et cotidie perfundant ante missa una hora: et hec versiculi conscripti sint in ipsis, per unumqueque duo et.*
>
>> *Mystica hinc Domini sumuntur hunc sacramenta.*
>> *O filii! quod sumitis amplectimini me.*
>> *Sumitur huic sanguis Domini de corpore fusus.*
>> *Qui bibis hinc potum cum magno sumere tremore.*
>> *Vodilo nomen habens haec vasa patraverat abbas.*
>> *Heinrici regis et munere contulis aris.*

Albers, I, 183. There are corruptions in this text. *Haec* may be suggested for *hunc, hinc* for *huic*. *Intinctio* was practiced at Cluny. See Udal., III, 14, *P.L.* 149, 758 and Ber., I, 35, 225 and 1, 24, 191. J. Evans, *Cluniac Art of the Romanesque Period*, (Cambridge, 1950), p. 13 makes reference to these verse inscriptions but offers no discussion of their significance.

62. *P.L.* 159, 862.

63. *P.L.* 142, 904.

64. P. E. Schramm, *Herrschaftszeichen, gestiftet, geschenkt, verkauft, verpfändet,* (Nachrichten der Akademie der Wissenschaften in Göttingen Phil. Hist. Kl. 1957, no. 5), p. 161, 226. No mention is made of the liturgical vessels in the Cluniac source.

65. *Ibid.,* p. 175.

66. Albers, I, 71.

67. *Ibid.*

68. Albers, I, 57. See also I, 44. Also Conrad II sent the royal insignia to Cluny as a gift and a delegation from Cluny was present at his coronation, *ibid.,* p. 178, n.

69. Albers, I, 86-87.

70. J. Wollasch has criticized the concept of a "Platonic" and merely personal relationship of the Saxon and Salian rulers to Cluny found in the works of Sackur, Hallinger, Tourlier, and Schieffer. Such views indicate misunderstanding in varying degrees, not only of the complementary roles of empire and monastery, but of the profoundly religious basis of their union as well. "Kaiser Heinrich in Cluny," *FS,* 3, 1969), p. 332.

71. J. Wollasch, *ibid.,* p. 337; K. J. Benz has opposed his argument and conclusion in two articles, "Heinrich II in Cluny," *FS,* 8, (1974), pp. 155-178 and "Heinrich II und Cluny," *RB,* 54, (1974), pp. 313-337, although he does affirm (p. 331) that there was an inner relationship between Henry II and the monastery "more or less". Cf. Wollasch's brief reply in *op. cit., FS,* 9, (1975), p. 2, n. 4.

72. J. Wollasch, "Kaiser Heinrich II" etc., p. 338f. The sequence of events is important to keep in mind when comparisons are made between the *consuetudines* of Cluny and those of imperial monasteries. Since Hallinger, *Gorze-Cluny,* ignores the process of "imitation by contrast" that occurs following the imperial visit to Cluny, he has left the way open to an almost infinite number of abstract comparisons that give far too much weight to mere differences of monastic observance.

5. Jerusalem Visio Pacis

Cluny was seen as an earthly image of the heavenly city, a second Jerusalem. Odilo was described as another Abraham leaving his country and friends in order to enter the promised land of Cluny.[1] Conversely the goal of his pilgrimage on earth was to find peace in the holy city.[2] The purpose of Majolus' life is defined as leading souls out from darkness and the shadow of death and setting them on the right path which would take them to the celestial city.[3] Peter Damian tells us that, thanks to the prayers of the Cluniacs, Pope Benedict VIII came to enter supernal Jerusalem.[4] And in the mass for All Souls Day which we possess, the same unmistakable accents reoccur: "We shall be consoled in Jerusalem",[5] "Lead them from darkness into the paradise of light".[6] The construction of the church at Cluny under St. Hugh, the famous Cluny III, celebrated in the entire Western world,[7] represented the architectural embodiment of all these aspirations, "because the church building there had a transcendent role to play. To the monks whose devotion centered there, it was an earthly representative of the celestial Jerusalem--'a place where the dwellers on high would tread, if it could be believed that human abiding-places of this sort are pleasing to them'...." The completed exterior "actually looked like medieval symbolic drawings of the Holy City".[8] In a similar vein, as J. Sauer tells us, Cluny adopted the *crux gemina* for the form of its basilica.[9] This form of the cross had an unknown Eastern origin but was adopted in the West where

t was desired to emphasize the remembrance of Jerusalem and
he "true" cross of Christ.

A simple enumeration of the liturgical chants chosen to
elebrate the anniversary dedication of a church[10] shows that
central theme pervades the selection of texts. Following
he lighting of candles, the readings from the gospels, the
erse of the Apocalypse 21, 2 *Vidi civitatem sanctam* was in-
oned in Chapter before the Responsory *Fundata est*. The hymn
rbs beata was sung followed by the Collect *Deus qui nos per
ingulos* which preceded the Responsory *Bene fundata est* and
erses said by the priest *Domus mea*. *Dominus vobiscum*, then
rayers appropriate to the day found their place at this
oint. *Domum Dei decet sanctitudo* was chanted, the *Urbs
eata* then repeated for the second time. After readings and
esponsories applicable to the day, the Antiphon *Hodie huic
omui* was chanted as well as the psalms, *Laetatus sum, Nisi
ominus, Lauda Hierusalem dominum*. Two candles were then
laced before the main altar, two behind and fifteen *in
ertica*.[11] Following Lauds, the hymn *Angularis fundamentum*
as sung before the Responsory *Domum tuam decet*. The litur-
ical components of Matins and their selected passages in-
luded: the Office *Terribilis est*, the Oration, *Deus qui
os per singulos annos*, the Epistle *Vidi civitatem sanctam*,
he Responsory *Locus iste a deo est Alleluja, Adorabo*, the
ospel, *Erat vir nomine*. At vespers antiphons and psalms
lternated with one another, beginning with the Antiphon
rit mihi dominus and the Psalm *Dixit dominus*, then followed:
ntiphon *Cum evigilasset*, Psalm *Laetatus sum*, Antiphon *Non
st hic aliud*, Psalm *Nisi dominus*, Antiphon *Vidit Jacob*,
salm *Lauda Hierusalem*, all preceding the final hymn *Urbs
eata* and the Oration *Deus per singulos annos*.

The theme of the anniversary celebration is that of the holy city recreated in the house of God. To be noted is the choice of the verse from Apocalypse 21, 2 to introduce the day long anniversary; it is sung twice. Psalm 147, 12 *Lauda Hierusalem* is also sung twice, while the hymn *Urbs beata* honors the occasion, as well as identifying it, by being sung three times.[12] All of these texts have as their central motif the first verses sung in Chapter: "And I, John, saw the holy city, new Jerusalem, coming down from God out of heaven, prepared as a bride adorned for her husband." Psalm 147, 12 reads: "Praise the Lord, O Jerusalem; praise thy God, O Zion. Earlier verses (2-6) of the Psalm identify the holy city more precisely as to what the building of the city consists: "The Lord doth build up Jerusalem: he gathereth together the outcasts of Israel. He healeth the broken in heart, and bindeth up their wounds. He telleth the number of the stars; he calleth them all by their names. Great is our Lord, and of great power: his understanding is infinite. The Lord lifteth up the meek: he casteth the wicked down to the ground." Therewith, the preeminent place given to the beautiful hymn *Urbs beata* becomes readily understandable. Few will find disagreement with Walpole's assertion that the main idea is taken from Revelation, 21, 2, some of its imagery from Isaiah, 28, 16 and I Peter, 2, 5f.[13] Its first line, *Urbs beata Ierusalem dicta visio pacis,* may be said to weave together all the various threads of Cluny's liturgical inheritance of this Biblical vision transmitted by the Church and culminating in the recreation on earth by the Cluniac *societas* of the heavenly model. It was Jerusalem that contained and embodied the vision of peace.

On a bronze vessel now in the Art Museum in Halle, whose origin is probably Magdeburg,[14] is an image of a crowned em-

peror placed in the center of a cross and identified solely
by the name Otto, most likely either Otto I or Otto II. That
this vessel is a liturgical vessel leaves no doubt since on
it we find a circular inscription which repeats the hymn sung
for the dedication of a church, at Cluny and of course elsewhere, *Hierusalem Visio Pacis*.[15] Moreover the vessel itself
is either a *patena chrismalis* for the holy oil (chrism for
catechumen oil) or a saucer for the oil receptacle (*chrisma-
torium, ampulla, pyxis*).[16] In Otto's left hand is the ampulla
itself, in his right the dove of the Holy Spirit.[17] Here we
find united in a single representation the emperor's unique
character within the Church: his special place at the center
of the cross, the presence of his name on liturgical vessels,
assuring commemoration of his name and role within the history of salvation, reaching here the stage of blasphemy in
portraying him as the very carrier of the Holy Spirit himself, as contained in *Hierusalem visio pacis*. Jerusalem as
the vision of peace was then represented at Cluny as well as
in the incarnate presence of the sanctified monasticized emperor, placed in the center of the cross as a Christlike
figure.

Further confirmation of the soundness of this conclusion
is provided by the content of the Cluniac text for the reception of a king,[18] therefore applicable to a visit of Henry II.
Leaving aside the festive activity associated with the greet-
ing and procession, let us focus on the very pertinent and
characteristic choice of the Biblical text: *Ecce mitto angelum meum*.[19] This text has a long history, connected with the
derivation of the imperial *adventus* from Oriental and Hellen-
istic-Roman tradition, whereby the ruler's reception on arrival
in a city possessed a deeply solemn and religious character.[20]
For St. Paul the same term for receiving an emperor is applied

to the eschatological return of Christ. Later in its Christian form every city on earth preparing itself for one anointed becomes a holy city, Jerusalem, celebrating the arrival of one in the likeness of Christ. "The *adventus* of the monarch reflects, or even stages....the Lord's entry into Jerusalem."[21] Hence,"the emperor on his arrival was received like the Redeemer whom he represented". And among the *Ordines ad regem deducendum* the passage in the Farfa costumal presents one of the earliest examples, since none appear to antedate the eleventh century.[22] However,the Messianic import of "Behold I send my angel before thee" does not mean that the emperor is the messenger of God but rather that "as the Lord at his Coming was preceded by the 'messenger', so shall the emperor at his Advent be preceded by an angel".[23] That we find this same text in the Mainz *ordo* chanted at the beginning of the coronation ceremony,while the King is being led to the Church,[24] might now be expected because of its earlier imperial associations. But that this antiphon appears in both sources indicates that Henry II was received at Cluny as an eschatological figure intimately bound up with the embodiment of the life of the cross, the descent of the heavenly Jerusalem on earth, preparing the way for the coming of Christ at Easter in his resurrection. We have already seen how the Masses for All Souls Day which we possess anticipate in their liturgically dramatic form the Last Day of universal resurrection.[25]

The celebration and adoration of the Holy Cross, present in the oldest Cluniac customaries, may be seen in connection with the emperor's eschatological function. The famous hymns, *Vexilla regis prodeunt, Pange lingua* and *Crux benedicta* by Venantius Fortunatus[26] were sung on these feast days when the cross was adored and contemplated.[27] Theodulf of Orléans' *Gloria, Laus et Honor*, an acclamation to Christ on his royal

try into Jerusalem on Palm Sunday[28] was sung at Cluny on
at day, as were the *Vexilla regis* and *Pangue lingua*, while
e royal insignia were borne in procession.[29]

As C. Erdmann indicates,[30] the *imperium Romanum* was
rected by a "Kaiser der Zukunft", one who fulfilled a
ique eschatological role of utmost importance as a bulwark
ainst the times of the Antichrist. In the abbot Adso's
ok on the Antichrist, written ca. 950,[31] we find the Frank-
h kings as heirs of the imperial dignity and from this line
all come one who will hold the empire together. Yet he is
Christian emperor entertaining a vision of Jerusalem where
shall lay down his sceptre and crown in the mount of Olives
fulfillment of the Scriptures which foretell the time of
e end.[32] It is to be stressed that a religious unity inte-
ating the Empire with the spread of the Christian faith is
the base of a terminology found in the oldest liturgical
xts where the themes of *pax, securitas, libertas Romana*
se themselves with the destiny of the Church.[33] The 82nd
rmon of Leo the Great, which defines the function of the
man Empire as that of preaching the Gospel, remained the
sential characteristic of Otto III's political program.[34]
s campaign to the north against the Slavs aimed to realize
e Kingdom of God on earth.[35] However all these studies
erlook the depth and extent of Cluny's entire adhesion to
is imperial intent and function,[36] not only in the *consuetu-
nes,* particularly those of Farfa, but preeminently in the
itings and vocabulary of Odilo as well.

NOTES

1. *P.L.* 142, 899.

2. *Ibid.*, 914.

3. *P.L.* 137, 759.

4. *P.L.* 144, 938.

5. Ps. 64, 1, WB, p. 280.

6. *Ibid.*, p. 263.

7. *P.L.* 159, 898f. and *ibid.*, 884.

8. K. J. Conant, *Carolingian and Romanesque Architecture 800-1200*, (London, 1959), p. 115. Already in 1043 the monastery could shelter some 400-450 souls. In 1245 due to extended building and enlargements some 2,000 visitors could be accomodated on the occasion when Pope Innocent IV, Louis IX, king of France, and the Emperor of Constantinople met there. The number of monks resident under Peter the Venerable was from 300-400. See G. Constable's edition of the *Statuta Petri Venerabilis Abbatis Cluniacensis IX* in *Consuetudines Benedictinae Variae*, VI, (*Corpus Consuetudinum Monasticarum*), Siegburg, (1975), note to Statute 55, p. 85. See also his instructive note to Statute 52, p. 82 on the circles of candles known as *coronae* which were meant to represent the heavenly Jerusalem.

9. *LTK*, VI, 606f. The *crux gemina* had two arms of unequal length, the lower arm being the longer of the two.

10. Albers, I, pp. 131-132. Also Ber., II, 10, pp. 298-299.

11. This was a kind of rood screen used to display ornaments of special significance.

12. If not four. The fifth verse of *Urbs beata* begins *Angularis fundamentum*.

13. A. S. Walpole, *Early Latin Hymns,* (Hildesheim, 1966), p. 377. The hymn was written in the 6-8th centuries. J. Leclercq, "L'Ecriture sainte" etc., pp. 127-128, has indicated the need for a *Biblia liturgica* which would provide an inventory of the Biblical texts as to their place and date in the old liturgies. This entire component of the Cluniac sources well deserves investigation,also as regards the particular circumstances for which they were composed. The choice of liturgical texts and scriptural quotations was certainly one undertaken with thoroughness and learning.

14. See particularly M. Sauerlandt, "Ein ottonisches Bronzebecken im städtischen Museum für Kunst und Kunstgewerbe im Halle a.d.S.," *Zeitschrift für christliche Kunst,* XXXII, Heft 4, (1919), pp. 49-58. Also J. Deér, "Das Kaiserbild im Kreuz," *Schweizer Beiträge zur allgemeinen Geschichte,* vol. 13, (1955), pp. 61ff. and P. E. Schramm, "Die Magdeburger Patene mit dem Bilde Otto des Grossen," *Thüringisch-Sächsische Zeitschrift für Geschichte und Kunst,* vol. 17, (1928), pp. 1-8. See also Eugen Rosenstock-Huessy, *Out of Revolution,* p. 488. An almost identical vessel has been found in Riga. Sauerlandt (pp. 55-56) dates it from around the year 1000. Schramm, *loc. cit.,* hypothesizes the 1130's, Deér feels sure that it originates at least a century earlier.

15. Sauerlandt, p. 57.

16. *Ibid.*

17. This artistic symbolism advances a claim of far greater spiritual import than the words of the King's coronation ceremony: *ipse per praesentem sacri unguinis infusionem Spiritus Paraclyti super caput tuum infundat,* P. E. Schramm, "Die Krönung in Deutschland," *op. cit.,* p. 316.

18. *Ad regem deducendum,* Albers, I, p. 170, which would apply to any king.

19. Cf. Exodus 23, 20, Malachi 3, 1, and Mark 1, 2.

20. E. H. Kantorowicz, *Selected Studies,* (New York, 1965), pp. 37-75.

21. *Ibid.,* p. 42f.

22. *Ibid.*

23. *Ibid.*

24. P. E. Schramm, *Die Krönung in Deutschland*, p. 311.

25. Odilo's three sermons devoted to the theme of the resurrection, *P.L.* 142, 1004-1011, indicate how central it was to the core of inner life at Cluny and its outward expression. To ignore its central place is to leave out the essential. For the resurrection symbolism built into the architecture of Cluny III see K. J. Conant, "Systematic Dimensions in the Buildings," *Speculum*, vol. 38, (1963), p. 12. His misgivings that this might be a coincidence may be put aside.

26. See B. M. Peebles, "Fortunatus, Poet of the Holy Cross," *New American Church Monthly*, (1935), pp. 152-166. The poet refers to the Merovingian Childert I as "our Melchisedech, rightly King and Priest," K. Morrison, *Imperial Lives*, p. 10.

27. Albers, I, 64, 110. Ber., II, 31, Herrgott, p. 348-349. For commentary on these hymns see A. Walpole, *op. cit.*, pp. 164-181 and J. Neale, *Medieval Hymns and Sequences*, (London, 1851).

28. E. H. Kantorowicz, *Laudes Regiae*, p. 72, n. 25.

29. Albers, I, 42-45. These hymns of course were sung in other churches and monasteries, which does not detract from their import at Cluny. However, a special study should be devoted to all Cluniac hymns, antiphons, psalms in light of the imperial connotations in the liturgical texts.

30. "Das ottonische Reich als Imperium Romanum," *DA*, vol. 6, (1943), pp. 412-441.

31. E. Sackur, *Sibyllinische Texte und Forschungen*, (Halle, 1898), pp. 104-113.

32. *Ibid.*, p. 110. The forcefulness with which this imperial vision sought to incarnate itself is evident from the report that only his premature death prevented Otto III from abdicating his imperial office and going as a pilgrim to the city of the Holy Sepulchre, P. E. Schramm, *Kaiser, Rom, Renovatio*, I, p. 180. For the reading of Adso's text during the Crusade cf. C. Erdmann, *Die Entstehung*, pp. 278-279.

33. G. Tellenbach, *Römischer und christliche Reichs-gedanke, loc. cit.*

34. *Ibid.*, pp. 8-9.

35. H. Hirsch, *op. cit.*

36. Although final proof is lacking that the imperial *laudes* were sung at Cluny, the fact that they are present in those mass texts which we do possess for All Souls Day points in that direction. Near the end of the mass previous to the procession to the cemetery, the naive victory shout of the Franks, *Xristus uincit, Xristus regnat, Xristus imperat,* was voiced three times by the priest and repeated three times by the choir, "after the ikon of the Lord is turned towards God the Father", says the Saint Vaast text, WB, p. 278. After the pronouncement of the words *Xristus regnat* in the Saint-Amand version, a procession with a crucifix took place around the church, while the poor were being fed, WB, 278, n. 1. Further, as E. de Moreau indicates in his *Historie de l'Eglise in Belgique,* vol. 2, 2nd ed., Brussels (1945), p. 178f., Saint-Vaast belonged to that group of monasteries which adopted Cluniac *consuetudines* without submitting to the jurisdiction of the Burgundian abbey. Although opposed to the centralization of Cluny, such monasteries were ready to accept its strong emphasis on liturgy and prayer, cf. infra, p. 109, n. 31. Saint Amand does not appear to have developed such strong links to Cluny as Saint-Vaast and Saint Bertin; however, along with the last-named monastery, it was renowned as a scriptorium for copying manuscripts, de Moreau, p. 302. Richard of Saint-Vannes was the head of Saint Amand from 1013-1018, idem, p. 165. Saint-Benoît-sur-Loire (Fleury) also adopted Cluniac consuetudinaries while remaining juridically independent, Hunt, pp. 6, 22, 159. For Fleury see also Sackur.

6. Cluny and the Imperial David
in the Service of
Saints Paul and Michael

(a) Servus Jesu Christi

Another avenue of Cluniac research which remains thus far
untravelled is that linking both the monastery and the empire
to the service of particular saints. Here once again a much
longer and a detailed study is called for than is presently
possible. We shall confine our remarks here largely to the
significance of the Apostles, Saints Peter and Paul, particularly the latter, and St. Michael. However, any number of
saints might well be investigated in this connection, particularly the "imperial saints", Mauritius and Lawrence for
example, along the general lines indicated.

Odilo's Sermon on the Nativity[1] provides us with the
most striking passage in the Cluniac sources demonstrating
Cluny's link to the Western imperial tradition. He begins
the sermon by introducing a number of Christmas themes, those
of joy, jubilation, the homeless birth of the Saviour. He
then develops his reflections on Jesus' words to the dis-
ciples saying that he shall be with them until the consumma-
tion of time. Especially emphasized is Christ's presence at
Christmas in conformance with the words of the prophets:
"him who Solomon showed to have existed before all ages.
Isaiah affirmed that the Lord was absent from no place. It
is impossible for him to be absent from us. I have daringly
said: It is not possible. Effectually this is not possible.
Such is the impotence of omnipotence. That impossibility is

the highest possibility."[2] This theme of Christ's eternal
presence and his existence before Abraham leads then to the
temporal part of the sermon which outlines the realization
of the divine presence in the flesh and on earth. Although
Christ existed before Abraham, he wanted to be born of the
seed of Abraham *temporaliter*.[3] At this point appears a
series of Scriptural quotations, eight of them, the purpose
of which is to provide edifying commentary to God the
Father's promise to Abraham: "In your seed all the people
of the earth are blessed." This promise is realized for
Odilo, as we realize from his quotations: Ps. 131, 11, Jer.
23, 5, Is. 4, 2, summed up in Matthew 1, 1 which tells how
Christ was generated as the son of David and son of Abraham
according to the flesh (Is. 41, 8). This tradition is then
placed on the foundation of three quotations from St. Paul,
the first from Hebrews 2, 16 which again emphasizes the
fleshly aspect of Christ's generation: "For verily he took
not on himself the nature of angels but the seed of Abraham."
And because, says Odilo, Christ was born of the seed of David,
the apostle said: Paul, a servant of Jesus Christ..., made
of the seed of David according to the flesh (Rom. 1, 3).
II Tim. 2, 8 provides the concluding quotation: "Remember
that Jesus Christ of the seed of David was raised from the
dead according to my Gospel." Odilo summarizes the point
of all the foregoing for his monks in unequivocal fashion:
"And since in the Gospel the Son of God is identified with
the Son of David, not only spiritually but physically, Christ
wished to be called by such a name because he knew there was
no other name by which it was possible for the world to be
saved: *quia scit non esse aliud nomen in quo possit mundus
salvari*.[4] Therefore, most beloved brothers, so that we deserve to be saved by him who is Saviour, we say together,

we say singly: O Lord, son of David, have mercy on us.
Amen." His meaning is clear. David's name is indispensable
for salvation. Here in a literary nutshell is displayed
Cluny's union with the Davidic tradition introduced and embodied by the Carolingian kings, then transmitted to their
heirs, the Holy Roman Emperors of Saxon and Salian stock.
The *Codex Carolinus* contains a number of varied references
to Charlemagne as a second David.[5] This identification of
the Roman Emperors with the anointed kings of the Old Testament must be kept in mind as a living tradition which in-
spires Odilo's words. As the son of David, Christ's presence
is real, indeed he finds it essential that it be expressed in
this form. At the same time Christ's presence is announced
and signalled by his imperial vicar and representative to whom
Odilo refers in one of his resurrection sermons as *sanctus*
David.[6] This reverence for David extended into the sign
language of the monks.[7] To indicate the Psalter one joined
his finger tips in such a way as to represent the form of a
crown placed on one's head, "because of the similarity to the
crown the King wears and because the author of the Psalms,
David, was a king".[8]

In the Mainz *ordo* the emperor receives the *virga
aequitatis* in remembrance of St. Paul's words addressed to
Christ, "a sceptre of righteousness is the sceptre of thy
kingdom", addressed in the epistle to Christ himself.[9] And
just as Christ said, "I am the door, he who enters through
me shall be saved (Jn. 7, 9), it is asked that this door of
faith (Acts 14, 27) be opened to the king. And he who is
the key of David (Apoc. 3, 7) and the sceptre of the house
of Israel (Jer. 1, 19), who opens and no one closes, who
closes and no man opens (Apoc. 3, 7), he who leads you out
from the shadow of death (Ps. 23, 4), is to be followed in

ll things. And imitating him, *imitando ipsum,* in accordance
with the word of David the prophet you love justice and hate
injustice, therefore you are anointed with the oil of glad-
ness (Hebr. 1, 9)."[10] Similarly we find in Odilo's sermons
further references substantiating his acceptance of Old Testament regal symbolism, inspired by the same tradition developed
in the Cambridge Songs which chant the glory of the imperial
name.[11]

This tradition of the imperial David now came to be
used under the Saxon kings with the authority bestowed by
the apostle Paul. The tradition of Peter bound exclusively
to Rome has overshadowed the moment when St. Paul came to the
forefront of imperial policy. In his mission of gaining new
souls for the Christian faith Otto III assumed a new title
whose presence we have already encountered in Odilo's
Nativity sermon. During his pilgrimage to the tomb of St.
Adalbert in Gnesen, the emperor assumed the title *servus
Iesu Christi.*[12] It was as another apostle that the emperor
came to undertake his *renovatio* of the Roman Empire, moving
from one part of it to the other. Thus by the new title the
emperor indicated his assumption of a universal function inside the Church which would compensate for the purely local
character of tenth century Petrine symbolism. Otto III was
summoned to Rome as a second Paul.[13] "Whereas Peter gave
Rome a monopoly, Paul was both Roman and universal."[14]
Sanctus Paulus Romanus et non Romanus est is a remark of
Pope Victor III.[15] The new symbolism is still retained in
an impressive ivory relief, stylistically associated with the
imperial monastery of Echternach. It was inscribed with the
apostle's confident words: *Dei gratia sum id quod sum* (I
Cor. 15, 10).[16] Indeed this *Dei Gratia,* by the grace of
God, was the formula on which imperial sovereignty was

based.[17] God's grace came directly to the emperors without intermediaries, which they never hesitated to emphasize. Even Adelaide's humble version of her role, *ex se peccatrix dono Dei imperatrix* implies no other possibility.[18] Then in the year 1001 when Poland had been won as a kingdom for the Papacy, since elevated in respect by the appointments of Gregory V (996-999), and Sylvester II (999-1003), Otto III assumed a new title, *servus apostolorum*, referring to himself as a servant of Saints Peter and Paul. By this means the "apostolic" emperor brought honor to the prince of the apostles as well.[19] Under Henry II a famous miniature shows the apostolic emperor and empress presented by the Apostles Peter and Paul and crowned by Christ himself.[20]

It is of course well known that Cluny was dedicated to the apostles Peter and Paul. However, it appears that no other church before 964 bears this dual name, nor even that of St. Paul alone.[21] The foregoing examples may serve as an explanation for this exceptional state of affairs. They show that the names of the apostles are the unique form by means of which the renewal of the Church expresses itself, principally through Cluny and the Empire, while not forgetting the link with the tradition passing through Petrine Rome. However, Odilo himself had felt it necessary to stress that "Paul is not inferior to Peter although the latter is the foundation of the Church".[22] There would seem to be little doubt that Paul was given special attention at Cluny. Odilo's writings are full of his quotations. Ulrich tells us that Chrysostom's commentary to Paul's Epistle to the Hebrews was also read as a supplement to the other readings from St. Paul.[23] Also Odilo presented Henry II with the special gift of St. Augustine's commentary to St. Paul's letters.[24] The recurrent theme of *Paulus servus Jesu Christi*

is found in the earliest customaries.[25] Later at Cluny it
came to be sung at the vigil of Christmas Eve in chapter to
the Responsory of *Judaea et Hierusalem.*[26] Bernard tells us
the Letters of Paul were read during the Octave of Christmas
beginning with *Paulus Servus Jesu Christi.*[27] In all of these
examples the link of the imperial David to the New Testament
was supplied by the Pauline symbolism. The feast-days of the
apostles themselves of course were celebrated with full
festivity at Cluny as one of the main events of the liturgical
year. On that day the imperial insignia were carried in procession, as at Christmas, with the exception of the ikon portraying Christ and the Virgin.[28]

(b) Princeps militiae coelestis

By anticipation of a Last Judgment hovering over all men
making them liable for their actions and deeds in their own
time, Cluny marked the soul of Western man.[1] Cluny's deepest
experience that the times shall be judged is foreign to the
joyous, self-contained harmony of God's already redeemed universe, so ardently expressed in the stones of the Hagia Sophia.
For the Western Christian, ever since Cluny, seeks freedom and
struggles for it in militant soldierly fashion. It is the
appearance of Saint Michael, the imperial archangel, in the
Cluniac liturgy which indicates the depth of the transformation.

Saint Michael, the standard bearer of the heavenly hosts
who in the Apocalypse conquers the dragon, is reverenced first
of all in the Orient before appearing in the West.[2] When he
does so, as Erdmann tells us, it is as the patron-saint of the
Holy Roman Empire: "His image was on the military banner with

which Henry I and Otto the Great campaigned against the Hungarians and at the same time a mass for St. Michael was celebrated in order to bring victory. Simultaneously, he of course remained the conqueror of the dragon, that is of Satan, as characterized in the Apocalypse; that his struggle had a spiritual meaning was always present to the consciousness of the Church."[3] At Cluny we find masses for St. Michael in the earliest customals. Later it was marked out as one of the principal feast-days to be celebrated with all the pomp and ceremony of Christmas, Easter, Pentecost, the birth of the Virgin, the feast of Majolus, etc.[4] The theme of the verse from the Apocalypse, 12, 7 is stressed throughout.[5] Here divine and earthly military service, *militia Dei* and *militia saecularia* are united for the first time--as a prince of the heavenly hosts, *princeps militiae coelestis,* Michael leads the soldiers into battle as well as the monks in their struggles for the salvation of their souls.[6]

However the saint had an even greater significance for Cluny. Saint Michael the Archangel, the soldier of God, enters the liturgy of All Souls.[7] After the opening prayers on All Saints Day, thanks is given to God for this feast of all the perfect. All Souls is then indicated as the feast of the imperfect who, however, too, are faithful.[8] Since it is not within man's power to judge them, it is Christ himself who, according to the characteristic close found uniquely in this office, has come to judge the living and the dead and the age by fire. Christ is then addressed as king of the angels before the tones of judgment again resound in the close, "by fire". The first invocation of the priest is *Gloriosus desu in sanctis suis* to which the Chorus replies *Mirabilis in maiestate tua.* The priest's second invocation at the start of the ceremony is *Animae omnium fidelium defunctorum* to which the chorus answers *Requiescant in pace*. The third invocation,following the first two orations to God the Father and God the Son,is to the Archangel Michael, who has this important place in the mass as the *Dei nuntius de animabus iustis*. By virtue of St. Michael's intercession and that of the Lord's celestial army supplication is made *to free souls* from the prince of darkness. Here at the very beginning of the office we see that St. Michael in the Cluniac liturgy is to lead the souls to freedom. This presence of the intercessory saint in this capacity reoccurs throughout the day-long ceremony of All Souls accompanying the themes of judgment and freedom.[9] And in the litany Michael is invoked as the first of the saints after the Virgin, as the standard-bearer of God.[10] *Mitte archangelum sanctum Michahelem...ut ille perducat eas...in lucem sempiternam.*[11] Hence the saint acquires a new function as God's messenger and standard bearer. He becomes the leader of souls seeking freedom. The struggle of the Apocalypse instead of belonging to the past becomes transformed into a future task.[12] The history of salvation is newly conceived, the Church no longer rejoices but trembles before the condition of the world as it really is.[13] It prays for freedom. Saint Michael who appears on the banners of the imperial army becomes the guide of souls seeking freedom before the seat of judgment. The archangel's appearance in the Cluniac liturgy complements his role as the patron-saint of the emperor's sword. By this unity of the secular army and the spiritual army both Cluny and the apostolic Emperor combine in their separate ways to make the belief in the Last Judgment a reality. They supplement one another. Both the sword of the Emperor,bringing Justice,and the tears and prayers of Cluny,invoking repentance as a condition for the soul's freedom, make present a coming judgment on this earth.

It should be clear by now that the vision of totality of all souls introduced by Cluny shares a common faith in the unity and universality of the Holy Emperor's function.[14] For in the Holy Roman Empire of the West since its beginnings under Charles the Great *heaven and earth form one unity*.[15] There is no "Church" and "State" but the bridge between the two spheres of life heavenly and earthly, spiritual and temporal was bridged by the person of the priestly king. The function of the Emperor's army is to conquer and convert the infidels, a sacred task.[16] The Emperor is a living embodiment of eternity; through him and his empire heaven and earth are one. In Cluny this same unity is acknowledged. As a monastery in spiritual union with the king, it develops an authentic religious spirit and brings it into the lives of the peoples by its own initiative. Many mistakes of historical interpretation would be avoided if this truth, valid until 1075, were made central.

NOTES

Servus Jesu Christi

1. *P.L.* 142, 991f. is the source of what follows.

2. *Ille qui semper est et ubique non potest nobis deesse. Audenter dixi: non potest. Potenter hoc non potest. Talis impotentia est omnipotentia. Ista impossibilitas est summa possibilitas.* P.L. 142, 993.

3. *Ibid.,* 994.

4. *Ibid.,* 994.

5. E. Rosenstock-Huessy, "Die Furt der Franken und das Schisma," in *Das Alter der Kirche,* (co-author J. Wittig, Berlin, 1927) and E. Kantorowicz, *Laudes Regiae,* pp. 56f. On David, as the prefigured ancestor of Christ, P. E. Schramm, "Das Alte und das Neue Testament in der Staatslehre und Staatssymbolik des Mittelalters," *La Bibbia,* p. 236.

6. *P.L.* 142, 1007. The significance of Gregory VII's being hailed as both *virum de plebe* and the new David in stark opposition to this imperial claim is invariably misunderstood by all who see him as a reformer, H. E. J. Cowdrey, *op. cit.,* p. 137.

7. On this mute means of communications introduced to maintain silence in the monastery see G. de Valous, *Le Monachisme Clunisien,* I, pp. 391-396.

8. Ber., I, 17, Herrgott, p. 172.

9. P. E. Schramm, *Die Krönung* etc., p. 318. Note the prominent use of Biblical quotation in what follows. The quotation from St. Paul is taken from Hebrews 1, 8. See pp. 313-314, *ibid.,* for references in the ceremony to Abraham, Moses, Josiah, Solomon.

10. It is in opposition to this Pauline word, derived from Ps. 4, 8 that Gregory VII spoke the words on his death

bed: "I have loved justice and hated injustice, therefore I die in exile." The fact that the Psalm is the older reference misleads historians. Gregory's summary of his life controverts the meaning of the imperial coronation more than it does that of the Psalmist. Beginning with the great innovator, as Caspar calls him, the life of the spirit became opened for all who in the world were willing to pay the price of exile from it. In the same sense universities could be born out of the earthly failure of Peter Abelard, the very opposite of a John the Scot who philosophized at the royal court.

11. *P.L.* 142, 1002; K. Strecker, *Die Cambridger Lieder.*

12. P. E. Schramm, *Kaiser, Rom, Renovatio,* I, p. 144.

13. F. Novati, *L'influsso del pensiero latino sopra la civiltà Italiana,* (Milan, 1899), pp. 173f. P. E. Schramm, *ibid.,* pp. 151-152.

14. E. Rosenstock-Huessy, *Out of Revolution,* p. 505.

15. *Ibid.* Also p. 766.

16. A. Goldschmidt, *Die Elfenbeinskulpturen aus der Zeit der karolingischen und sächsischen Kaiser,* no. 25, (Berlin, 1914). Paul wears a priest's stola, a complement to Deshman's evidence (v. i, p. 175, n. 5) regarding imperial adoption of priestly attributes begun by Otto III in *imitatio Christi*; in the Montecassino Gospels Henry II is portrayed as the first ruler to wear the stola of a Christian priest himself.

17. Ullmann, *op. cit., La Bibbia,* p. 191: "The most characteristic symptom of all theocratic rulership, that the king was *rex Dei gratia,* found its model in the Bible. *Gratia Dei sum id quod sum* one read in the Pauline epistle."

18. See also the reference to Rom. 7, 25, Paulhart, p. 43.

19. P. E. Schramm, *ibid.,* p. 145f.

20. G. Leidinger, *Das Perikopenbuch Kaiser Heinrich II,* clm 4452, (Miniaturen aus Handschriften der Kgl. Hof- und Staatsbibliothek in München, 5), Munich, 1914. P. E. Schramm and F. Mütherich, *Denkmale der deutschen Könige und Kaiser: Ein Beitrag zur Herrschergeschichte von Karl der Grosse bis Friedrich II, 768-1250,* (Veröffentlichung des Zentralinstitutes für Kunstgeschichte in München, 2), Munich, 1962, pp.

156-157, no. 110, p. 326, Pl. 110. Henry II is crowned by
the patrons of the "Bamberger Dom", Peter and Paul: H.
Wölflin, *Die Bamburger Apokalypse*, Munich, 1921, Pl. 51-52.
According to Rosenstock-Huessy, *Die europaïschen Revolution-
en*, p. 565, Henry II is called apostolic in a hymn of the
cathedral.

21. W. Jorden, *op. cit.*, p. 39. However, subsequently,
Bamberg was dedicated to Peter and Paul. And a remark of
Mercier, *op. cit.*, p. 21, should be noted: "Toute la philosophie de la peinture clunysienne se résumera...dans ce
culte clunysien de dévotion à saint Pierre et saint Paul...."

22. *P.L.* 142, 1022.

23. Udal., I, 1, *P.L.* 149, 645.

24. O. Ringholz, *op. cit.*, p. LVII.

25. BB[1], p. 6; C, p. 36, Albers, II.

26. Albers, I, 7.

27. Ber., II, 7, 293.

28. Albers, I, 86. Cf. infra, p. 152, n. 33.

Princeps militiae coelestis

1. The abandonment of this tradition by both historians
and theologians alike, proud of being scientific, has led to
shallow and naïve discussions where eschatology is concerned.
By anticipating the dangers of the end and acting to prevent
it, the Cluniacs brought about consequences on the political,
social and economic levels, as did the Emperors. Compare
their faith with the following example of nineteenth century
self-satisfaction written by an authority on medieval eschatology.

> Die pessimistischen Stimmen des Mittel-
> alters sind schon längst verklungen, die
> bangen Ahnungen desselben wie Schatten
> beim Anbruch des Tages geflüchtet. Wie
> aus einem langen, unruhigen Traum erwacht,

> schaut der moderne Zeitgeist bei dem Licht
> einer immer gesteigerten Aufklärung sich
> kritisch um, findet aber nirgends irgend
> welche Zeichen des Endes und spricht sich
> deshalb zuversichtlich ein: es ist Friede,
> es hat keine Gefahr (I Thess. 5, 3).
> E. Wadstein, "Die eschatologische Ideen-
> gruppe: Antichrist, Weltsabbat, Weltende
> und Weltgericht," *Zeitschrift für wissen-
> schaftliche Theologie*, vol. 39, (1896),
> p. 291.

Eighteen years later this total misunderstanding of St. Paul
was to be called to account with a very violent end of a
world prophesied by one who had to take the mantle of Anti-
Christ on himself to represent the extent of the danger,
Friedrich Nietzsche.

2. C. Erdmann, *Die Entstehung des Kreuzzugsgedankens*,
pp. 17-18.

3. *Ibid.*, p. 18. See also R. Jenkins, "A Cross of the
Patriarch Michael Cerularius" with an Art History Comment by
E. Kitzinger, *Dumbarton Oaks Papers*, no. 21, pp. 235-249.
Jenkins translates from "The Miracles of the Archangel Michael"
by Michael Psellus, an 11th century contemporary who wrote on
the miracles worked from the seventh to the eleventh centuries
by a cross dedicated to St. Michael by the Emperor Heraclius:
"So then that excellent Emperor (Heraclius) in accordance with
this custom dedicated this divine and unconquerable shape to
the Archangel Michael and gave it his name; and what was seen
was the Victorious Cross, and what was heard was the Archangel
Michael. And it failed of neither name, or rather it acquired
the power of both: for by its form it at once dismayed the
barbarians and by the divine Archangel and general it put
their ranks to flight" (p. 235).

4. Albers, I, pp. 115f., 133. However, it was in a lower
category than Easter, Pentecost, etc.

5. *Ibid.*, p. 116.

6. C. Erdmann, *loc. cit.*

7. WB, pp. 261f.

8. The contrast is marked by transposing the joyful mood
of All Saints immediately into the somber tones of All Souls.

9.   WB, see 261, 262, 264, 273, 275, 279, 281, 282.

10.   *Ibid.*, pp. 273, 279.

11.   *Ibid.*, p. 281, n. 7, which is the counterpart to: *Libera me domine de morte aeterna in die illa tremenda*, *ibid.*, p. 272.

12.   E. Rosenstock-Huessy, *Die europäschen Revolutionen*, p. 125.

13.   *Ibid.*

14.   The Carolingian emperor Louis the Pious was already referred to as *almus* and *sanctus*, Herrgott, p. 23.

15.   Cf. Chapter II.

16.   "The subjection to the king was the subjection to God himself based on Biblical references." W. Ullmann, *art. cit.*, p. 201. Problems of historical interpretation must turn naturally on the concrete manifestations of such a central truth, particularly where artistic symbolism is concerned. Henry IV, for example, was a suffragant in the monastic brotherhood of Echternach, A. Schulte, (infra p. 176, n. 24) p. 170, maintaining the links to this monastery in succession to his Saxon forebearers. However, K. Oettinger's attempt, "Der Elfenbeinschnitzer des Echternacher *Codex Aureus* and die Skulptur unter Heinrich III (1039-1052)," *Jahrbuch der Berliner Museen*, 2, (1960), pp. 34-54, to date the Echternach ivory relief into the reign of Henry III on solely stylistic grounds disregards the historical context in favor of overly abstract considerations, cf. infra pp. 157-158, 164, n. 16, n. 17.

CHAPTER III

CLUNY, HUGH, HENRY III, HENRY IV

1. Henry III, Caput ecclesiae

Sackur sagaciously decided to end his study of the Cluniac movement with the year 1049, marked by the death of Odilo.
By doing so he made it clear that the founding period of
Cluny's history had come to a close and with the advent of
the abbot Hugh a new phase had begun. Thanks to this methodological approach, based on sound historical instinct, he was
able to stake out his conclusions on the solid ground of a
period of time foreign to the outbreak of the struggle initi-
ated by the Roman popes against the Roman emperors. Erroneous
premises as to the Cluniac origin of principles advanced by
reformers concerned mainly with the growth of papal power and
the issues of simony, uncanonical marriage and the celibacy
of priests were thereby set aside.[1] Cluny's support of the
Papacy and its desire for popes that would protect its acquired privileges[2] could be rightfully affirmed without con-
tradicting the monastery's links to the German emperors and
imperial reform policy within the Church.[3] Indeed our own
study has shown that Cluny during the reigns of Majolus and
Odilo was independent of both Empire and Papacy, free in its
own Christian creativity, nonetheless lending support to the

leading reformers of the Church, the emperors themselves, and allied with them in the fulfillment of their eschatological and redemptive mission. Any appraisal of Cluny's role or position during the reigns of later abbots, particularly those of Hugh, Pontius and Peter the Venerable, shall have to recognize the force of conclusions valid during the period 964-1049.

To what extent did Cluny maintain, oppose or modify its traditional stance during the following years? When did changes occur and what form did they take? Did change in Cluny's role, importance and function come initially from within or without? In what historical context does it develop? Primarily, it would seem, our interest should focus on the reign of St. Hugh for there is no question that historical circumstances during the period 1049-1109 became radically altered. Scholarly research has for the most part limited itself to the question of Cluny's relationship to the reform popes and to the Gregorian Papacy in particular.[4] The result is that biographies are written of Odilo embarrassed by the abbot's "imperialism" or "Caesaropapism",[5] but nonetheless sure that the Roman Pontiff is the unique and immediate superior of the abbot, which only represents the wishful thinking of a later age.[6] Studies are made of Cluny based on the false and misleading premise of Odilo's deference "pour les grands", as de Valous' Gregorian view would have it.[7] M. de Valous has in turn been the dominant influence on a full-length study of the reign of St. Hugh whose author, unaware of the emperors' spiritual role in the Church at the accession of the abbot, gives them short shrift, while her reports on the German monarchs are at times deficient.[8] With regard to the reigns of Majolus and Odilo the answer is clear: since there was no Gregorian papacy in existence at this time, 964-1049, nor had one even been conceived, Cluny's relationship to authority in the Church was necessarily dependent on that inherited by German kings from the Carolingian legacy. Additionally, since there was then no struggle on Gregorian terms possible between *Regnum* and *Sacerdotium*, the question of Cluny's neutrality towards them does not arise. Only during the reign of St. Hugh does the question of neutrality become relevant at all. Similarly, the relationship of Cluny to the Papacy must take into account the changed social movements in European life beginning with the middle of the eleventh century.

We have already committed ourselves to one aspect of this question by our own usage of the *consuetudines*. Although two of these were composed during the reign of St. Hugh, they are obviously a continuance of observances from the earlier period. Hence they tell a story of continuity in the life of the abbey and all together represent Cluny's basic orientation despite their individual differences. For this reason they should be seen in their totality. They, too, of course reveal the presence of change occurring during Hugh's reign and it is with both aspects, that of tradition and adaptation to it, that we must now be concerned.

Disengaged from the affairs of the world, the saint-to-be received the two murderers of one of his brothers at Cluny where in that asylum of peace they became monks, one of them permanently.[9] His power to heal body and soul was given numerous illustration.[10] By his power of prayer he freed Alphonso of Spain from his prison whence his brother restored him to his kingdom.[11] To Anselm of Canterbury in exile he foretold the death of William Rufus thanks to the gift of prophecy also attributed to Majolus.[12] Hugh's pious works, especially his alms to the poor,[13] are seen as an awesome feat, as are the list of his miracles.[14] Like his predecessor, he

was addressed as an "archangel of the monks".[15] In his final
words when the old abbot sums up his reign describing the
spread of the Cluniac order beyond the bounds of Burgundy into the many regions of Christian Europe he assesses his life
in terms of Cluny's constant theme, *pro animae meae remedio*
in the day of Judgment.[16] We have already considered the
consuetudines of Bernard and Ulrich as being a more detailed
description of Cluniac observances. Under Hugh, the customaries
attained their final form and, as Sackur has pointed out, the
statutes became fixed and the impulse to expansion more con-
trolled and organized.[17]

With regard to Hugh's relationships to the Emperor Henry
III the sources are again unanimous respecting the continuity
of the monastery's traditional union with the imperial House.
The evidence of the customaries has already been noted. Hildebert informs us that Hugh was at the imperial court when ap-
prised of Odilo's death.[18] He returned bringing large gifts
from the king for the beautification of the abbey.[19] We are
expressly told that Hugh, like his predecessors, found especial favor with the emperor who desired his presence and
wished to see his face.[20] A charter reaffirming Cluny's
rights to Payerne reinforces the view that the change of
abbots affected in no way the spiritual bonds of confraternity
present between the monastic congregation and the Roman Emperors.[21] The charter is dated December 4, 1049. Here Henry
III (1039-1056) states that the necessity of providing for the
poor and the servants of God is a requirement of the imperial
dignity and profession.[22] Hence Hugh's petition for the control of the monastery is granted because of traditional confraternity and love which he and his forerunners entertained
with Henry's royal and imperial predecessors, "praying to God
for the stability of kingdoms and the Empire".[23] Here we see

once again that the divine order of the Cluniac liturgy, its commemorative anniversaries and intercessory prayers were a stabilizing force of the entire feudal and social order at the summit of which was the eschatological figure of the Imperial dignity.[24]

We also possess a letter written by Henry III to Hugh regarding the birth of his son, the future Henry IV.[25] After acknowledging his joy at the reception of letters from the abbot, which have been lost, he humbly asks for Cluny's prayers for the public good, for the honor of the whole kingdom, for his salvation and those belonging to him so that prosperity will be bestowed on them all by God. May peace and tranquillity of the churches and of all the people be possible, he asks. He continues: What wise man would not desire your prayers and those of your monks?[26] Who would hesitate to be bound in the chains of indissoluble charity with those whose prayers are the purer as they are removed from the agitation of the age, all the more worthy being closer to divine presence? The letter ends with a request to Hugh, the future godfather of Henry IV, to come to Cologne for Easter.[27] Some years later, the Empress Regent Agnes writes to the abbot, following the death of her spouse in 1056.[28] Agnes, born to a family influential in Burgundy, was a descendant of the House of Aquitaine and, therefore, an heiress of the tradition binding her family to Cluny through its founder, Duke William. Burgundy itself had become subject to the Empire during the reign of Conrad II[29] and Henry's marriage to Agnes was intended to cement that union, making Burgundy therewith part of a triune kingdom whose other parts were Germany and Italy.[30] It may therefore well be, as Lehmann concludes, following Giese-brecht, that Henry III's choice of Hugh as godfather was

intended to benefit his son thanks to the abbot's extensive
influence in that part of his kingdom.[31] By the same token
Hugh was interested in receiving imperial favor. Agnes'
letter lends itself to this interpretation, confirming in
all events that the ties between Cluny and the Imperial
House had in essence remained the same. After commending
the soul of her husband to the prayers of the monks, she asks
that Hugh obtain for the emperor's fatherless son, also the
abbot's through baptism, long years as his heir and that he
be worthy of God. "Try," she writes, "by your counsel to
still any troubles that might arise in the parts of the kingdom in your vicinity."[32] Later events indicate that her concern was not unfounded. Indeed she and her two grandsons
were themselves to become a source of anguish for the future
king.

NOTES

1. Sackur, II, 445f.

2. Sackur, II, 444. Cluny was also protected by an *advocatus* during this first period of growth (see G. Duby, *La société* etc., pp. 110f.) who did not present problems for the monastery; cf. J. Richard, *op. cit.*, p. 69 and N. Bulst, *op. cit.*, p. 200f. Emancipation from lay control was not present in the sense indicated by H. Hoffman, "Von Cluny zum Investiturstreit," *Archiv für Kulturgeschichte*, 45, (1963), pp. 165-209.

3. Sackur, II, 449f.

4. The study of the subject by H. Cowdrey, *op. cit.*, begs the question by its anachronistic references to "lay" rulers; to brand kings as laymen did not constitute reform.

5. J. Hourlier, *S. Odilon*, p. 183. For numerous references to the king as *imago dei*, K. Hoffmann, *Taufsymbolik im mittelalterlichen Herrscherbild*, (Düsseldorf, 1968). More recently, R. Deshman, "*Christus rex et magi reges:* Kingship and Christology in Ottonian and Anglo-Saxon Art". I herewith express my thanks to Professor Deshman for making his preliminary draft available to me before publication in *FS*, vol. 10, (1976).

6. Hourlier, *idem*, p. 178.

7. *DHGE*, vol. 13, 37.

8. N. Hunt, *op. cit.*, p. 24, has Henry II confused with Henry III, who could not have visited Cluny in 1014.

9. *P.L.* 159, 904-905.

10. *P.L.* 159, 873f.

11. *P.L.* 159, 866.

12. Gilo, *Vita Hugonis*, L'Huillier, p. 588. Also Hugh's conduct while captured on a voyage is compared with Majolus' retention by Saracens. *P.L.* 159, 864-865.

13. *P.L.* 159, 895, 912. Gilo, L'Huillier, pp. 584-585.

14. L'Huillier, *op. cit.*, pp. 371-390.

15. By Peter Damian, R. L. Lehmann, *Forschungen zur Geschichte des Abtes Hugo I von Cluny*, (Göttingen, 1869), p. 91.

16. *Imprecatio B. Hugonis*, *P.L.* 159, 951-952.

17. Sackur, I, vi-vii.

18. *P.L.* 159, 862.

19. *Ibid*.

20. *P.L.* 159, 864.

21. Bruel, IV, no. 2977, pp. 171-172.

22. *Ut a nobis exigit imperialis dignitas et professio.*

23. *Ibid.*, p. 172. The expression was also used in Carolingian times.

24. It might be mentioned in this connection that the Necrologium of the Domkirche in Speyer indicates Henry III's deep piety and concern for the souls of his dead parents by prayers meant to remember their anniversary. A. Schulte, "Deutsche Könige, Kaiser, Päpste als Kanoniker an deutschen und römischen Kirchen," *Historisches Jahrbuch*, vol. 54, Heft 2, (1934), p. 169. Speyer was the mausoleum of the royal house. The German kings had no imperial capitol but a "city of the dead", p. 148.

25. *Henrici Imperatoris Cognomento Nigri ad S. Hugonem*, *P.L.* 159, 931-932.

26. See *P.L.* 159, 864 where the same sentiments are reported by Hildebert.

27. *P.L.* 159, 932.

28. *Imperatricis Agnetis, Henrici Nigri Uxoris ad S. ugonem, P.L.* 159, 932.

29. Baethgen, *op. cit.*, p. 37.

30. That Henry III viewed his empire as a triune kingdom composed of Germany, Italy, Burgundy is indicated by his possession of a seal for each of them. P. E. Schramm, *Herrchaftszeichen*, II, (Stuttgart, 1955), p. 681.

31. *Op. cit.*, pp. 105-106.

32. *P.L.* 159, 932.

2. Henry IV, <u>A</u> <u>seculo</u> <u>inaudite</u> <u>et</u> <u>horribilis</u> <u>traditionis</u> <u>nostre</u>

As far as the Regency goes, there is no evidence in the
Cluniac sources which indicates any basic change in the relationships between abbot and king. Nor would one expect any
in view of the king's adolescence. Despite the growing
strength of the Papacy under Leo IX (1049-1054) and Nicholas
II (1059-1061), the boy-king was far too young to be cognizant
of the significance of events marked by the papal election
decree of 1059 or the bonds of fealty sworn by Robert Guiscard
to the Roman See. The dispute surrounding the election of
Alexander II (1061-1073) forced, however, the realization on
the papal party that without imperial support the pope's claim
to authority could not be firmly established. For this reason
it would be surprising if Cluny's spiritual alliance with the
emperors had been affected in any substantial way during his
pontificate. However, we have no sure way of knowing, from
Cluniac sources at least, that protests against imperial
authority in the Church beginning with Wazo of Liège and
taking various forms had any effect on Cluny's basic relationship to the imperial house, particularly throughout the period
1049-1073.[1] Also it is the present view, which revised manuscript editing may cause to be modified, that the available
editions of Ulrich and Bernard were composed after the death
of Alexander II.[2] Hence the extent to which changes were introduced before or after his pontificate could be open to
question. Not to be overlooked of course is Cluny's relationship to the long series of popes beginning with Bruno of Toul

or which we have evidence that they were of Cluniac origin hemselves or strongly bound to Cluny.[3] Certain aspects of his development, which requires further research, are outined in an addendum,[4] supplemented by some observations on he evidence that Gregory VII was a Cluniac monk.[5]

In addition the admission that Gregory VII's attack on he "liturgical king" in the Church and society was revoluionary in nature is not willingly conceded by the majority f scholars. Yet the *Dictatus Papae* are totally foreign to he period of Odilo's relations with emperors, indeed they re newly conceived in diametrical opposition to the spirit f imperial responsibility for the welfare of the Church and o the judicial tradition of the Church as well. The whole urport of these 27 dictates asserts the pope to be the urisdictional head of the Church, not the emperor.

A simple example might be cited, however, to illustrate ow deep the misunderstanding goes. Gregory's attack on the ld order of things was succinctly summarized in his very articular interpretation of Christ's words, affirming that he Lord did not say, *Ego sum consuetudo sed: veritas.*[6] n this manner the pope established a principle to justify is attack on imperial claims which were not based on canon aw, but only on tradition of *consuetudo*. However, this word onsuetudo is usually translated as tradition, custom, usage, nd therefore interpreted as being a way of doing things hich is familiar and even habitual. An admonition by a pecialist in medieval constitutional law[7] against this reading of the word goes unheeded and ignored.[8] *Consuetudo* never eans a mere habit in the sense of a hum-drum, routine custom Schlendrian). *Rather it is unwritten law as opposed to ritten law.*[9] Oral law was then the only aspect of law there as. Hence to consider this oral law as mere traditional

usage, or custom, is to ignore that it was the only form that
objective law had assumed before the written codifications of
the canon lawyers. In those days only subjective laws were
confirmed in writing and they were regarded with reverence
as Bernard tells us. He wrote for his fellow monks, *ut a*
sanctarum Consuetudinum tramite non recedant.[10] The "custom
of the land" is always "good custom" whereas acts contrary
to this subjective law were then called *prava, falsa consuetu-*
do. Therefore it is correct, and indispensable for the historian's understanding, to translate the word *consuetudo* by
"law".[11]

In the right translation of this one word we can see how
closely the Roman emperor and Cluny were similarly bound to
legal commitments within the social framework. Hence, Gregory'
version of Christ's words quite pointedly aimed at an overthrow of the established legal order expressed in all *consuetu-*
dines, since there was no *consuetudo* by which the pope could
rule the Church. The rise and development of written canon
law[12] urged with all haste by Gregory VII, then assiduously
compiled, dialectically conceived, argued and expurgated,
thereby became a necessary invention of the new party of
spirituales, later imitated in its written, objective codifications by all national states. The new systematizing of law
by overthrowing the old tradition inevitably caused turmoil,
as in every revolution, one in which neither Cluny nor the
emperors could be initiators, bound as they were to previous
law.

It may be well to recall that Odilo, too, was acquainted
with Christ's pronouncement that He was the way, the life and
the truth,[13] but the abbot did not conceive the dictum polem-
ically, only reminding his monks that they should flee a false
and blind life and hearken to Christ's words. Gregory's intro

duction of the polemical, contradictory element into his reading of these words raised a new issue. In one's efforts to resolve the meaning of the pope's sentence, he must not forget that the number of things not said by Christ are numerous indeed and He certainly did not say that he was either a reformer or a revolutionary, meaning that those so designated may not be evaluated solely in Christian terms. In this vein one may note that neither did Christ say, *Ego sum jus canonicum sed: veritas*. A formulation of this kind reveals what is at stake in that of the pope. For it is not only the content of *Non dixit ego sum consuetudo sed: veritas* that deserves attention. The central issue is rather who has the authority to enunciate such a rejection of *consuetudo* and all that it implies. Not only what is said, but who says it, is essential here because the very practical and unavoidable question of who is to mediate between *veritas* and *consuetudo* in all matters of the Church is thereby posed for the first time. Since that mediator was to be no one but the Roman Pope himself, the rejection of *consuetudo* according to his decision was to be the content of the first of revolutionary upheavals in the history of the West. Hence it is not surprising that works on Gregory VII, none of which are satisfactory, alternate between the extremes of Macdonald,[14] for whom he can do no right, and of Arquillière[15] for whom, as Erdmann remarks,[16] he can do no wrong. Much more has been written on the *Sanctus Satanas,* as his friend Peter Damian termed him, and the "great innovator who stands by himself alone"[17] than on Henry IV, but for the latter, too, the pious defender of the old order, a fair appraisal is wanting. As Schramm says: Henry's image is distorted by the slander of his opponents and the evil rumours that surrounded him.[18] Yet this image

is fully belied by his *vita* and his letters, including those
to Hugh of Cluny.

Of the letters that passed between Henry IV and Hugh
we have three extant.[19] All were written by the emperor at
the end of his life. They indicate the hope that the pious
faith inherited from his forefathers may be restored by the
aid of his Cluniac godfather. In all of these letters Henry
indicates that he writes as a spiritual son to his spiritual
father. In one of them he assures his most beloved father
and the monks of Cluny of the tender affection of a son, the
devoted obedience of a brother, even of a slave.[20] From the
earliest of the three,[21] dated 1102, we learn that the frequent visits of the abbot of former days have ceased[22] and
that the sick man which Henry calls himself, no longer receives the consolation of the abbot's care. However, the note
of penitence is apparent: the separation between the two,
he says, is to be laid to the account of the king's sins and
perhaps Hugh wishes to avoid an unfruitful tree. The people
of Israel was punished by the Lord when it sinned but was
pardoned when it became penitent, which he illustrates by examples from the Old Testament as prototypes for his own experience. Have we not borne the Lord's anger, he asks, by
the destruction of ecclesiastical religion and can we not
hope for compassion by restoring this same religion? He then
declares his intent to heal the schism and the ruin of the
Church brought about through his own sins by restoring peace
and justice. Also, when he is able to unite as one again the
kingship and the priesthood, he promises to go on pilgrimage
to Jerusalem.[23] The letter concludes with a request to the
abbot and the monks for prayers.

Of the two remaining letters dated four years later in
the year of Henry's death, 1106, the longer of these[24] relates

in detail the betrayal of his own son. Caught in the midst
of an unnatural choice,he turns to Hugh and Cluny for support
because he has always been assured of the abbot's piety and
paternal solicitude. The liturgical prayers for the king he
says have freed him, he believes, from many dangers and therefore, as to one after God most dear, he has recourse to Hugh
as if to his only refuge in a time of need, humbly seeking
solace in his misery. Would that it be granted to see the
abbot's angelic face so that the head which was taken from
the baptismal font could be pressed against the abbot's
knees and laid in the holy father's lap where the emperor's
sins could be confessed.[25] Hugh is beseeched not to dis-
dain his letter but to accept his words as true. Henry recounts the story of being imprisoned by his own son, his
loss of the imperial dignity by treason and blackmail, his
treatment, worse than a slave at the hands of barbarians,
he says, in the presence of the papal legate,Richard of Al-
bano.[26] Now that he has escaped the hands of his persecutors
he writes to Hugh,trusting entirely to his counsel with all
the force and desire of his soul. Once again he pleads for
peace and unity with the Roman Church,hoping to break the
spell of the papal excommunication. Hugh is asked to hasten
to give him counsel.

The last letter[27] recalls once again the unheard of
betrayal[28] and asks for Hugh's support. He promises to do
whatever the abbot would propose as an intermediary as long
as his honor is preserved. The last words commit him to the
confraternity and its prayers now chanted in a world transformed by a new vision, the Crusades.[29]

Henry's repeated requests to be remembered by the abbot
and the entire Cluniac confraternity indicate that it was his
desire to maintain the traditional bonds uniting the imperial

to the monastic world. Throughout his life to the very end
his confidence in Hugh remains unquestioned. We have a
charter[30] of July 27, 1072, just before the outbreak of the
papal offensive, where Henry confirms the gift of a chapel
by a certain Hesso to Cluny expressing his desire through
good works to be a participant in Cluny's prayers. We find
the same concern and desire at the end of his life. However,
the repentance of the conscientious king reflects the inner
anguish of a man stunned inwardly by the course of events for
which he was not prepared. He seeks accomodation with the
Pope, although any reconciliation with the new types of men
who have appeared on the historical scene[31] is not possible
during his reign. Never before had emperors been excommunicated. Gregory's act was to launch the whole series of bans
laid on them for the next centuries, which step by step dis-
allowed the significance of their anointment as *Christi
Domini*,[32] until the emperor's adoption and ordination by the
Church came to precede his anointment as a *filius specialis*
of the Apostolic See, a title bestowed on him formally by the
Pope.[33] Henry IV died banned from communion and burial in
the Church, his empire lost. Prayers for the emperor at
Cluny continued within the confraternity but they could no
longer insure the stability of kingdoms. The change, great
as it was, occurred as the result of historical forces external to both Hugh and Henry IV. At Cluny the change was
not only perceived, but accepted. Cluny was forced to draw
back from its close spiritual alliance with the Empire and
recognize the successful challenge to its spiritual base by
a third force, a revolutionary Papacy bent on overturning
the bases of previous church law and tradition. The papal
claims to precedence in the Church combined with the intent

o recast for the first time the structure of the Church in
its entirety could neither be ignored,nor withstood.

Following the death of Gregory VII in 1085 there was
uncertainty about the appointment of his successor.[34] The
choice finally settled on the abbot of Monte Cassino, De-
siderius, who was to take the name of Victor III after a
year-long refusal to assume the papal office. He was a
compromise candidate meeting such outspoken opposition from
two ardent Gregorians, the archbishop Hugh of Lyon and the
abbot Richard of St. Victor in Marseilles, that he excommunicated them both at the Synod of Benevento in 1087. The
Cluniacs, who had entered into bonds of confraternity with
Monte Cassino, respected this excommunication and thereby
drew upon themselves the archbishop's wrath,expressed following the early death of the pontiff September 16, 1087. The
monks were violently criticized for their excesses and injustice because of their prayers for the excommunicated
Henry IV on Good Friday.[35] The intensity of the criticism
is highly instructive,as were the consequences. First of
all,it reveals the influence of the prayers of the Cluniac
confraternity on contemporaries in the midst of the struggle.
Secondly,it indicates Hugh's good will towards the banned
emperor and the willingness to recognize his traditional
allegiance to the Burgundian community,once Gregory VII had
passed from the scene. It is Lehmann's supposition that these
prayers had been interrupted during Gregory's pontificate,
otherwise their presence in the Cluniac liturgy would not have
caused such a stir.[36] If this is so, which appears highly
probable, Hugh felt himself free to reintroduce them during a
period when there was no pope on the papal throne, namely on
April 3, 1086.[37] In support of this argument we might recall

that Hugh's commerce with the excommunicated German king did not escape Gregory's censure as early as 1076 when the abbot received papal absolution for so doing.[38] Hence it cannot be far from the mark to assume that Hugh of Lyon's bitter indignation also expressed the late pontiff's attitude. By the same token St. Hugh's own decision to reintroduce the Good Friday prayers for the emperor indicates his reluctance to accept Gregory's views unequivocally, at least in the form in which they were presented to him. His chief benefactor was by this time no longer the German emperor, plagued with a civil war and treason within his own family, but the Spanish Emperor Alphonso VI (1066-1109). Cluny III was built with funds supplied by this monarch, his chief support in Spain and one who in 1077 had doubled the cens promised by his father Ferdinand.[39] Hugh was to decree a series of liturgical prayers and high masses as part of the reception of this king into the *societas* in excess of those enumerated for German emperors.[40] Consequently, the wily abbot in his reply to criticism of his prayers *pro imperatore* could reply that the prayers were for any emperor: *orationem illam pro imperatore quolibet se dixisse*.[41] Nonetheless, there is little doubt that the prayers were intended for Henry IV. Hugh's answer to the archbishop, however, indicates that Henry IV had lost his spiritual base at Cluny while under the ban of excommunication. The emperor's authority to depose popes, present at Sutri some forty years previously and recognized by the Cluniac abbot, was therewith supplanted by the pope's newly recognized authority to excommunicate an emperor and to ban his name from the liturgical prayers of the largest independent monastic congregation of the eleventh century. The abbot's reply was no less than the implicit recognition of the pope's authority to rule the universal Church.

Under Urban II (1088-1099) Gregory VII's hopes were
realized in irrevocable fashion.[42]   More moderate in his
policies and dealings than his great predecessor, Urban II
was to reconcile many of the conflicting tensions present
during the reign of Victor III[43] while supplying an irresist-
ible impulse to papal hegemony by calling the Crusades, the
first revolutionary movement in the West. Both Richard of
St. Victor in Marseilles and Archbishop Hugh were restored
to papal grace, their excommunication lifted.[44]   The latter
was to become a papal legate again, his friendship with Hugh
of Cluny restored and acknowledged at his death by the abbot.[45] A letter from St. Hugh to the pope written in 1097
contains words which would have gladdened the heart of Gregory VII. He writes: "O Lord Father, many for just and necessary reasons desire to be in your worthy presence but they
are prevented from doing so by various difficulties standing
in the way. They and others come at least to us as to your
servants:" *ad domesticos vestros.*[46]   And he closes with a
wish that the Lord preserve the pope's most beloved paternity
for him and--his terminology is new for the Cluniac sources--
the universal Church. The universal Church was no longer
identified with the Emperor. On the contrary Hugh now found
himself deeply moved by the tragic fate of kings, little sus-
pecting that Cluny, too, would have to adapt to the new
papacy.[47] He wrote in 1106 to Philip of France encouraging
his desire to enter a monastery since the king might well be
terrified by the lamentable deaths of his two contemporaries
William,king of England,and the emperor Henry IV: the latter
died overwhelmed with anguish and grave troubles.[48]   Therefore learn to fear God, he is told, lest he finish like these
princes. "Behold the princes of the apostles Peter and Paul,
judges of emperors and kings and of the earth who are prepared

to receive you in this his house which our fathers have named an asylum of penitence."[49] We are very far here from the days when Otto III was seen to be crowned by the apostles, forging spiritual links of the emperor to the papacy. Hugh does not say that the Apostles are judges of popes.[50]

Under the reign of Hugh, then, the relationship of the abbot to the emperor Henry IV becomes radically changed by his acceptance of the emperor as a schismatic. The abbot thereby accepts a different principle from that constituting the spiritual pre-eminence of the emperor in the pre-Gregorian order of things.[51] Hugh of course does not take sides in the struggle, as his biographer Reynald is quick to point out,[52] but by recognizing the existence of the Roman Church detached forever from the domination of the Roman Emperor he has acknowledged the passing of a world in which the Cluniac confraternity came to birth.[53] The basis of the spiritual and social resurgence in the pre-Gregorian Church had been the *Renovatio Romani Imperii*. Now the future was to see this same *renovatio* revolutionized and transformed. In the Crusades the imperial and Cluniac visions of Jerusalem were transformed into a vision calling forth worldly conquest inviting every Christian to bear his cross in the world. No longer was the cross the philosophy of emperors. But henceforth everyone was to be marked more and less by its demanding revolutionized version, *Crux christianorum philosophia.*

NOTES

1. Udal., I, 25, *P.L.* 149, 672, says that Hugh introduced many changes.

2. K. Hallinger, "Kluny's Braüche" etc., p. 110f.

3. Cf. infra, pp. 118-121.

4. Cf. infra, pp. 203f. Mehne's work (see infra, p.
83, n. 9) will certainly contribute to casting light on this
whole subject, as far as bishops are concerned.

5. Cf. infra, pp. 217f.

6. P. Jaffé, *Bibliotheca Rerum Germanicarum*, vol. II,
(reprint of 1865 edition, Aalen, 1964), no. 50, p. 576.

7. E. Rosenstock-Huessy, *Königshaus und Stämme*, pp. 42f.
for the discussion that follows.

8. Hence Gregory VII's decision to overthrow the reign-
ing social order is still seen as a mere break with an out-
moded tradition,reinforced by Christian principles of reform
and renewal. The commitment of the pope to war on the issue
of the freedom of the Church may have been necessary at a
moment when the emperor could be considered as possessing the
Holy Spirit himself but the magnitude of the change may not
be minimized,as it is in the discussion of the pope's words
by G. Ladner, "Two Gregorian Letters. On the Sources and
Nature of Gregory VII's Reform Ideology," *SG*, 5, (1956), pp.
221-242, and G. Tellenbach, *Church, State*, p. 164. Ladner
fails to see that Gregory's references to Christ's words are
made in a political context and are meant to have a political
effect. See infra, p. 193, n. 42, relative to Urban II's call
to the Crusades, a radical appeal to revolutionary action.

9. E. Rosenstock-Huessy, *op. cit.*, p. 43. Cf. infra,
p. 20, n. 37 and p. 195, n. 53.

10. Ber., Prae., p. 135.

11. E. Rosenstock-Huessy, *ibid.* Before Gregory VII's
particular application of *veritas*, all the reform papacy

could conceive was to imitate the imperial model of the *regalia*
by introducing the *regalia s. Petri* which led to papal success
in the secular area, viz. J. Fried, "Der Regalienbegriff im 11.
und 12. Jahrhundert," *DA*, 29, (1973), pp. 450-528. This symbolism was not developed further, as the author expects it
might have been (p. 512), because of the preferred development
of written law, culminating in Gratian, which released the
papacy from dependence on *consuetudo*. Cf. on the *regalia s.
Petri*, the *papatus Romanus* and the early oaths of fealty to the
Holy See which showed a deviation from feudal norms, E. Kantorowicz, *The King's Two Bodies*, (Princeton, 1957), pp. 185, n.
293. A. Nitschke, "Die Wirksamkeit Gottes in der Welt Gregors
VII," *SG*, 5, (1956) is also pertinent: Human will was only
free when it agreed with the will of the Pope (p. 213). It is
characteristic for Gregory's world that religion, law, morals,
and custom were not separated into different compartments (p.
217), a characteristic, it might be added, of all revolution-
aries. Further on *consuetudines*, defined by J. F. Lemarignier
for the eleventh century as, "l'ensemble des droits de la puis-
sance publique", "La dislocation du 'pagus' et le problème des
'consuetudines' (Xe-XIes.)" in *Mélanges d'histoire du moyen âge
dédiés à la mémoire de L. Halphen*, (Paris, 1951), p. 404. Also
Nitschke, *art. cit.*, p. 217, "Dass im frühen Mittelalter Recht
und Sittlichkeit weitgehend zusammenfallen ist allgemein be-
kannt"; hence for Gregory the source of law lay in the true
Christian's experience of God's justice. With regard to
Cluny's decline, the *consuetudines* ceded to a more legalistic
organizational principle advanced by the Cistercians and Pre-
monstratensians, P. Hofmeister, "Cluny und seine Abteien,"
StMGBO, 75, (1964), p. 186. Rudolph Glaber makes clear in
the middle of the eleventh century that king, pope and monks
follow as law the *antiqua consuetudo*. M. Vogelsang, "Der
kluniacenzische Chronist Raoul Glaber: Ein Beitrag zur kluniazensischen Geschichtsschreibung," *StMGBO*, 67, (1956), p. 37.

12. See P. Fournier and G. Le Bras, *Histoire des collections canoniques en Occident depuis les fausses decrétales
jusqu' au décret de Gratien*, (Paris, 1932) for examples of the
new spirit opposing that of the *consuetudines*. "The systematic
establishment of the law is the overwhelming and unmistakable
characteristic of the Reform", and Petrine Supremacy is the
constitutive principle, as there were no official law books:
R. Knox, "Finding the Law: Developments in Canon Law during
the Gregorian Reform," *SG*, 9, (1972), pp. 422f., 464, and
passim. That "Roman Primacy guarantees the active presence
of the Holy Spirit in the Church" (*ibid.*, pp. 427-428) may
have been a necessary position to take in order to free the

Church from the kingdoms of this world but the conflict, as in all revolutions, was not confined to a reform of abuses.

13. *P.L.* 142, 1001, hence also aware that the Lord "definitely never said: I am custom", Ladner, *art. cit.*, p. 225.

14. A. J. MacDonald, *Hildebrand, a Life of Gregory VII*, (London, 1932).

15. H.-X. Arquilliere, *Saint Grégoire VII*, (Paris, 1934). Also engaging in apologetics at times, A. Fliche, *La Réforme grégorienne et la Reconquête chrétienne*, (Paris, 1940). Cf. K. Hampe, *Deutsche Kaisergeschichte in der Zeit der Salier und Staufer*, (F. Baethgen edition, Heidelberg, 1963[11]), p. 50, n. 2 and Tellenbach in *Libertas*, Appendix VI, p. 212.

16. C. Erdmann, *Die Entstehung* etc., p. 134, n. 3.

17. E. Caspar, "Gregor VII in seinen Briefen," *Historische Zeitschrift*, vol. 130, (1924), p. 30.

18. P. E. Schramm, *Kaiser, Könige, Päpste*, II, p. 301.

19. *Quellen zur Geschichte Kaiser Heinrichs IV in Ausgewählte Quellen zur deutschen Geschichte des Mittelalters*, (ed. R. Buchner, vol. 12, Berlin, 1963), Letters no. 31, 37, 38, pp. 100f. and 112f.

20. *Ibid.*, Letter no. 37, 112. In Letter no. 34, 107f., written to Pope Paschal II, Henry writes that he would address the pontiff as a son his father if peace and concord reigned as formerly during the time of the monk-popes (viri religiosi) Nicholas II and Alexander II. This complaint makes it clear that the first open attack on the imperial role in the Church originated with Gregory VII.

21. Letter no. 31, *op. cit.*

22. See H. Diener, "Das Itinerar des Abtes Hugo von Cluny," *NF*, pp. 353-393. P. Segl, "Zum Itinerar Abt Hugos I von Cluny (1049-1109)," *DA*, 29, (1973), pp. 206-219.

23. In direct inheritance of Otto III, cf. p. 152, n. 32.

24. Letter no. 37, *op. cit.*

25. *Ibid.*, pp. 112, 114.

26. *Ibid.*, p. 118. See also *Vita Heinrici IV Imperatoris*, *ibid.*, c. 10, pp. 446f. It should be recognized that the humiliation suffered by the king at this time (December 1105-January 1106) was real, unlike that at Canossa. For the historic meeting in 1077 see W. v. d. Steinen's insufficiently appreciated *Canossa*, (Munich, 1957).

27. Letter no. 38.

28. *A seculo inaudite et horribilis traditionis nostre.* *Ibid.*, p. 120.

29. "For the first time since the passing of the Roman Empire a united aspiration and common ideal were put before Europe." L. Smith, *Cluny in the Eleventh and Twelfth Centuries*, p. 295.

30. No. 3449, Bruel, IV, 558.

31. "This time in comparison with many misfortunes of human life brought forth a certain kind of man who differs so much from the ways and the integrity of life of the previous age that one scarcely knows if it is an aberration of nature or if this kind of man did not derive its lineage at all from the stock of that prior age." *Petri Crassi Defensio Heinrici IV Regis*, MGH, *Libelli de Lite*, I, p. 434.

32. E. Eichmann, "Das Exkommunicationsprivileg des deutschen Kaisers im Mittelalter," *ZRG, KA*, 1, (1911), p. 164.

33. *Ibid.*, p. 194.

34. Abbé Rony, "L'election de Victor III," *RHEF*, 14, (1928), pp. 145-160.and H. Diener, "Das Verhältnis Clunys zu den Bischofen," *NF*, pp. 273f.

35. R. Lehmann, "Ueber den die Excommunication des Erzbischofs Hugo von Lyon durch Papst Victor III betreffenden Brief des Ersteren an die Graefin Mathilde," *Forschungen zur deutschen Geschichte*, VIII, pp. 641-648. Also H. Diener, *loc. cit.* The source is found in Mansi, *Sacrorum Conciliorum nova et amplissima collectio*, (Florence and Venice, 1759-1798), vol. 20, 634.

36. R. Lehmann, *op. cit.*, p. 646.

37. *Ibid.*

38. H. Diener, "Das Itinerar" etc., *NF*, p. 366.

39. *P.L.* 159, 938.

40. *P.L.* 159, 945-946. J. Bishko, *loc. cit.*, fails to note that Cluny's interest in Spanish emperors was a response to a crisis of first magnitude. Alphonso was, so to speak, the only "Holy Emperor" available. He called himself *servus servorum Dei*, a title reserved for popes, hence he, too, found himself subject to Gregory VII's strictures. By turning to the Spanish kingdom Cluny indicated that its relationship to the German Emperors was a vulnerable one. The quantity of prayers for the Spanish monarch was the attempt to keep a threatened tradition alive. The enormous number of prayers for the nephew of Henry of Winchester, L. Champly, *op. cit.*, pp. 118-119, is but another chapter in Cluny's descent from the pinnacle of the spiritual world. Statistics, in this case the number of prayers, are far from infallible guides here. Alphonso's letter is in Bruel IV, no. 3441, 532. On Cluny in Spain cf. C. J. Bishko, "Fernando I y los origenes de la alienza castellano leonesa con Cluny," *Cuardenos de Historia de España*, vols. 47-48, (1968), pp. 31-135 and vols. 49-50, (1969), pp. 50-116 and now P. Segl.

41. Mansi, *loc. cit.* The indignation of his Gregorian opponents was to no avail. He refused to repent his action.

42. A. Becker, *Papst Urban II*, (Stuttgart, 1964), pp. 15-16. Exalted by his French journey, this pope expressed his Gregorian faith anew the following year: *quod minimus clericulus de ecclesia Dei est maior quolibet rege mortali*, *ibid.*, p. 226. In 1088 he wrote to Alphonso VI of Spain explicitly asserting the superiority of the priestly dignity to the royal power, p. 227f. He called the Crusades by invoking Christ's words: "Whoever does not take up his cross and follow me, cannot be my disciple," C. H. Brakel, "Die vom Reformpapsttum geförderten Heiligenkulte, *SG*, 9, (1972), p. 306, a doctrinaire Biblical reading foreign to Cluny, cf. n. 31.

43. H. Diener, "Das Verhältnis Clunys" etc., *NF*, p. 274.

44. *Ibid.*

45. *Ibid.*, p. 276.

46. After Urban's death his anniversary was to be celebrated as though Urban were an abbot of the cloister; Fechter,
p. 114f., includes other references to the relationship between Urban and Hugh. Also Becker, p. 41f.

47. H. Wolter, *Ordericus Vitalis, Ein Beitrag zur klunia-
zensisches Geschichtsschreibung,* (Wiesbaden, 1955), points out
that although Cluny was preeminent in a monastically oriented
world (p. 2), it fell prey to the forces which wished to trans-
form the Church into an *ecclesia spiritualis* (p. 148). The
enthusiasm of *Ordericus* for the Crusades signals the end of
that preeminence (p. 150). The confraternities were subjected
to increasing criticism during the twelfth and thirteenth centuries, Duhr, *op. cit.* The Lateran council of 1180 reproached
these religious associations of weakening the episcopal authority, p. 473. During the thirteenth century their vows were
condemned by the ecclesiastical hierarchy which saw in them a
narrow 'esprit particulariste' based on clannish rather than
universal loyalties, p. 466f. Indeed, Duhr concludes, p. 477,
"l'autorité de l'Eglise ne les a jamais ni sanctionnés, ni
même tolérés", i.e. the basic divergence of outlook endured.

48. *P.L.* 159, 930. No *sanctus* David comes into question
any longer. Under Hugh, and the exact point in time remains
to be determined, although it does not precede the pontificate
of Gregory VII, Cluny switches spiritual allegiance from emperor to pope.

49. *Ibid.*

50. Gregory VII on his death-bed "absolved and blessed
all those who firmly believed that, in the place of the
apostles Peter and Paul, he had power to do so," H. Mann,
The Lives of the Popes, vol. 7, (London, 1925), pp. 167-168,
whose source is Paul of Bernried's *Vita Gregorii,* c. 110.
See *AA SS*, V, May, 1741 under May 25. Also Paul of Bernried
relates a vision of St. Paul appearing to Hildebrand asking
him to clear up the filth left by cattle in the cloisters,
A. Stacpoole, *art. cit., Downside Review,* p. 262. Compare
with our reference in Novati, p. 164, n. 13.

51. T. Schieffer, "Cluny et la querelle des investitures,"
Revue Historique, vol. 225, (1961), p. 55, states that there
was no "hostilité de principe" on the part of Cluny against
the emperor. However, the abbot's neutrality indicates that
the opposite became true, at least to the extent which Hugh
felt himself obliged to choose. However, it needs to be

stressed that the scholarly obsession to view Cluny mainly
in terms of the "Investiture Contest" introduces a false historical perspective. See Chapter II.

Under Urban II Cluny and the Holy Emperors became
subject to a new principle, based on the division between
spiritual and temporal, hence their relationship in these
terms is a totally different matter even though the words
seem to mean the same. Prayers for the emperor continue
for example.

52. *P.L.* 159, 903.

53. I am pleased to report that this historical view of
the revolutionary birth of modern legal systems is now being
taught at Harvard Law School by Professor Harold Berman, viz.
"The 'Papal Revolution'...led to the creation of a new kind
of law for the church as well as new kinds of law for the
various secular kingdoms." "The canon law of the later Middle
Ages...was the first modern legal system of the West," *The
Interaction of Law and Religion,* (Nashville, New York, 1974),
p. 56f. Further in "The Crisis of the Western Legal Tradition," *Creighton Law Review,* vol. 9, no. 2, (1975), pp. 252-
265 and "The Religious Foundations of Western Law," *Catholic
University Law Review,* vol. 24, no. 3, (1975), pp. 490-508.
A layman in the business world, R. McFalls, sent these publications to me as a matter of contemporary interest, just before submission of the final proofs. I would like to take
this occasion to thank him for his persistent efforts to dis-
tribute writings of significance.

With respect to the larger historical problem of the
legal usages which preceded the radical change (cf. p. 179f.),
J. Stiennon, "Cluny at Saint-Trond au XIIe Siècle," in *Ancien
Pays et Assemblés d'Etats,* VIII (Louvain, 1955), describes the
consuetudinaries as "la loi non-écrite," p. 66. Also a supple-
mentary index to a manuscript copy of Bernard's *Ordo Cluniacensis* states that ecclesiastical *consuetudines* have the force
of divine law unless in conflict with the Bible, *ibid.,* p. 79.
To ignore the significance of the change by insistence on the
"Gregorian Reform" (see infra pp. 189-190, notes 8, 12, 13, 15)
blocks the way into the future for the Roman Church, as well as
the law schools, since its defenders assume the continuance of
an ecclesiastical structure that does not do justice to the believing layman. The controversy about Hans Küng, whose writings signal the end of the "canon law mentality", of an overly
clericalized church is a case in point. Compare for example
his *"Alle* Glaubenden sind Gottesvolk: eine Klerikalisierung
der Kirche ist ausgeschlossen," p. 151f., and "Alle Christen

als königliche Priesterschaft," p. 439f. of *Die Kirche*, Freiburg i.B., (1967), with our reference to *regale sacerdotium*, p. 61, for an indication of the necessary change in historical perspective forced on Rome.

CHAPTER IV

DONUM LACRIMARUM

What influence did Cluny exert on society with regard to its own claim to be an asylum of penance and in what form did the monastery express its deepest faith both within and without the abbey?

Cluny's main concern was for the dead and the souls of the dead. As such, it follows an impulse in the long tradition reaching back to the very beginnings of mankind's history, the lamentation of man's end in death and his consciousness of it. "The lament for the dead was originally a loud wail....in the place of this wild wailing tears appear. The wailing cry and the invocation of the dead change into a singing that induces the grief-stricken to weep. The lament becomes a pious duty, disregard of which is detrimental to the dead and those left behind."[1] Thanks to the inspired invention of the feast of All Souls, the widespread diffusion of masses for the dead, which infused the huge monastic congregation with a single spirit, and the example of its abbots, Cluny was able to permeate Western society with a consciousness of the cleansing and penitential gift of tears, *donum lacrimarum*.[2] The *vitae* of our three abbots are sown with references to their possession of this gift. On journeys Majolus would withdraw from his companions for several days and water the earth with his tears.[3] At his return from his capture by the Saracens all wept, "gushing tears abundantly which do not extinguish the

fire of love but rather arouse it".[4] Having no food for the
poor in a time of famine Majolus prayed more intensely *solutus
in lacrymas pauperibus*.[5] We are told on another occasion that
he had recourse to a familiar remedy, which was: *in oratione
curvatus aures Domini suspiriis lacrymosis everberat*.[6] Fore-
telling the death of Otto the Great he shed tears.[7] Odilo's
biographer speaks of his *affluentia lacrymarum*[8] and his eyes
are described as having a particular brilliant splendor, in-
spiring both fear and admiration and continually filled with
tears, because of the virtue of compunction.[9] Odilo shed tears
in contemplating the cross just before his death.[10] And if
you wish to know, he says, what the mother of God was doing
after the Lord's resurrection, but before his ascension, she
frequented the places of his passion, burial and resurrection
shedding tears.[11] On the occasion of Odilo's *dies natalis* on
January 1 everyone weeps at the news[12] and on Hugh's return he
finds the entire community in tears.[13] In the lives of Hugh
the same theme is present. When a Cluniac monastery was
threatened by a local tyrant, Hugh committed the whole matter
to St. John the Baptist, demanding immediate aid which was
granted thanks to tears and groans.[14] Tears are shed as Pope
Stephen IX expires in Hugh's arms.[15] Tears are designated as
the insignia of piety.[16] Before Hugh's death it was revealed
to him that he would enter heaven because he waited *in lacrymis*
and both he and Anselm of Canterbury are said to have earned
eternal joy after their tears on earth.[17] Ulrich of Cluny was
also said to have this gift.[18] Indeed tears are seen by Peter
the Venerable as the essence of Cluny, an integral part of its
custom,[19] allowing the monks at their feasts as at Christmas to
"solemnize with the angels".[20]

The gift of compunction was of course not confined to
monasteries and its tradition in the Christian Church is

long.[21] However in this period as Neander tells us: "We see a new awakening of religious life break out among the peoples. Amidst raging passions and the crude outbreaks of force a powerful feeling of penitence is awakened. The call to the Crusades finds therein its point of annexation and furthers this stimulus even further."[22] It has been observed that "durch Cluny eine Welle der Selbsterniedrigung ueber das Abendland ging, die durchaus selbstverständlich und auszeichnend war".[23] Evidence of this wave of feeling could be illustrated in the lives of popes, emperors, nobles, knights and common people. The outbreak of tears evidenced by Otto II and his mother Adelaide at the moment of their reconciliation is one example.[24] The penitential conduct of Henry IV at Canossa is another, the letters of both the emperor and his papal adversary to Hugh are other forms of the same gift emanating from Cluny, *donum lacrimarum*.

NOTES

1. M. J. Hengstl, *op. cit.*, p. 1.

2. U. Berlière, *L'Ascèse bénédictine*, pp. 209f. has seen the essential importance of this element in Cluniac life and has mentioned it briefly in a few moving pages. Also O. Ringholz, *op. cit.*, p. LXIIIf.

3. *P.L.* 137, 758.

4. Nalgod, *Vita S. Majoli, AA SS*, May, II, 664 D.

5. *Ibid.*, 659.

6. *Ibid.*, 664. *P.L.* 137, 762.

7. Nalgod, *op. cit.*, 665. *P.L.* 137, 771.

8. *P.L.* 142, 901. Also Peter Damian following Jotsald, *P.L.* 144, 928.

9. *P.L.* 142, 901. See Berlière on this virtue, *loc. cit.*

10. *P.L.* 142, 910.

11. *Sermo XII, De Assumptione Dei Genetricis Mariae, P.L.* 142, 1026-1027.

12. *P.L.* 142, 897.

13. *P.L.* 159, 862.

14. *P.L.* 159, 881. The devotion to John the Baptist prominent in the Middle Ages and particularly so at Cluny is no doubt connected with Cluny's role as an asylum of penance (*P.L.* 159, 931-932).

15. Gilo's *Vita Hugonis, op. cit.*, 578 and *ibid.*, p. 378. Also *P.L.* 144, 928.

16. *P.L.* 159, 879, 887, 888.

17. *P.L.* 159, 892.

18. U. Berlière, *L'Ascèse bénédictine*, p. 211.

19. *Mos*, not *consuetudo*.

20. *"Quod longe praestantius est, speciali devotione, multaque lacrymarum profusione, cum angelicis spiritibus alacriter solemnizare,"* Quid beatus Hugo narraverit in capitulo vigilia Natalis Domini, (Ex Petro Venerabili, lib. I Mirac, cap. 15), *P.L.* 159, 953.

21. The most profound commentary I know on the subject is the chapter "Tears in Holy Scripture" in the beautiful book of the great French Catholic Ernest Hello, *Paroles de Dieu*, (Paris, 1919). Anglo-Saxon writers raised in a Puritan tradition have had to supply explanations when mentioning the *donum lacrimarum* viz. "The 'gift of tears' which the Church came to regard as a special grace is by no means the accompaniment of a weak character; Ignatius Loyola had it, and in more recent times, Frederick Temple." L. Elliot Binns, *Innocent III*, (London, 1931), p. 10, n. 1.

22. A. Neander, *Der heilige Bernhard und sein Zeitalter*, (Gotha, 1865), pp. 1-2.

23. H. Mikoletzky, *Kaiser Heinrich II und die Kirche*, (Vienna, 1946), p. 56.

24. H. Paulhart, *op. cit.*, p. 34. H. von Eicken, *Geschichte und System der mittelalterlichen Welt*, (Stuttgart, 1887), p. 318f., has written with insight on the gift of tears and its relevance for understanding the contemporary frame of mind, noting that all noble religious natures possessed this gift to a greater or lesser degree.

ADDENDUM

1. Any definitive attempt to evaluate Hugh's relationship to Henry IV first requires a detailed investigation of
the increasing claims of the renovated Papacy to authority
over Cluny's autonomous role, secured under Odilo. Although
there is no question of undertaking this enterprise here, a
short survey supplementing the main text may venture to show
that the abbacy of Hugh presents contrasts with that of his
predecessor in this regard. Papal reform was given its initial
impetus by the emperors themselves as a function of their role
within the Church. Imperial concern for placing suitable occupants on the papal throne had been an essential aspect of
church policy from the days of the Ottos. The high point of
this imperial reform movement was reached some years later in
1046 at the council of Sutri called by Henry III who sat in
judgment on the three papal claimants for the chair of St.
Peter and declared them legally deposed.[1] The emperor's own
choice was the bishop of Bamberg who took the name of Clement
II indicating by this name a hearkening back to the times of
Clement I, who in some papal lists is designated as the successor to St. Peter himself. This action and choice of the
emperor was welcomed by the Cluniacs; Henry III acted in his
capacity of being *caput ecclesia,* head of the Church.

Of his four imperial appointees the most significant was
Bruno of Toul who became Leo IX in the year 1049. With him a
period of papal initiative begins a new era for the papacy.
In the same year Odilo had died at the age of 87, fulfilling

his duties to the last by attendance at the emperor's coronation three years previously, a long journey in those days,
particularly at that age. Richard of St. Vannes, his disciple,
Poppo of Stablo,[2] and Odilo's friend, Isarnus of the monastery
of St. Victor, had all died within the past three years. Henry
III's death in 1056 left behind his sole heir, a boy of six.
Hence at the same time that this boy, the future Henry IV, was
coming of age under the conditions of a turbulent regency, the
Papacy and its single-minded reformers felt themselves prepared
to begin undertaking the reform of the Church and to question
the role of the emperor in that process, especially with regard
to papal elections. By the time of the accession of Hildebrand
to the papal throne in the year 1073, the pope was a man of
some fifty years of age, as was Hugh. Both consequently attained full adulthood during a series of pontificates whose
papal representatives were forcing the issues of simony, lay
investiture and the development of canon law to the forefront
while, from the point of view of the boy emperor at least, the
imperial tradition, based on the king as the anointed of the
Lord, remained constant and unquestioned. The outbreak of the
conflict in 1075 made irrevocable the presence of two parties
in conflict, the imperial and the papal. It is in terms of
these two irreconciliable opponents that Hugh's stand is
generally analyzed. Tellenbach and his school have carried
out assiduous research, the conclusion of which points towards
Hugh's position above the parties, tied in his choices and decisions to neither of them.[3] Stacpoole summarizes the present
general consensus:

> There are those who argue that the Gregorian
> Reforms were incubated within the walls of
> the Burgundian monastery....and above all they
> see in Hildebrand, as a Cluniac monk, the
> linchpin between Cluny and the papacy. But

this is a weak case. Cluny was of course in
sympathy with the pope--its own authority,
indeed, spread throughout Europe--and required a strong papacy for its undisturbed
existence. Yet Cluny hesitated to draw upon
itself the wrath of the pope's adversaries,
notably the emperor, in the stormy years of
the Gregorian Reform. Abbot Hugh chose rather
a cautious neutrality than a full-blooded es-
pousal of the papal cause, knowing well that
Cluniac privileges over the course of time had
provoked many jealous prelates, who waited
only for the moment of Cluniac weakness. To
these, the enemies of his House, he was reluc-
tant to add those of the papacy. Cluny, therefore, sat on the fence: and the tone of Pope
Gregory's letters--a tone of impatient reproach
--bears witness to it: Gregory VII complained
that there were occasions when the abbot's
holiness shunned trouble, and when he was
slothful in answering demands of business.[4]

Convincing though these arguments may be in themselves,
they are incomplete with regard to their significance for our
understanding of Cluny. Let us restate the evaluations of the
Sellenbach school and Dom Stacpoole in terms of our present
investigation and then supplement their conclusions. For Cluny
to maintain a position of neutrality between the parties and
therefore towards the emperor involved a basic change from her
previous position; hence Hugh's relationship to the papacy,
and consequently that of Cluny, can only be adequately determined by historical contrast with the monastery's traditional
bonds to the imperial House. These bonds linked both to a
common cause, the renewal of the Church. A neutral position
taken by Hugh can only represent a retreat from Cluny's unquestioned earlier stance with regard to the Empire and an
acceptance of papal authority absent in Odilo's concurrence
with the rejection of Gregory VI in 1046. Hence, not only does
the influence of the monastery on the series of Cluniac popes

named in the necrologies of the confraternity deserve attention, but its corollary as well, the influence of the Reform
Papacy in forcing Cluny into a previously unheard-of neutrality regarding the imperial claim to full spiritual supremacy
in the Church. With regard to the question of who was to be
head of the Church *Tertium non datur.*

At the council of Rheims[5] called in 1049 the abbot was
interrogated as to his simoniacal intentions and he admitted
to the temptation before the assembly. Although his prompt
denial cleared him of the charge, it had become evident that a
new critical and spiritual force invoked by the papal reform
party had come into existence. In the years following, Hugh
acted as a papal legate of Leo IX to Hungary in 1051 or 1052,
of Nicholas II in 1060 to Avignon and in 1062, when he held a
synod at Toulouse.

However, the pressure on the abbot to comply with papal
claims reached its high peak of intensity during the pontificate of Gregory VII when the attempt was made by its author
to put into practice the revolutionary pronouncements of the
Dictatus Papae.[6] Since the contents of this document are all
directed against the emperor's role inside the Church, the
reason for Gregory's reproaches to Hugh is not far to seek;
it is Cluny's allegiance to the customary role of the emperors
in the Church. Already at the Lenten synod of 1073[7] the monks
of Cluny had accused Hugh Candidus of simony which indicates
that support of reform party doctrine was present in the monastery. In his instructions of April 30, 1073 to the papal
legates in France the pope made it clear that Cluniac travel-
ing companions were not to take precedence over the papal
representatives.[8] In a similar vein the following year the
Pope wrote to the abbot: "Welcome and sweet to us are your
words: but they would give us far greater satisfaction if

your affection toward the Roman Church were more ardent."[9]
However, it is in his letter of January 22, 1075 that we find
a sure indication of Gregory's differences with Cluniac monasticism and his attempt to sever it from its links to royal
tradition:

> And because we ought to use either hand as a
> right hand in crushing the savagery of the
> wicked, it becomes our duty, when there is no
> prince to care for such matters, to keep watch
> over the lives of religious men. We enjoin
> upon you in brotherly love that so far as you
> are able, you lend your aid with watchful zeal,
> warning, urging and exhorting those who love
> St. Peter, that if they really wish to be his
> sons and his soldiers, they do not prefer the
> princes of this world to him. For these can
> yield them only what is wretched and transient,
> while he promises eternal blessings, absolving
> them from all their sins and leading them into
> their heavenly home by the power committed to
> him.
>   I desire to know more clearly than the
> day who are really faithful to St. Peter
> (Gregory had doubts about Hugh's allegiance!)
> and who are no less devoted to that heavenly
> prince for the sake of their glory than to
> those to whom they are subject for temporal
> and miserable rewards.[10]

Here we see that in a world and a time when the temporal
and spiritual were indissolubly joined, in a period of history
where pope and emperor both embodied vital needs inside the
Church, where the emperor was clothed with an ecclesiastical
responsibility, where indeed he had been addressed as *caput
ecclesiae*, Gregory's attitude was necessarily oblique. Cluny's
community of prayer could not be attacked, only its relationship to emperors and its recognition of the emperor's privi-
leged status supported by the presuppositions and organization

of the imperial church system. Gregory states unhesitatingly
in this last letter that it becomes the duty of the Roman
Church to keep watch over the lives of monks. It is obvious
from this letter that Gregory wished to destroy the very basis
of the spiritual bonds uniting Cluny to Henry IV because the
emperor in his view was to be regarded as a member of the
temporal order. However, the question as to who was to be the
head of the Church was not Cluny's direct concern, important
though the historical answer given to this question was. All
Souls excludes no one. Consequently, although Hugh could lend
his authority to the new papacy in the midst of the civil war
by acting occasionally as a papal legate, Cluny's widespread
confraternity of prayer and property was too autonomous and
too large for Rome to accept as a model of monastic life.
The result of this dissatisfaction was the creation by Gregory
VII of St. Victor of Marseilles as a counterweight to Cluny.[11]
Its abbot in the days of Odilo, Isarnus (1022-1047), had been
on friendliest terms with the Cluniac abbot, whereas under
Durandus (1060-1064) the monastery of Saint-Ferréol in Vienne,
once placed upon Odilo's advice under the jurisdiction of St.
Victor, was now returned to Cluny at the demand of Hugh and
the papal legate Cardinal Stephen. Under the abbot Bernard
(1064-1079), Saint Victor, working by then hand in hand with
papal policy received a statement of privileges from the pope
modeled on that accorded to Cluny. However, with the appointment of Richard as abbot by Gregory, St. Victor of Marseilles
was to follow a policy setting it at odds with Cluny in Spain.
Richard was sent there as papal legate in 1080 where he came
into conflict with the Cluniac monk Robert about whom he complained to the pope. Gregory's subsequent letter to Hugh concerning the controversy should leave little doubt that Hugh no
longer retained the freedom of action or unassailable dignity

209

eyond criticism of his abbot predecessor. Hugh's representa-
ive Robert is called evil, an imitator of Simon Magus, one in
ebellion against the authority of St. Peter leading 100,000
ersons back into error. Hugh is reminded that in the past he
as shown himself to be of one mind with the pope as to the
onor of the Holy Roman Church and one who has preserved his
reedom to execute righteousness. Hugh is even threatened
hat extreme hostility could be the result without the re-
traint of papal persuasion, then warned to discipline his
ubordinates and ordered particularly to exclude Robert from
pain. King Alphonso VI was threatened with excommunication
or having sided with Cluny and,more, the pope would consider
oing to Spain to take severe measures against the king as an
nemy of the Christian faith if his orders were not obeyed.
onks scattered throughout Spain were to be returned to their
wn houses.[12] In short Spain was meant to become Rome's
phere of influence.[13]

The offensive thrust of Gregory's position is clear here.
f its result was to neutralize Hugh's influence in its col-
aboration with emperors,it had already achieved great suc-
ess.[14] Hugh must have been hard put at times despite the
ope's affection and admiration displayed on various occa-
ions for the abbot and the congregation.[15]

More amenable, it would seem, to St. Hugh's preferences
as Gregory VII's successor on the papal throne, Victor III,
he former abbot,Desiderius of Monte Cassino.[16] In 1083 their
ongregations had entered into the bonds of confraternity.
lso the outspoken opposition to the new pope of the two un-
ompromising Gregorians, Hugh of Lyon and the aforementioned
bbot Richard of St. Victor, ran counter to a papal candidate
ell-disposed towards Cluny. In August 1087 the excommunica-
ion of the abbot from Marseilles and archbishop of Lyon indi-

cated a rejection of the extremist Gregorian position and the apparent triumph for Cluny over its Rome-oriented competitor.[1] Yet with Victor III's early death the following month a new turn was given to all these internal conflicts. The new pope Urban II was a "Gregorian in the dress of a Cluniac,".... "however one to be understood in the context of the new forces that were to shape the coming century: the popular religious movements, the spiritual authority of canon law, the idea of the Papacy as the head of Christendom."[18] An independent Papacy freed of imperial domination is above all Urban's contribution to history.[19] It is under this pope that Hugh of Cluny was to accept his new allegiance. Urban II was the first pope to visit Cluny. Hugh was present at Clermont when the first Crusade was called. Hugh of Lyon and Richard of St. Victor were reconciled to papal policy which, unlike that of Gregory VII, refrained from attacks on Cluny. What further need was there to do so? Hugh received the gift of papal vestments and wore them at high feasts.[20] Rome had entered the Cluniac liturgy with full force. Hence, by the time of Urban's death in 1099, the die was cast between the priestly king and Cluny. We have the emperor's moving letters to Hugh, but no record of any replies of the abbot. A comparative study of those written by Henry IV to Hugh with the correspondance exchanged between popes and the abbot beginning with Gregory VII would be revealing. Henry IV approaches Hugh as a suppliant seeking the source of his spiritual base in the pre-Gregorian, non-revolutionary world of monastic confraternity. Hugh as a submissive neutral has withdrawn his full commitment to the imperial cause and his letter to Pope Urban II indicates where his deepest allegiance now lies. In the year of Henry IV's death on August 7, 1106 Paschal II was to spend Christmas at Cluny and he was also there the following February.[21]

Cluny's next abbot Pontius, the godson of the same pope, was to request and receive from his godfather the privilege of wearing the mitre, dalmatic, gloves and sandals at the eight principal festivals.[22] Although Pontius was to incur the rebuke of the papal chancellor John of Gaeta, the future Gelasius II, for calling himself the "abbot of abbots", he was to receive this pope and his retinue of cardinals and bishops at Cluny where the exiled pope was to die after a short pontificate. Gelasius' successor, Guy of Vienne, was elected at Cluny as Pope Calixtus II.[23] This pope was to address Cluny as "his own and especial monastery" and decree that its abbot was always and everywhere to fulfill the office of Roman cardinal.[24] In sign that belonging to the abbot and Pope alone Cluny was never to be subjected to any other jurisdiction, he invested Pontius with his own ring.[25] At the council of Rheims in 1119 when under attack Pontius defended the monastery by proclaiming that Cluny was subject to the Roman Church alone and to the pope.[26] And with Hugh's canonization on January 6, 1120 the bounds of papal authority were extended even further. Pope Calixtus refused to accept the testimony of documents regarding Hugh's sanctity without confirming witnesses who could attest in person as to what they had seen and heard.[27] Sainthood itself was becoming subject to a process of inquiry no longer satisfied with conclusions, however true, if not subjected to canon law.[28]

NOTES

1. See G. Tellenbach's discussion of Henry III's church policy in *Libertas*, Appendices IV and VI.

2. Sackur, II, 291f.

3. *NF*.

4. A. Stacpoole, *art. cit.*, p. 147.

5. *P.L.* 159, 866, 903 and C. Hefele, *Histoire des Conciles*, v. 4, pt. 2, p. 1019, n. 1.

6. The hypotheses of K. Hoffman, "Der 'Dictatus Papae' als eine Index Sammlung?," *SG*, 1, (1947), pp. 531-537 and G. Borino, "Un ipotesi sul 'Dictatus Papae' di Gregorio VII," *Archivio della Deputazione Romana di Storia Patria*, vol. 67, (1944), pp. 237-252, which affirm that the *Dictatus Papae* were chapter headings for a lost canonical law collection have no foundation in fact. These papal dictates possess a meaning intrinsic to themselves. They were Gregory VII's, hence the Papacy's, Bill of Rights. For further bibliography, H. Mordek, "*Proprie auctoritatis apostolice sedis:* Ein zweiter *Dictatus Papae* Gregors VII?," *DA*, 28, (1972), p. 105, n. 3.

7. Hefele, *ibid.*, pp. 1287f.

8. E. Caspar, *Das Register Gregors VII*, (Berlin, 1955), pp. 8f.

9. *Ibid.*, p. 90, translation from E. Emerton, *The Correspondence of Gregory VII*, (New York, 1966), p. 28.

10. *Ibid.*, p. 190, Emerton, p. 65.

11. P. Schmid, "Die Entstehung des Marseiller Kirchenstaates," *Archiv für Urkundenforschung*, vol. 10, (1928), pp. 176-207 for what follows.

12. E. Caspar, *op. cit.*, pp. 517-518, Emerton, pp. 160-161.

13. P. Schmid, *art. cit.*, pp. 193f.

14. "Cluny...konnte seine Ausnahmestellung nur mit lfe des wiedererstärkten Papsttums halten." E. Werner, *. cit.*, p. 99.

15. See A. Stacpoole, *art. cit.*, p. 154.

16. "Eine vermittelnde Persönlichkeit." A. Becker, *. cit.*, p. 83.

17. P. Schmid, *art. cit.*, p. 197.

18. A. Becker, *op. cit.*, pp. 15-16.

19. *Ibid.*

20. H. Cowdrey, *op. cit.*, p. 59, who for this moment of luniac history comes into his own. I have reached my own onclusions independently with regard to the relationship etween Hugh and Urban II.

21. *NF*, p. 373. Six years earlier Paschal II had nnounced in a papal bull Cluny's adherence to the Apostolic ee: *Inconcussa charitatis unitas qua inter procellas omnes di Apostolicae adhaesistis.* L'Huillier, *op. cit.*, p. xvi. f. infra, p. 82, n. 2.

22. L. H. Champly, *Histoire de l'Abbaye de Cluny,* (edi- ion of 1878, Paris, 1930), pp. 89f.

23. *P.L.* 159, 919.

24. L. Smith, *Cluny in the Eleventh and Twelfth Centuries,* *. 251f.

25. *Ibid.*

26. *Ibid.* It was the conflict between Pontius and Peter le Venerable, however, that settled the matter of Cluny's edience to the Roman Papacy once and for all. That was the ssue as Zerbi, *art. cit.*, has pointed out in the debate with redero. Also to be noted is that the financial crisis of luny appeared about this time when needs began to exceed re- ources, G. Duby, *La société* etc., pp. 484-487. Under Hugh luny had turned from a manorial economy to a monetary economy lich led to a forty-year period of opulence, *idem,* "Economie

domaniale et économie monétaire: Le budget de l'abbaye de Cluny entre 1080 et 1155," *Annales*, 7, (1952), pp. 155-171.

27. *P.L.* 159, 919.

28. E. W. Kemp, *Canonization and Authority in the Western Church*, (Oxford, 1948), p. 70f. Urban II was moving in the same direction, *ibid.*, p. 67.

2. Cluniac necrologies make it clear that the question of the Cluniac origins of the reform and revolutionary popes has to be restudied. Since one otherwise excellent investigation devoted to this topic, particularly as it concerns Hildebrand, has not taken the witness of obituary notices into consideration, its conclusions regarding the series of Cluniac popes appearing on the papal throne have been erroneous. Dom Stacpoole's monograph, however invaluable in other respects, concludes that only Hildebrand in a secondary way and Urban II, no question here, were indisputably Cluniac.[1] He is willing to admit,[2] based on Cluny's assistance as a source of financial aid[3] and capable men for papal administrative tasks, that essential links between the papacy and monastery were forged by wealth and talent, but he is adamant in his denial of other direct Cluniac influence seated on the papal throne. A later evaluator of his work has gone even further and reaffirmed the doubts of many scholars by stating bluntly that there is no direct evidence that Gregory VII was ever a monk of Cluny.[4] The entries of papal names in the Cluniac obituary lists present testimony that the entire series of popes beginning with Leo IX and lasting throughout the reign of Gelasius II (1118-1119) were members of the Cluniac confraternity. That is the meaning of the appearance of their names there. Moreover the necrological lists were drawn up in such a way as to make marked distinctions between the various entries. The names of professed monks of the congregation compose the overwhelming number of entries and are listed separately from those of benefactors. Consequently, the discovery of a pope's name among the obituary entries for deceased monks on that particular day in the calendar provides the assurance that

he was a Cluniac monk. In addition further distinctions were often, if not always, made among the professed members of the entire congregation. At St. Martial de Limoges for example we find that the pope Alexander II was listed apart, under the *peregrini*, meaning that he was not a member of the monastic community at Limoges but had expressed his allegiance elsewhere. Since St. Martial had had a tradition of its own under a lay abbot before it was transferred to Cluny in 1062 under quarrelsome circumstances,[5] it follows that the local tradition of Limoges was differentiated from the more comprehensive one of Cluny. Thus we often find additions to the main entries indicating the monastic allegiance of the monks by the addition of l, le or c, cl.[6] A comparison of such entries with those of the nun's cloister at Marcigny indicates not surprisingly that those indicating a Cluniac allegiance show a clear degree of correlation. Most entries indicating a monk's allegiance to Limoges are not found in the largest Cluniac necrology of all, that of Marcigny. The same is true for Moissac.[7] Since the Marcigny necrology was found at Muenchenwiler and was originally thought to come from that small Swiss priory, we find that of some 10,000 entries 106, a small percentage, indicate monastic burial in Switzerland.[8] By the same token, since Marcigny and the mother abbey were tightly knit forming together a single unit, the names of monks and nuns are indiscriminately mixed under the main rubric of a single monastic congregation.[9] A comparison of the obituary notices of bishops in the necrology of Marcigny with those of other necrologies indicates the greatest degree of correlation with that of St. Martin-des-Champs.[10] In view of the foregoing, the reason soon becomes clear. While St. Martial's subjection to Cluny resulted in the clash of two traditions, the Parisian monastery presented no such difficulties. The latter was

founded only in 1059 as a foundation for canons until transferred to Cluny twenty years later as a priory by Philip I.[11]
This monastery consequently was brought under Cluniac influence
quite speedily as one ready to accept its tenets without offering resistance. It is in the necrology of this Cluniac priory
that the name of Gregory VII appears, which can only mean that
he was a member of the Cluniac confraternity either as a benefactor or a monk.[12] The pope Victor II was indeed listed as a
benefactor but, as a pioneering monograph indicates, both Cluny
and Marcigny had a special reason to do so.[13] Hugh had asked
for a special papal privilege to be awarded to the sister
cloister which was bestowed by the Pope and acknowledged by
the nun who authored the Marcigny necrology, Elsendis, through
the inclusion of his name as a benefactor of Marcigny. S.
Martin-des-Champs on the other hand was a creation of the
French king Philip I, not of Cluny itself, as was Marcigny.
The king, less autonomous than his father, found it impossible
to resist the Gregorians.[14] And in the drive against simony
it was probably the monasteries who benefited the most. Consequently, there is no foundation for believing that the three
popes named in the necrology would be designated as special
benefactors of the particular priories since they extended
their privileges and protection to the mother abbey itself
as the head of the entire congregation.

Although special studies devoted to the Cluniac connections of each of the popes, based on the evidence contained in
these documents, are called for, the strong influence of Cluny
in papal policy and politics is irrefutable. The appearance
of prayers for the popes in the customaries of Bernard and
Ulrich indicates their renewed historical status. Humbert,[15]
the biographer of Bruno of Toul, relates that Odilo appeared
in a dream to the future Leo IX and explained to him an enig-

matic vision as follows: one night the pope-to-be saw an ugly
hag standing before him and, filled with fear, he made the
sign of the cross on her forehead. She fell down as one dead,
then arose transformed into a beautiful woman. Odilo explained
that her soul had been saved from death. This revelation indicated that Odilo was the saint chosen by Providence to presage
the mission of the future pope--to restore the Church to its
pristine beauty.[16] Also, we now know that Pope Stephen IX, although continuing to administrate the abbey of Monte Cassino
during his pontificate, took a second vow to become a professed
monk of Cluny *in extremis*,[17] that the election of Nicholas II,
also a former monk of Cluny, was an outcome of his designation
by the dying pope[18] and that the Cluniacs participated directly
in the election.[19] As for the newly introduced papal policy,
breaking with imperial nominations, whereby the pontiffs came
to designate their successors, it can only have had one source,
one model, the procedure followed at Cluny.[20] The result was
a series of monk-popes occupying the papal throne.[21]

The most famous of these is of course the pontiff who
reached the heights of greatness in his meeting with the Emperor Henry IV and Hugh of Cluny at Canossa. There is no need
to repeat the evidence assembled by Borino[22] and Stacpoole
that Gregory was a monk of Cluny. However, as an addition to
our present information, Bonizo of Sutri's statement in reference to the year 1048 merits a brief comment: *Quo* (Gregory VI)
*mortuo et in pace sepulto, venerabilis Hildeprandus Cluniacum
tendens, ibi monachus effectus est, et inter religiosos viros*
(monks) *adprime philosophatus est.*[23] Scholars have almost un-
animously rejected this clear proof of Hildebrand's profession
at Cluny partly because of an unwillingness to accept Bonizo
as reliable in view of errors found elsewhere in his book and
his one-sided Gregorian position. However, the evidence of the

uthor's shortcomings elsewhere is a weak basis for denial
hat he is here speaking the truth. L. Smith has sought to
ring reinforcement to this critical stance by a judgment
hat needs to be rectified. She rejects Bonizo's testimony
t its source by saying that one did not go to Cluny to study
hilosophy. However, she has misunderstood the meaning of the
ord philosophy in this context. The sentence means that
ildebrand went to Cluny in order to become a monk, a *philosophus Christi*, like the abbot himself. Just as Cluny once
raised the philosophy of emperors as bearers of the cross,
aking monks as their models, so, too, do popes embody mon-
sticism on the papal throne. As heirs to this Cluniac phil-
sophy these popes aim to monasticize the clergy by imposing
elibacy. Cluny's special reverence for St. Henry II, the
onk-emperor, who voluntarily allowed his dynasty to expire
y having no children, reveals Cluny's essential mission, as
o the monk-popes. However, the latter were better placed and
ualified to impose the Cluniac model on the world.[24]

NOTES

1. *Hildebrand, Cluny and the Papacy, loc. cit.*, p. 264.

2. *Ibid.*, pp. 264-269.

3. Following D. B. Zema, "Economic Reorganization of the Roman See during the Gregorian Reform," *SG*, 1, (1947), pp. 137-168.

4. N. Hunt, *op. cit.*, p. 143.

5. C. de Lasteyrie, *L'Abbaye de S. Martial de Limoges*, (Paris, 1901), pp. 84f. and 427.

6. *MN*, p. 426. Wollasch, who has broken new ground in his analyses of these lists, is being followed throughout this brief sub-section where indicated apart from the conclusions.

7. *Ibid.*, p. 433.

8. *Ibid.*, p. 412.

9. *Ibid.*, p. 423f.

10. J. Wollasch, "Die Ueberlieferung cluniacensischen Totengedächtnisses," *loc. cit.*, p. 394f.

11. According to J. Fr. Lemarignier, *Le gouvernement royal aux premiers temps capétiens 987-1108*, (Paris, 1965). S. Martin-des-Champs became a Cluniac priory in 1079, not in 1077 as reported by Wollasch, *ibid.*, p. 395, n. 20. See *P.L.* 159, 899 for mention of its change of status.

12. The same is of course true for Pascal II and Gelasius II. See infra, p. 189, n. 4.

13. J. Wollasch, "Die Wahl des Papstes Nikolaus II," *op. cit.*, p. 210.

14. See n. 11 above for references.

15.   Wibert's authorship has been rejected. For the references see Stacpoole, *loc. cit.*, p. 269.

16.   P. Jardet, *op. cit.*, pp. 770-771.

17.   J. Wollasch, "Die Wahl des Papstes Nikolas II," *op. cit.*, p. 216.

18.   *Ibid.*, pp. 207f. Cf. D. Hägerman, "Zur Vorgeschichte des Pontifikats Nikolaus II," *ZKG*, 81, (1970), pp. 352-361.

19.   *Ibid.*, p. 219.

20.   *Ibid.*, p. 220. Nonetheless, Odilo did not nominate Hugh directly, nor did Hugh appear to nominate Pontius at all. However, the principle is valid.

21.   *Ibid.*

22.   G. Borino, "Quando et dove si feci Monaco Ildebrando," *Miscellanea Giovanni Mercati*, V, *Studi et Testi*, 125, (Citta del Vaticano, 1946), pp. 218-262.

23.   Bonizo, *Liber Ad Amicum*, c. 5, Jaffé, II, 630-631.

24.   In no way should it be inferred from the foregoing that Gregorian principles were derived from Cluny simply because Hildebrand was a professed monk at Cluny, any more than one would be justified to infer that Thomas Becket inherited his commitment to an entirely new office and responsibility from the king's entourage. Indeed the undeniable connections between Cluny and the Papacy present since the reign of Leo IX shall have to be reevaluated in the realization that the doctrines of both the Reform and revolutionary Papacy originate elsewhere than at the Burgundian monastery. The "Renaissance of Papal Names" (Rosenstock-Huessy, *Out of Revolution*, p. 521f.) was a weapon in the struggle and should be investigated. Hildebrand, for example, took his new name as Gregory VII, recalling the first monk-pope Gregory I, while at the same time legitimizing the pontificate of Gregory VI. This entire process is separate from Cluny, whether or not the popes were professed monks there, or had been a Cluniac abbot, as was Gregory VII of the monastery, St. Paul's-Outside-the-Walls. On the other hand Cluny did transmit its centralizing and organizational corporative principle to the Roman Church.

BIBLIOGRAPHY

I. Sources

Acta Sanctorum Bollandiana, (Brussels and elsewhere, 1643ff.).

Alphonsi Regis Hispaniarum ad S. Hugonem, P.L. 159, 938-939.

Ausgewählte Quellen zur deutschen Geschichte des Mittelalters, ed. R. Buchner, vol. 12, (Berlin, 1963).

Bernard of Cluny, *Ordo Cluniacensis* in Herrgott, 133-371.

Bibliotheca Cluniacensis, ed. Dom M. Marrier and A. Quercatenus, (Paris, 1614).

Bibliotheca Rerum Germanicum, vol. II, *Monumenta Gregoriana,* ed. P. Jaffé, (Berlin, 1865).

Bonizo, *Liber ad Amicum* in *Bibliotheca Rerum Germanicum,* II, 577-689.

Bullarum Sacri Ordinis Cluniacensis, ed. P. Simon, (Lyon, 1680).

Capitula Monachorum ad Augiam Directa monitum in Herrgott, 18.

Capitulare Aquisgranense de Vita et conversatione monachorum monitum in Herrgott, 22.

Caspar, E., *Das Register Gregors VII,* (*MGH,Epistolae Selectae,* Berlin, 1955).

Concordantium Universae Scripturae Sacrae Thesaurus, (Paris, 1939).

Consuetudines Monasticae, ed. Dom B. Albers, (Stuttgart and Monte Cassino, 1900-1912): Vol. I, *Consuetudines Farfenses*. Vol. II, *Consuetudines antiquiores*. Vol. IV, *Consuetudines Fructuarienses*.

Corpus Consuetudinum Monasticarum, ed. K. Hallinger, (Siegburg, 1963f.), esp. *Consuetudines Benedictinae Variae*, Tomus VI, 2. *Statuta Petri Venerabilis Abbatis Cluniacensis*, IX, (1146/7), Recensuit: Giles Constable, (1975).

Crassi Petri, Defensio Heinrici Regis, MGH, Libelli de Lite, I, 432.

Delisle, L., *Rouleaux des morts du IXe au XVe siècle*, (Société de l'Histoire de France, Paris, 1866).

_____, *Rouleau mortuaire du b. Vital*, (Paris, 1909).

Diplomate ad Hugonem abbatem anno 1098, Bibl. Clun., 250.

Du Cange, C., *Glossarium ad scriptores mediae et infimae latinitatis*, (Paris, 1883-1886).

Electio S. Maioli in *Abbatem Cluniacensem*, P.L. 137, 707-708.

Electio S. Odilonis, P.L. 142, 777-780.

Epistola Adsonis ad Gerbergam Reginam de Ortu et Tempore Antichristi, E. Sackur, *Sybyllinische Texte und Forschungen*, (Halle, 1898), 97-113.

Epistola Hugonis Lugdunensis archiepiscopi ad Mathildem Comitissam, Mansi, vol. XX, 634f.

Epistolae Henrici IV. See under *Ausgewählte Quellen*, ed. R. Buchner, 52-141.

Ermini, F., "Il Pianto di Jotsaldo per la morte di Odilone," *Medio evo latino*, (Modena, 1938), 199-213.

Ferotin, Dom, "Une lettre inédite de S. Hugues, Abbé de Cluny, à Bernard d'Agen, archévêque de Tolède (1087)," *Bibliothèque de l'Ecole des Chartes*, vol. 61, (1900), 339-345; vol. 63, (1903), 682-686.

Gerberti Acta Concilii Remensis ad Sanctum Basolum, MGH, SS, III, 658-686.

Glaber, Rodulfus, *Historiarum sui temporis Libri Quinque*,
P.L. 142, 611-698.

*Gregorius papa Wimundo episcopo Aversano scribit, consuetu-
dinem veritati postponendam esse* in *Bibliotheca Rerum
Germanicarum*, 576, no. 50.

Hückel, G. A., *Les poèmes satiriques d'Albéron*, (Bibliothèque de la faculté des lettres de Paris, 13, 1901).

*Hugonis, S. Abbatis Cluniacensis, Commonitorium ad succes-
sores suos pro sanctimonialibus Marciniacensibus*, P.L.
159, 949-952.

_____, *Epistolae*, P.L. 159, 927-932.

　　　Ad Willelum I Anglorum Regem

　　　Ad Moisacenses Fratres

　　　Ad Anastasium Eremitam

　　　Ad Urbanum II Papam

　　　Ad Philippum Regem

　　　See also under Férotin.

_____, *Exhortatio ad sanctimoniales apud Marciniacum Deo
serventes*, P.L. 159, 947-948.

_____, *Imprecatio*, P.L. 159, 951-954.

_____, *Quid beatus Hugo narraverit in capitulo vigilia
Natalis Domini*, P.L. 159, 953-956.

_____, *Statutae*, P.L. 159, 945-948.

　　　*Pro Alphonso rege Hispaniarum tanquam insigni
benefactore.*

　　　*Recipit Lambertum abbatem S. Bertini veluti
proprium Cluniaci monachum.*

_____, *Vitae: auctore anon. Bibl. Clun.*, 447-462.

　　　auctore Hildeberto Cenomanensi Episcopo,
P.L. 159, 857-892.

226

    auctore Hugone Monacho, P.L. 159, 916-923.

    auctore Raynaldo Abbate Vezeliacensi,
       P.L. 159, 893-905.

    Epistola Gilonis in L'Huillier, 574-618.

    Synopsis Vitae Metrica Auctore Raynaldo,
       P.L. 159, 905-910.

Henrici Imperatoris Cognomento Nigri ad S. Hugonem, P.L. 159,
   931-932.

Hesbert, Dom R. J., "L'office de la Commemoraison des Défunts
   à Saint-Benoît-sur-Loire au XIIIe siècle," *Miscellanea
   Liturgica in honorem L. Cuniberti Mohlberg,* II, (1949),
   392-421.

Imperatricis Agnetis Henrici Nigri Uxoris ad S. Hugonem, P.L.
   159, 932.

Inguanez, D. M., "'Dies Irae' in un codice del sec. XII,"
   Miscellanea Cassinese, (Monte Cassino, 1931).

*Jotsaldi Planctus de transitu domni Odilonis abbatis Clunia-
   censis, P.L.* 142, 1043-1046.

Mabillon, J., *Sancti Maioli Elogium, P.L.* 137, 709-744.

_____, *Sancti Odilonis Elogium, P.L.* 142, 831-896.

Maioli, S. Abbatis Cluniacensis, Vitae: *auctore Nagoldo,*
   Acta SS, May, II, 658-668.

    auctore Syro, P.L. 137, 746-778.

    See also under Odilo.

Mansi, J. D. *Sacrorum Concilorum nova et Amplissimo Collectio,* vol. 20, (Florence and Venice, 1759-1798).

Molinier, A., ed., *Obituaires de la Province de Sens,* vol. 1,
   (*Recueil des historiens de la France,* Paris, 1902).

Molinier, E., *Documents historiques bas-latins, provençaux et
   français concernant principalement la Marche et le
   Limousin,* I, (Limoges, 1883).

Morin, Dom G., "Un opuscule inédit de S. Odilon abbé de Cluny," *RB*, vol. 16, (1899), 477f.

Odilonis, S. Abbatis Cluniacensis, Carmina Sacra et Preces, P.L. 142, 1035-1038.

    Hymnus in Assumptione Sanctae Mariae.

    Inc. Oritur sydus inclitum.

    Ad Crucem Adorandam Oratio.

_____, *Credulitas, P.L.* 142, 1035-1036.

_____, *Epistolae, P.L.* 142, 939-944.

    Ad Fulbertum Carnotensem Episcopum.

    Ad Paternum Abbatem.

    Ad Domnum Garseam.

    Ad Matronam R.

    (Ad imperatorem Henricum): see under Sackur.

    (Ad Stephanum regem): in Ringholz, xxxv.

    (Ad Patriarchum Aquileae): see under Morin.

_____, *Epitaphium Ottonis Magni Imperatoris, P.L.* 142, 967-968.

_____, *(Donum ad imperatorem Henricum) Inc. Hoc. opus egregium coeleste nectare plenum* in Ringholz, xlvii.

_____, *Hymni Quatuor in Vigilia Beati Maioli, P.L.* 142, 961-964.

_____, *Inc. Omne quod est plangat quod posse plangere constat.* (Epitaphium Henrici imperatoris), *P.L.* 142, 967-968.

_____, *Sermones, P.L.* 142, 991-1034.

    de Nativitate Domini Salvatoris.

    de Epiphania Domini.

de Purificatione Sanctae Dei Genetricis Mariae.

de Incarnatione Dominica.

de Resurrectione Domini.

de eadem Resurrectione Domini.

de eadem Resurrectione.

de Ascensione Domini Salvatoris.

in die Pentecostes.

de admirabili praecursoris Christi Joannis Baptistae Nativitate.

in Vigilia Apostolorum Petri et Pauli.

de Assumptione Dei Genitricis Mariae.

de Nativitate Beatae Mariae Virginis.

de Nativitate Beatae Mariae.

de Sancta Cruce.

_____, *Statutum de Defunctis, P.L.* 142, 1037-1038.

_____, *Vita Beati Maioli Abbatis, P.L.* 142, 943-962.

_____, *Vita Domnae Adalheidae.* See under Paulhart.

_____, *Vitae: auctore Jotsaldo, P.L.* 142, 898-940.

auctore Petro Damiano, P.L. 144, 926-944.

Patrologia Cursus Completus, Series Latina, ed. J. P. Migne, (Paris, 1844-1864).

Paulhart, H., ed., *Die Lebensbeschreibung der Kaiserin Adelheid von Abt Odilo von Cluny, (Cluniacensis abbatis Epitaphium domine Adelheide auguste), MIÖG,* Erganzungsband XX, Heft 2, 1962.

Recueil des Chartes de l'Abbaye de Cluny, ed. A. Bernard and A. Bruel, vols. III, IV, V, (*Documents inédits sur l'histoire de France,* Paris, 1876-1903).

Recueil des historiens de la France, (published by the
 Académie des Inscriptions et des Belles Lettres since
 1899. *Obituaires.* 5 parts in 7 vols., Paris, 1902-
 1951).

S. Joannis Chrysostomi, de Coemeterio et de Cruce, P.G.
 391-398.

_____, *de Cruce et Latrone duae Homiliae,*
 P.G. 399-418.

Sackur, E., "Ein Schreiben Odilo's von Cluni an Heinrich
 III vom October 1046," *NA,* vol. 24, (1899), 728-735.

Schmitt, Dom P. S., "Neue und alte Hildebrand-Anekdoten aus
 den *Dicta Anselmi,*" *Studi Gregoriani,* vol. 5, 1-18.

Schnürer, G., *Das Necrologium des Cluniacenser--Priorates*
 Münchenwiler, (*Collectanea Friburgensia,* Neue Folge,
 X, 1909).

Schramm, P., "Die Krönung in Deutschland bis zum Beginn des
 salischen Hauses, 1028," *ZRG, 55, KA,* 24, (1935), 307-
 332.

Spicilegium, ed. L. D'Achery, 3 vols., (Paris, 1723).

Strecker, K., *Die Cambridger Lieder,* (*MGH Carmina canta-*
 brigiensa, Berlin, 1926).

Ulrich of Zell, *Antiquiores consuetudines Cluniacensis Mon-*
 asterii, P.L. 149, 643-778.

Vita Heinrici IV imperatoris. See under *Ausgewählte Quellen,*
 ed. R. Buchner, 52-141.

Walpole, A. S., ed., *Early Latin Hymns,* (1922; reprinted
 Hildesheim, 1966).

William of Hirsau, *Constitutiones Hirsaugienses* in Herrgott,
 371-571.

Wilmart, Dom A., and Brou, Dom L., "Un office monastique pour
 le deux novembre dans le Nord de la France au XIe siècle,"
 Sacris Erudiri, vol. 5, (1953), 247-330.

II. Scholarly Works

"Actes du Colloque International de Moissac 3-5 mai 1963," *Annales du Midi*, vol. 75, no. 64, (1963).

Adel und Kirche. Festschrift für Gerd Tellenbach, ed. J. Fleckenstein and K. Schmid, (Freiburg, 1968).

Albers, B., "Les *Consuetudines Sigiberti abbatis*," *RB*, (1903), 420-433.

_____, "Le plus ancien coutumier de Cluny," *RB*, vol. 20, (1903), 174-184.

_____, *Untersuchungen zu den ältesten Mönchsgewohnheiten*. Ein Beitrag zur Benediktinerordensgeschichte des X-XII Jahrhunderts, (Veröffentlichungen aus dem Kirchenhistor-ischen Seminar München. II Reihe, no. 8, Munich, 1905), xii-132.

Arquillière, H.-X., *Saint Grégoire VII*, (Paris, 1934).

Auf der Maur, I., *Mönchtum und Glaubensverkündigung in den Schriften des hl. Johannes Chrysostomos*, (Fribourg, Switzerland, 1959).

Baethgen, F., "Das Königreich Burgund in der deutschen Kaiserzeit des Mittelalters," *Medievalia*, (*Schriften der MGH*, vol. 17/1, Stuttgart, 1960).

Barbetti, B., "Adalbert von Prague und der Glaube an den Weltuntergang im Jahre 1000," *Archiv fur Kulturgeschichte*, vol. 35, (1953), 123-141.

Bartelink, G. J. M., "'Philosophie' et 'philosophes' dans quelques oeuvres de Jean Chrysostom," *RHS*, 36, (1960), 487-492.

Becker, A., *Papst Urban II*, (*Schriften der MGH*, 19/1, Stutt-gart, 1964).

Benz, K. J., "A propos du dernier voyage de l'impératrice Adélaïde en 999," *RHE*, 67, (1972), 81-91.

_____, "Heinrich II in Cluny?," *FM*, 8, (1974), 155-178.

_____, "Heinrich II und Cluny," *RB*, 84, (1974), 313-337.

Berlière, U., *L'ascèse bénédictine des origines à la fin du XIIe siècle*, (Paris, 1927).

_____, "Les confraternités monastiques au Moyen-Age," *Revue liturgique et monastique*, vol. 11, (1925-1926), 134-142.

_____, "Coutumiers monastiques," *RB*, vol. 29, (1912), 357-367.

_____, "Les Coutumiers monastiques," *RB*, vol. 23, (1906), 260-267.

_____, "Les fraternités monastiques et leur rôle juridique," (*Academie royale de Belgique*, Classe de lettres et des sciences morales et politiques. Mémoires 2 sér., t. 11, fasc. 3, Bruxelles, 1920), 1-26.

_____, "Le nombre des moines dans les anciens monastères," *RB*, 41, (1929), 231-261, and 42, 19-42.

_____, *L'ordre monastique des origines au XIIe siècle*, 3rd ed., (Lille, 1924).

Berthelier, S., "L'expansion de l'ordre de Cluny et ses rapports avec l'histoire politique et économique du Xe au XIIe siècle," *Revue archéologique*, 6e série, 11, (1938), 319-326.

Beumann, H., and Buttner, H., *Das Kaisertum Ottos des Grossen*, (Munich, 1963).

Biehl, L., *Das liturgische Gebet für Kaiser und Reich*, (Goerres-Gesellschaft, Heft 75, Paderborn, 1937).

Bishko, C. J., "Fernando I y los origenes de la alianza castellano leonesa con Cluny," *Cuadernos de Historia de España*, vols. 47-48, (1968), 31-135 and vols. 49-50, (1969), 50-116.

232

_____, "Liturgical Intercession at Cluny for the King-Emperors of León," *Studia Monastica,* vol. 3, (1961), 53-76.

Bishop, E., *Liturgica Historica,* (Oxford, 1918).

_____, "Some Ancient Benedictine Confraternity Books," *Downside Review,* vol. 4, (1885), 2-14.

Boehm, L., *Geschichte Burgunds,* (Stuttgart, 1971).

Borino, G. B., "Ildebrando non si fece monaco a Roma," *SG,* 4, (1952), 441-456.

_____, "Quando et dove si feci Monaco Ildebrando," *Miscellanea Giovanni Mercati,* V, (*Studi et Testi*), vol. 125, (Citta del Vaticano, 1946).

_____, "Un' ipotesi sul *'Dictatus Papae'* di Gregorio VII," *Archivio della Deputazione Romana di Storia Patria,* vol. 67, (1944), 237-252.

Bornscheuer, L., *Miseriae Regum. Untersuchungen zum Krisen- und Todesgedanken in den herrschaftstheologischen Vorstellungen der ottonisch-salischen Zeit,* (Arbeiten zur Frühmittelalterforschung, 4, Berlin, 1968).

Boye, M., "Die Synoden Deutschlands und Reichsitaliens von 922-1059," *ZRG, KA,* vol. 18, (1929), 131-284.

Brackmann, A., "Die politische Wirkung der kluniazensischen Bewegung," *HZ,* vol. 139, (1929), 34-47.

_____, "Die Ursachen der geistigen und politischen Wandlung im 11.Jahrhundert," *HZ,* vol. 149, Heft 2, (1934), 229-239.

_____, *Zur politischen Bedeutung der kluniazensichen Bewegung,* (Darmstadt, 1955).

Brakel, C. H., "Die vom Reformpapsttum geförderten Heiligenkulte," *SG,* 9, (1972), 239-311.

Bredero, A. H., "Cluny et Cîteaux au XIIe siècle: les origines de la controverse," *Studi Medievali,* (Centro Italiano di Studi Sull' Alto Medioevo, III s., 12, Fasc. 1, Spoleto, 1971), 135-175.

_____, See also under J. Leclercq.

Bresslau, H., *Jahrbücher des deutschen Reiches unter Konrad,* II, vol. 1, (1879).

Brou, L., See under Wilmart (Sources).

Bulst, N., *Untersuchungen zu den Klosterreformen Wilhelms von Dijon (962-1031),* (Pariser Historische Studien, 11, 1973).

Bulst, W., "Eine Sequenz auf Otto II," *Nachrichten der Gesellschaft der Wissenschaft zu Göttingen,* Phil.-Hist. Kl., vol. 4, NF, II, 3, (1937), 67-85.

Buttner, H., See under Beumann.

Cantor, N. F., "The Crisis of Western Monasticism," *American Historical Review,* vol. 65, no. 1, (1960), 47-67.

Caspar, E., "Gregor VII in seinen Briefen," *HZ,* vol. 130, (1924), 1-30.

Chagny, A., *Cluny et Son Empire,* (Paris, 1938).

Chalandon, F., *Histoire de la Domination Normande en Italie et en Sicile,* (2 vols., 1907; reprinted, New York, 1960).

Champly, L. H., *Histoire de l'Abbaye de Cluny,* (edition of 1878, Paris, 1930).

Conant, K. J., *Carolingian and Romanesque Architecture, 800-1200,* (Baltimore, 1959).

_____, *Les Eglises et la Maison du Chef d'Ordre,* (publication no. 77 of the Mediaeval Academy of America, Macon, 1968).

_____, "Mediaeval Academy Excavations at Cluny," *Speculum,* vol. 29, (1954), 1-45.

_____, "Systematic Dimensions in the Buildings," *Speculum,* vol. 38, (1963), 1-45.

Congrès scientifique de Cluny 9-11 Juillet 1949 en l'honneur des Saints Abbés Odon et Odilon, (Société des Amis de Cluny, Dijon, 1950).

Connally, R. H., "Liturgical Prayers of Intercession," *Journal of Theological Studies,* vol. 21, (1920), 219-232.

Constable, G., "Monastic Possession of Churches and *'Spiritualia'* in the Age of Reform," in *Il Monachesimo e la Riforma Ecclesiastica (1049-1122),* Mendola, (1968).

Cowdrey, H. E. J., *The Cluniacs and the Gregorian Reform,* (Oxford, 1970).

_____, "Cluny and the First Crusade," *RB,* 83, (1973), 285-311.

_____, "Unions and Confraternity with Cluny," *Journal of Ecclesiastical History,* vol. 16, (1965), 152-162.

Cucherat, M. F., *Cluny au onzième siècle, son influence religieuse, intellectuelle, et politique,* (Autun, 1873).

Curtius, E. R., *Europaïsche Literatur und Lateinisches Mittelalter,* (Bern and Munich, 1961[3]).

Dawson, C., *The Formation of Christendom,* (New York, 1967).

_____, *The Making of Europe,* (Cleveland, 1964).

Deér, J., "Das Kaiserbild im Kreuz," *Schweizer Beiträge zur Allgemeinen Geschichte,* vol. 13, (1955), 48-110.

Delisle, L., *Inventaire des manuscrits de la Bibliothèque nationale, Fonds de Cluni,* (Paris, 1884).

_____, "Des monuments paléographiques concernant l'usage de prier pour les morts," *Bibliothèque de l'Ecole des Chartes,* 2e série, t. 3, (1846), 361-411.

Deshman, R., *"Christus rex et magi reges:* Kingship and Christology in Ottonian and Anglo-Saxon Art," (announced for publication in *FS,* 10, 1976).

Diener, H., "Das Itinerar des Abtes Hugo von Cluny," *NF,* 355-426.

_____, "Das Verhältnis Clunys zu den Bischöfen vor allem in der Zeit seines Abtes Hugo, 1049-1109," *NF*, 219-352.

Dorries, H., "Der Glaube Ottos des Grossen," *Jahrbuch der Gesellschaft für niedersächisische Kirchengeschichte*, vol. 47, (Sonderdruck, 1949).

Dressler, F., *Petrus Damiani, Leben und Werk*, (Rome, 1954).

Duby, G., "Economie domaniale et économie monétaire: Le budget de l'abbaye de Cluny entre 1080 et 1155," *Annales*, 7, (1952), 155-171.

_____, *L'économie rurale et la vie des campagnes dans l'Occident médiéval*, 2 vols., (Paris, 1962).

_____, *La société aux XIe et XIIe siècles dans la région mâconnaise*, (Paris, 1953).

Duchesne, L., *Les Premiers Temps de l'Etat Pontifical*, (Paris, 1904).

Duhr, J., "La confrérie dans la vie de l'église," *RHE*, 35 (1), (1939), 437-478.

Ebner, A., *Die klösterlichen Gebetsverbrüderungen bis zum Ausgang des karolingischen Zeitalters*, (Regensburg, 1890).

Eckhardt, F., *Introduction à l'histoire hongroise*, (Paris, 1928).

Egger, P. B., *Geschichte der Cluniazenserklöster in der Westschweiz*, (*Freiburger Historische Studien*, vol. 3, 1907).

Eichmann, E., "Das Exkommunikationsprivileg des deutschen Kaisers im Mittelalter," *ZRG, KA*, vol. 1, (1911), 160-194.

Ellard, G., "Devotion to the Holy Cross and a Dislocated Mass-Text," *Theological Studies*, vol. 11, no. 3, (1950), 333-355.

Emerton, E., *The Correspondence of Gregory VII*, (Records of Civilization XIV, New York, 1966).

Erdmann, C., "Die Anfänge der staatlichen Propaganda im Investiturstreit," *HZ*, vol. 154, (1936), 491-512.

_____, "Endkaiserglaube und Kreuzzugsgeschichte im 11. Jahrhundert," *ZKG*, 3. Folge, 51, (1932), 384-414.

_____, *Die Entstehung des Kreuzzugsgedankens*, (Stuttgart, 1935; reprinted 1955).

_____, *Forschungen zur politischen Ideenwelt des Frühmittelalters*, (Berlin, 1951).

_____, "Der Heidenkrieg in der Liturgie und die Kaiserkrönung Ottos I," *MIÖG*, vol. 65, (1932), 129-143.

_____, "Das ottonische Reich als Imperium Romanum," *DA*, 6, (1943), 412-441.

Evans, J., *Cluniac Art in the Romanesque Period*, (Cambridge, 1950).

_____, *Monastic Life at Cluny, 910-1157*, (London, 1931).

Fechter, J., *Cluny, Adel und Volk*, (Dissertation, Tübingen, 1966).

Fliche, A., *La Réforme grégorienne et la reconquête chrétienne, 1059-1123*, (Paris, 1940).

Fournier, P. and Le Bras, G., *Histoire des collections canoniques en Occident depuis les fausses décrétales jusqu' au décret de Gratien*, (Paris, 1932).

Freistedt, E., *Altchristliche Totengedächtnistage und ihre Beziehung zum Jenseitsglauben und Totenkultus der Antike*, (Liturgiegeschichtlichen Quellen und Forschungen, Heft 24, Münster, 1928).

Frend, W. H. C., *The Early Church*, (New York, 1966).

Fried, J., "Der Regalienbegriff im 11. und 12. Jahrhundert," *DA*, 29, (1973), 450-528.

Goldschmidt, A., *Die Elfenbeinskulpturen aus der Zeit der karolingischen und sachsischen Kaiser, VIII-XI Jahrhundert*, vol. II, (Berlin, 1918).

Hägermann, D., "Zur Vorgeschichte des Pontifikats Nikolaus II," *ZKG*, 81, (1970), 352-361.

d'Haenens, A., *Les invasions normandes en Belgique au IXe siècle. Le phenomène et sa répercussion dans l'historiographie médiévale*, (Louvain, 1967).

Hallinger, K., "Le climat spirituel des premiers temps de Cluny," *RM*, vol. 46, (1956), 117-140.

_____, "Cluny," *Enciclopedia Cattolicà*, vol. 2, (Vatican City, 1949), 1883-1893.

_____, *Gorze-Kluny. Studien zu den monastichen Lebensformen und Gegensätzen im Hochmittelalter*, (Rome, 1950-1951).

_____, "Kluny's Bräuche zur Zeit Hugos des Grossen (1049-1109)," *ZRG, KA*, vol. 45, (1959), 99-140.

_____, "Neue Fragen der reformgeschichtlichen Forschung," *Archiv für mittelrheinische Kirchengeschichte*, vol. 9, (1957), 19-32.

Halphen, L., "The Kingdom of Burgundy," *Cambridge Medieval History*, vol. 3, (Cambridge, 1957), 134-147.

Hampe, K., *Deutsche Kaisergeschichte in der Zeit der Salier und Staufer*, (F. Baethgen edition, Heidelberg, 1963[11]).

Harnack, A. von, "Die Bezeichnung Jesu als Knecht Gottes und ihre Geschichte in der alten Kirche," *Sitzungsbericht der Preussischen Akademie* Phil. Hist. Kl., (1926), 212-228.

Hauck, A., *Kirchengeschichte Deutschlands*, vol. 3, (Leipzig, 1920).

Hauviller, E., *Ulrich von Cluny*, (Kirchengeschichtliche Studien III, Heft 3, Münster i.W., 1896).

Heath, R. G., "The Western Schism of the Franks and the Filioque," *Journal of Ecclesiastical History*, vol. 23, no. 2, (April, 1972).

Heer, F., *Aufgang Europas*, (Vienna, Zürich, 1949).

_____, *The Medieval World,* (translated by Janet Sondheimer, New York, 1963).

Hefele, C. J. and Leclercq, H., *Histoire des Conciles,* vols. 4 and 5, (Paris, 1911).

Heimbucher, M., *Die Orden und Kongregationen der katholischen Kirche,* vol. 1, (Paderborn, 1907).

Hello, E., *Paroles de Dieu,* (Paris, 1919).

Hengstl, M. H., *Totenklage und Nachruf in der mittelalterlichen Literatur seit dem Ausgang der Antike,* (Dissertation, Würzburg. Munich, 1936).

Hirsch, H., "Der mittelalterliche Kaisergedanke, in den liturgischen Gebeten," *MIÖG,* vol. 44, (1936), 1-20.

Hlawitschka, E., "Gebetsverbrüderung," *LTK,* vol. 4, 554-555.

Hoffmann, H., *Gottesfrieden und Treuga Dei, (Schriften der MGH,* vol. 20, Stuttgart, 1964).

_____, "Von Cluny zum Investiturstreit," *Archiv für Kulturgeschichte,* vol. 45, (1963), 165-209.

Hoffman, K., *Taufsymbolik im mittelalterlichen Herrscherbild, Bonner Beiträge zur Kunstwissenschaft,* 9, Düsseldorf, 1968).

Hofmann, K., "Der 'Dictatus Papae' als eine Indexsammlung?" *SG,* 1, (1947), 531-537.

Hofmeister, P., "Cluny und seine Abteien," *StMGBO,* 75, (1964), 183-239.

Holtzmann, R., *Geschichte der sächsischen Kaiserzeit,* (Munich, 1955).

Hourlier, J., "Le Bréviaire de Saint-Turin," *Etudes Grégoriennes,* vol. 3, (1959), 163-173.

_____, *Saint-Odilon, Abbé de Cluny,* (Bibliothèque de la Revue d'Histoire Ecclésiastique, Fasc. 40, Louvain, 1964).

_____, "Saint-Odilon Bâtisseur," *RM,* vol. 51, (1961), 303-324.

_____, "Saint Odilon et la fête des morts," *RG*, 28, (1949), 209-212.

Hunt, N., *Cluny under Saint Hugh, 1049-1109*, (London, 1967).

I laici nella societas christiana di secoli XI e XII, (Settimane internazionale de studio, 3rd, Passo della Mendola, 1965, Milan, 1968).

Il Monachesimo e la Riforma Ecclesiastica (1049-1122), (Settimane internazionale de studio, 4th, Mendola, 1968, Milan, 1971).

Il Monachesimo nell' alto medioevo e la formazione della Civiltà occidentale, (Settimane de Studio del Centro di Studi sull' alto medioevo, IV, Spoleto, 1957).

I Normanni e la Loro Espansione in Europe Nell' Alto Medioevo, (Centro Italiano di Studi Sull' Alto Medioevo, vol. 16, Spoleto, 1969).

Jardet, P., Abbé, *Odilon sa vie, son temps ses oeuvres*, (Lyon, 1898).

Jenkins, R., "A Cross of the Patriarch Michael Cerularius," with an art history comment by E. Kitzinger, *Dumbarton Oaks Papers*, no. 21, 235, 249.

Jerome Biblical Commentary, (Englewood Cliffs, N.J., 1968).

Jorden, W., *Das cluniazensische Totengedächtniswesen*, (Münsterische Beiträge zur Theologie, Heft 15, Separate printing, 1930), 1-116.

Jungmann, J., *Missarum sollemnia: eine genetische Erklärung der römischen Messe*, (Vienne, 1962).

_____, *Die Stellung Christi im liturgischen Gebet*, (Liturgiegeschichtliche Forschungen, vols. 7-8, Münster, 1925).

Kantorowicz, E. H., *The King's Two Bodies*, (Princeton, 1957).

_____, *Laudes Regiae: A Study in Liturgical Acclamations and Medieval Ruler Worship*, (Berkeley and Los Angeles, 1946).

_____, *Selected Studies,* (New York, 1965).

Kemp, E. W., *Canonization and Authority in the Western Church,* (Oxford, 1948).

Kern, L., "Sur les rouleaux des morts," *Schweizer Beiträge zur allgemeinen Geschichte,* 14, (1956), 139-147.

Kirchberg, J., *Kaiseridee und Mission unter den Sachsen-könige und den ersten Saliern von Otto I bis Heinrich III,* (Berlin, 1934).

Kirchner, M., *Die deutschen Kaiserinnen in der Zeit von Konrad I bis zum Tode Lothars von Supplinburg,* (*Historische Studien,* ed. E. Ebering, Heft 78, 1910).

Knowles, D., *Cistercians and Cluniacs,* (Oxford, 1955).

_____, *From Pachomius to Ignatius: A Study in the Constitutional History of the Religious Orders,* (The Sarum Lectures, 1964-65. Oxford, 1966).

_____, *The Monastic Order in England,* (Cambridge, 1963).

Knox, R., "Finding the Law: Developments in Canon Law During the Gregorian Reform," *SG,* 9, (1972), 419-466.

Krause, H. G., "Das Papstwahldekret von 1059 und seine Rolle im Investiturstreit," *SG,* 7, (1960).

La Bibbia Nell' alto Medioevo, (Settimane di Studio del Centro Italiano di Studi Sull' Alto Medioevo, 10, Spoleto, 1963).

Ladner, G., "The Portraits of Emperors in Southern Italian Exultet Rolls and the Liturgical Commemoration of Emperors," *Speculum,* vol. 17, (1942), 181-200.

_____, "St. Gregory of Nyssa and St. Augustine on the Symbolism of the Cross," in *Late Classical and Medieval Studies in Honor of A. M. Friend,* ed. K. Weitzmann, (Princeton, N.J., 1955).

_____, *Theologie und Politik vor dem Investiturstreit,* (1936; reprinted, Darmstadt, 1968).

_____, "Two Gregorian Letters. On the Sources and Nature of Gregory VII's Reform Ideology," *SG,* 5, 221-242.

Lamma, P., *Momenti di storiografia cluniacense,* (Instituto Storico Italiano per il Medio Evo Studi Storici, vols. 42-44, Rome, 1961).

Lasteyrie, C. de, *L'Abbaye de S. Martial de Limoges,* (Paris, 1901).

Leclercq, H., Articles "Mort" and "Obituaire," *DACL,* vol. 12, 44-49 and 1834-1857.

Leclercq, J., "Cluny fut - il ennemi de la culture?," *RM,* (1957), 172-182.

_____, "La crise du monachisme aux XIe et XIIe siècles," *Bullettino dell' Istituto storico Italiano per il medio evo a Archivio Muratoriano,* no. 70, (1958), 19-41.

_____, "Documents sur la mort de moines," *RM,* vol. 65, (1956), 65-81.

_____, "L'Ecriture sainte dans l'hagiographie du moyen âge," *La Bibbia,* 103-128.

_____, Bredero, A. H., Zerbi, P., "Encore sur Pons de Cluny et Pierre le Vénérable," *Aevum,* 48, Fasc. 1-2, (1974), 134-149.

_____, *Etudes sur le Vocabulaire Monastique du Moyen Age,* (Studia Anselmiana, 48, Rome, 1961).

_____, "Pour une histoire de la vie à Cluny," *RHE,* 385-408; (3-4), 783-812.

_____, "Violence and the Devotion to St. Benedict in the Middle Ages," *Downside Review,* vol. 88, (1970), 344-360.

Lehmann, R., *Forschungen zur Geschichte des Abtes Hugo I von Cluny,* (Dissertation, Göttingen, 1869).

_____, "Ueber den die Excommunication des Erzbischofs Hugo von Lyon durch Papst Victor III betreffenden Brief des Ersteren an die Graefin Mathilde," *Forschungen zur deutschen Geschichte,* vol. 8, 641-648.

L'Huillier, A., *Vie de Saint Hugues Abbé de Cluny, 1024-1109,* (Solesmes, 1888).

Leidinger, G., (ed.), *Das Perikopenbuch Heinrichs II*, clm. 4452, (Miniaturen aus Handschriften der Kgl. Hof- und Staatsbibliothek in München, Heft 5, Munich, 1912).

Lemarignier, J.-F., "La dislocation du 'pagus' et le problème des '*consuetudines*' (X^e-XIe s.)," in *Mélanges d'histoire du moyen âge dédiés à la mémoire de L. Halphen*, (Paris, 1951), 401-410.

_____, "L'exemption monastique et les origines de la réforme grégorienne," *Congrès scientifique*, 288-340.

_____, *Le gouvernement royal aux premiers temps capétiens, 987-1108*, (Paris, 1965).

_____, "Structures monastiques et structures politiques dans la France de la fin du Xe et des débuts du XIe siècle," *Il monachesimo nell' alto medioevo e la formazione della civiltà occidentale*, (Spoleto, 1957).

Letonnelier, G., *L'Abbaye exempte de Cluny et le Saint Siège*, (Paris, 1923).

Lopez, R. S., *The Tenth Century: How Dark the Dark Ages?*, (New York, 1959).

Lortz, J., *Geschichte der Kirche in ideengeschichtlicher Betrachtung*, (Münster, 1948).

Lotter, F., *Die Vita Brunonis des Ruotger*, (Bonner Historische Forschungen, vol. 9, Bonn, 1958).

MacDonald, A. J., *Hildebrand, a Life of Gregory VII*, (London, 1932).

Mager, H.-E., "Studien über des Verhältnis der Cluniacenzer zum Eigenkirchenwesen," *NF*, 169-217.

Manitius, M., *Geschichte der lateinischen Literatur des Mittelalters*, vol. 2, (Munich, 1923).

Mann, H. K., *The Lives of the Popes in the Early Middle Ages*, vol. 7, (St. Louis, 1925).

Mehne, J., "Cluniacenserbischöfe," (announced for publication, *FM*, 11, 1977).

_____, "Eine Totenliste aus S. Martin-des-Champs," (announced for publication, *FM*, 10, 1976).

Mercier, F., *Les primitifs français. La Peinture Cluny-sienne en Bourgogne en l'époque Romane*, (Paris, 1931).

Meyer von Knonau, G., *Jahrbücher des deutschen Reiches unter Heinrich IV und Heinrich V*, 7 vols., (Leipzig, 1909).

Mikoletzky, H. W., *Kaiser Heinrich II und die Kirche*, (Vienne, 1946).

Millénaire de Cluny, (*Annales de l'Académie de Mâcon*, sér. 3, vol. 15, 1910).

Mitford, J., *The American Way of Death*, (New York, 1963).

Mitis, O., "Bemerkungen zu den Verbrüderungsbüchern und über deren genealogischen Wert," *Zeitschrift für schweizerische Kirchengeschichte*, vol. 43, (1949), 28-42.

Molinier, A., *Les obituaires français au moyen-âge*, (Paris, 1890).

Mordek, H., "*Proprie auctoritates apostolice sedis.* Ein zweiter *Dictatus Papae* Gregors VII?," *DA*, 28, (1972), 105-132.

Morrison, K. F. and Mommsen, T., *Imperial Lives and Letters of the Eleventh Century*, (New York and London, 1962).

Mortet, V., "Note sur la date de rédaction des coutumes de Cluny, dites de Farfa," *Millénaire de Cluny*, 142-145.

Mütherich, F., See under Schramm.

Neale, J., *Medieval Hymns and Sequences*, (London, 1851).

Neander, A., *Der heilige Bernard und sein Zeitalter*, (Gotha, 1865).

Neumann, R., *Hugo I der Heilige, Abt von Cluny*, (Frankfurt, 1879).

Nitschke, A., "Die Wirksamkeit Gottes in der Welt Gregors VII," *SG*, 5, (1956), 115-219.

Novati, F., *L'influsso del pensiero latino sopra la civiltà Italiana*, (Milan, 1899).

Ogerdias, Abbé L. J., *Histoire de S. Mayeul abbé de Cluny*, (Moulins, 1877).

Otto, Bishop of Freising, *The Two Cities*, (translated by C. C. Mierow, New York, 1928).

Paulhart, H., "Zur Heiligsprechung der Kaiserin Adelheid," *MIÖG*, vol. 64, (1), (1956), 65-67.

Peebles, B. M., "Fortunatus, Poet of the Holy Cross," *American Church Monthly*, vol. 38, (1935), 152-166.

Pfister, C., *Etudes sur le Règne de Robert le Pieux, 996-1031*, (Paris, 1885).

Philippeau, H. R., "Pour l'histoire de la Coutume de Cluny," *RM*, vol. 64, (1954), 141-151.

Pignot, J. H., *Histoire de l'ordre de Cluny depuis la fondation de l'Abbaye jusqu' à la mort de Pierre le Vénérable, 909-1157*, 3 vols., (Paris, 1868).

Poeschl, A., *Bischofsgut und Mensa Episcopalis*, 3 vols., (Bonn, 1908).

Poupardin, R., *Le royaume de Bourgogne, 888-1038*, (Paris, 1907).

Previté-Orton, C. W., *The Shorter Cambridge Medieval History*, 2 vols., (Cambridge, 1962).

Richard, J., *Les ducs de Bourgogne et la formation du duché du XIe au XIVe siècle*, (Publications de l'Université de Dijon, 12, Paris, 1954).

Ringholz, O., *Der heilige Odilo von Cluny*, (Münster, 1885).

Rony, Abbé, "L'election de Victor III," *RHEF*, 14, (1928), 145-160.

Rosenstock-Huessy, E., *Die europäischen Revolutionen und der Character der Nationen*, (Stuttgart and Cologne, 1951).

_____, "Die Furt der Franken," *Das Alter der Kirche,* (in collaboration with Joseph Wittig, Berlin, 1928).

_____, *Königshaus und Stämme in Deutschland zwischen 911 und 1250,* (Leipzig, 1914).

_____, *Out of Revolution,* (Norwich, Vt., 1964).

Rousset, P., "Raoul Glaber, interprète de la pensée commune au XIe siècle," *RHEF,* 36, (1), (1950), 5-24.

Sackur, E., *Die Cluniacenzer in ihrer kirchlichen und allgemeingeschichtlichen Wirksamkeit,* 2 vols., (Halle, 1892-1894).

Sauerlandt, M., "Ein ottonisches Bronzebecken im Städtischen Museum für Kunst und Kunstgewerbe im Halle a.d.S.," *Zeitschrift für christliche Kunst,* vol. 32, Heft 4, (1919), 49-58.

Schieffer, T., "Cluniazensische oder gorzische Reformbewegung?," *Archiv für mittelrheinische Kirchengeschichte,* vol. 4, (1952), 24-44.

_____, "Cluny et la querelle des Investitures," *Revue historique,* vol. 225, (1961), 47-72.

_____, "Heinrich II und Konrad II," *DA,* 8, (1950), 384-437.

_____, "Notice sur les Vies de S. Hugues, Abbé de Cluny," *Le Moyen Age,* vol. 7, (1936), 81-103.

Schmid, K. and Wollasch, J., "Die Gemeinschaft der Lebenden und Verstorbenen in Zeugnissen des Mittelalters," *FS,* vol. 1, (1967), 365-389.

_____, "Religiöses und sippengebundenes Gemeinschaftsbewusstsein in frühmittelalterlichen Gedenkbucheinträgen," *DA,* 21, (1965), 18-81.

_____, *"Societas et Fraternitas:* Begründung eines kommentierten Quellenwerkes zur Erforschung der Personen und Personengruppen des Mittelalters," *FS,* 9, (1975), 1-48.

246

_____, "Über das Verhältnis von Person und Gemeinschaft im frühen Mittelalter," *FS*, 1, (1967), 225-249.

_____, "Zur problematik von Familie, Sippe und Geschlecht Haus und Dynastie beim mittelalterlichen Adel," (*Zeitschrift für die Geschichte des Oberrheins*, 105, NF, vol. 66, 1957).

Schmid, P., "Die Entstehung des Marseiller Kirchenstaates," *Archiv für Urkundenforschung*, 10, (1928), 176-207.

Schmitz, P., *Histoire de l'ordre de saint Benoît*, 3 vols., (Maredsous, 1948).

Schnürer, G., *Kirche und Kultur im Mittelalter*, 3 vols., (Paderborn, 1929^2).

Schramm, P. E., "Das Alte und das Neue Testament in der Staatslehre und Staatssymbolik des Mittelalters," *La Bibbia*, 229-255.

_____, and F. Mütherich, *Denkmale der deutschen Könige und Kaiser: Ein Beitrag zur Herrschergeschichte von Karl der Grosse bis Friedrich II, 768-1250*, (Veröffentlichungen des Zentralinstitutes für Kunstgeschichte in München, 2, Munich, 1962).

_____, *Herrschaftszeichen: gestiftet verschenkt, verkauft, verpfändet*, (*Nachrichten der Akademie der Wissenschaften in Göttingen*, Phil. Hist. Kl., 1957, no. 5).

_____, *Herrschaftszeichen und Staatssymbolik*, 3 vols., (Stuttgart, 1954-1956).

_____, *Kaiser, Könige und Päpste: Gesammelte Aufsätze zur Geschichte des Mittelalters*, part 2. *Vom Tode Karls des Grossen (814) bis zum Anfang des 10. Jahrhunderts*, (Stuttgart, 1968).

_____, *Kaiser, Rom, Renovatio*, 2 vols., (Leipzig, Berlin, 1929).

_____, "Die Krönung in Deutschland bis zum Beginn des salischen Hauses, 1028," *ZRG*, 55, *KA*, 24, (1935), 184-332.

_____, "Die Magdeburger Patene mit dem Bilde Otto des Grossen," *Thüringisch-Sächsische Zeitschrift für Geschichte und Kunst XVIII*, (1928), 1-81.

_____, "Zur Geschichte der Buchmalerei in der Zeit der sächsischen Kaiser," *Jahrbuch für Kunstgeschichte*, vol. 1, (1923).

Schreiber, G., *Gemeinschaften des Mittelalters*, (Münster, 1948).

_____, *Kurie und Kloster im 12. Jahrhundert*, 2 vols., (Stuttgart, 1910).

_____, Review of Tomek's book in *ZRG, KA*, vol. 32, (1911), 356-373.

Schulte, A., "Deutsche Könige, Kaiser, Päpste als Kanoniker an deutschen und römischen Kirchen," *Historisches Jahrbuch*, 54, (1934), 137-177.

Schuster, I., "L'Abbaye de Farfa et sa restauration au XIe siècle," *RB*, vol. 24, (1907), 374-385.

_____, *Liber Sacramentorum: Geschichtliche und liturgische Studien über das römische Messbuch*, (translated by P. Bauersfeld, 10 vols., Regensburg, 1929-1932).

Schwarzmaier, H., "Das Kloster S. Benedetto di Polirone in seiner cluniacensichen Umwelt," *Adel und Kirche*, 280-294.

Segl, P., *Königtum und Klosterreform in Spanien. Untersuchungen über die Cluniacenserklöster in Kastilien--León vom Beginn des 11. bis zur Mitte des 12. Jahrhunderts*, (Kallmünz, 1974).

_____, "Zum Itinerar Abt Hugos I von Cluny (1049-1109)," *DA*, 29, (1973), 206-219.

Sheehan, M. M., "Necrology," *New Catholic Encyclopedia*, vol. 10, 296-297.

Sitwell, G., (trans. and ed.), *St. Odo of Cluny*, (New York, 1958).

Smith, L. M., *Cluny in the Eleventh and Twelfth Centuries*, (London, 1930).

_____, *The Early History of the Monastery of Cluny*, (London, 1920).

_____, "Ezelo's Life of Hugh of Cluny," *English Historical Review*, 27, (1912), 96-101.

Spiritualità Cluniacense, (Convegni del Centro di Studi, sulla Spiritualità medievale, 1958, Todi, 1960).

Sprengler, A., *Gebete für den Herrscher im frühmittelalterlichen Abendland und die verwandten Anschauungen im gleichzeitigen Schrifttum*, (Dissertation, Göttingen, 1950).

Stacpoole, A., "Hildebrand, Cluny and the Papcy," *Downside Review*, 81, (1963), 142-164; 254-272.

_____, "Hugh of Cluny and the Hildebrandine Miracle Tradition," *RB*, vol. 77, (1967), 341-363.

Stegmüller, O., "Diptychon," *RAC*, vol. 3, 1138-1149.

Steindorff, E., *Jahrbucher des deutschen Reiches unter Heinrich III*, (Leipzig, 1874-1881).

Steinen, W. von den, *Canossa*, (Munich, 1957).

_____, "Heilige als Hagiographen," *HZ*, 143, (1930), 229-256.

Strecker, K., "Dies irae," *Zeitschrift für deutsches Altertum und deutsche Literatur*, vol. 51, (1909), 227-255.

Szövérffy, J., "*Dies Irae*," *New Catholic Encyclopedia*, 4, 863-864.

Tellenbach, G., "La chute de l'abbé Pons de Cluny et sa signification historique," *Annales du Midi*, vol. 76, (1964), 355-362. Also in *QFIAB*, 42, (1964), 13-55.

_____, *Libertas: Kirche und Weltordnung im Zeitalter des Investiturstreites*, (Leipzig, 1936). Bibliographical additions in Appendix V of R. F. Bennett's translation, *Church, State and Christian Society at the Time of the Investiture Contest*, (Oxford, 1959).

_____, "Liturgische Gedenkbücher als historische Quellen," *Mélanges Eugene Tisserant V*, Biblioteca Vaticana, (1964), (*Studi e Testi*, 235), 389-399.

_____, (ed.), *Neue Forschungen über Cluny und die Cluniazenser*, (Freiburg, 1959).

_____, "Römischer und christliche Reichsgedanke in der Liturgie des frühen Mittelalters," *Sitzungsberichte der Heidelberger Akademie der Wissenschaften*, 1 Abhandlung, 25, (1934), 4-71.

_____, "Zum Wesen der Cluniacenser," *Saeculum*, vol. 9, (1958), 370-378.

Tomek, E., *Studien zur Reform der deutschen Klöster im 11. Jahrhundert*, (Studien und Mitteilungen aus dem Kirchengeschichtlichen Seminar, Vienna, 1910).

Ullmann, W., "The Bible and Principles of Government," *La Bibbia*, 181-227.

Valous, G. de, "Cluny," *DHGE*, vol. 13, 35-174.

_____, *Le Monachisme clunisien des origines au XVe siècle*, 2 vols., (Ligugé and Paris, 1935).

Van Dijk, S. J. P., "The Customary of St. Benedict's at Polirone," *Miscellanea Liturgica in honorem Cuniberti Mohlberg*, 2 vols. Vol. 2, (Rome, 1949), 451-465.

Vermeesch, A., *Essai sur les origines et la signification de la Commune dans le Nord de la France: XIe et XIIe Siècles*, (Etudes presentées à la Commission Internationale pour l'Histoire des Assemblées des Etats, no. 30, Heule UGA, 1966).

Vogelsang, M., "Der kluniazensische Chronist Raoul Glaber: Ein Beitrag zur kluniacensischen Geschichtsschreibung," *StMGBO*, 67, (1956), 25-38.

Wadstein, E., "Die eschatologische Ideengruppe; Antichrist-Weltsabbat-Weltende und Weltgericht," *Zeitschrift für wissenschaftliche Theologie*, vol. 39, (1896), 154f.

Warnack, V., "Das Mönchtum als 'Pneumatische Philosophie' in den Nilusbriefen," in *Vom christlichen Mysterium...zum Gedächtnis von O. Casel*, (Düsseldorf, 1951), 135-151.

Werner, E., *Die gesellschaftlichen Grundlagen der Kloster-reform im 11.Jahrhundert*, (Berlin, 1953).

White, H., "Pontius of Cluny, the 'Curia Romana' and the end of Gregorianism in Rome," *Church History*, vol. 27, (1958), 197-219.

White, L., *Latin Monasticism in Norman Sicily*, (Cambridge, 1938).

Wimmer, F. P., *Kaiserin Adelheid in ihrem Leben und Wirken von 931-973*, (Dissertation, Regensburg, 1897).

Wölflin, *Die Bamberger Apokalypse*, (Munich, 1921).

Wollasch, J., "Ein cluniazensiches Totenbuch aus der Zeit Abt Hugo von Cluny," *FS*, 1, 406-443.

_____, "Gemeinschaftsbewusstsein und soziale Leistung im Mittelalter," *FS*, 9, (1975), 268-286.

_____, "Gerard von Brogne im Reformmönchtum seiner Zeit," *RB*, vol. 70, (1960), 224-231.

_____, "Das Grabkloster der Kaiserin Adelheid in Selz am Rhein," *FS*, 2, (1968), 135-143.

_____, "Kaiser Heinrich II in Cluny," *FS*, 3, (1969), 327-342.

_____, "Königtum, Adel und Kloster während das 10. Jahrhunderts," *NF*, 19-165.

_____, "Qu' a signifié Cluny pour l'abbaye de Moissac?," *Annales du Midi*, 75, (1963), 345-352.

_____, "Die Wahl des Papstes Nicholas II," *Adel und Kirche*, 205-218.

_____, See also under Schmid, K.

Wolter, H., *Ordericus Vitalis. Ein Beitrag zur kluniazen-sischen Geschichtsschreibung*, (Wiesbaden, 1955).

Zappert, G., "Über sogenannte Verbrüderungsbücher und Nekrologien im Mittelalter," *SB der Akademie der Wissenschaften*, Phil. Hist. Kl., vol. 10, (1853), 417-463.

Zema, D. B., "The Economic Reorganization of the Roman See during the Gregorian Reform," *Studi Gregoriani*, vol. 1, (1947), 137-168.

Zerbi, P., "Intorno allo scisma di Ponzio, abate de Cluny," *Studi storici in onore di O. Bertolini*, vol. II, (Pisa, 1972), 835-891. See also under J. Leclercq.

Zoepf, L., *Heiligenleben im X Jahrhundert*, (Tübingen, 1908).

- - - - - - -

Kindly refer also to pp. 48 n. 16, 95 n. 53, 125 n. 52, 167 n. 16, 201 n. 24, 221 n. 24, for further works not listed in the Bibliography by H. Berman, H. Küng, E. de Moreau, K. Oettinger, E. Rosenstock-Huessy, J. Stiennon, W. Teske, H. von Eicken.

INDEX

ROBERT G. HEATH is a native of New Hampshire. He received his B.A. degree from Dartmouth College ('47); his diploma for French language and civilization from the Université de Lyon ('49); graduate work was done at the University of Munich (1950-51); and finally his Ph.D. in medieval history was earned at the University of California in Los Angeles (1971). He is now on the faculty at the California State University in Northridge.

Pittsburgh Theological
Monograph Series
Number 13

THE PICKWICK PRESS
5001 Baum Blvd.
Pittsburgh, Pa. 15213